DISCARDED

Encyclopedia

—— *of* ——

LIFE SCIENCES

Second Edition

Fibers – Hallucinogens

Marshall Cavendish
New York • London • Toronto • Sydney

Marshall Cavendish
99 White Plains Road
Tarrytown, New York 10591-9001

www.marshallcavendish.com

© 1996, 2004 Marshall Cavendish Corporation

Created by **The Brown Reference Group plc**

All rights reserved. No part of this book may be reproduced or utilized
in any form or by any means, electronic or mechanical, including
photocopying and recording, or by any information storage and retrieval
system, without prior written permission from the copyright holders.

Library of Congress Cataloging-in-Publication Data

Encyclopedia of life sciences / [edited by] Anne O'Daly.—2nd ed.
   p.   cm.
Summary: An illustrated encyclopedia with articles on
agriculture, anatomy, biochemistry, biology, genetics,
medicine, and molecular biology.
Includes bibliographical references (p.   ).
   ISBN 0-7614-7442-0 (set)
   ISBN 0-7614-7448-X (vol. 6)

   1. Life sciences—Encyclopedias. 2. Biology—Encyclopedias. [1.
Biology—Encyclopedias. 2. Life sciences—Encyclopedias.] I. O'Daly,
Anne, 1966–
   QH302.5 .E53   2003
   570'.3—dc21
                                    2002031157

Printed in Malaysia
Bound in the United States of America

07 06 05 04 03   6 5 4 3 2 1

Artworks by:
Darren Awuah, Bill Botten, Jennie Dooge, Dax Fullbrook,
and Mark Walker.

For The Brown Reference Group:
Project Editors: Caroline Beattie and Lesley Campbell-Wright
Editors: Richard Beatty, Robert Cave, Simon Hall, Rob Houston,
Jim Martin, and Ben Morgan
Designer: Joan Curtis
Picture Researcher: Rebecca Cox
Managing Editor: Bridget Giles
Design Manager: Lynne Ross
Indexer: Kay Ollerenshaw

For Marshall Cavendish:
Project Editor: Joyce Tavolacci
Editorial Director: Paul Bernabeo
Production Manager: Michael Esposito

Title page: fossils in amber (Frank Lane Picture Agency)

PICTURE CREDITS
Biophoto Associates: 726, 735, 737, 738, 743, 744, 745, 750, 753, 757, 761,
762, 763, 767, 775, 783, 784, 788, 789, 790, 795, 797, 799, 800, 823, 829, 835;
Bill Botten: 727, 736, 739, 748, 758, 760, 793, 803, 830, 831, 836, 839, 844t,
847, 847, 848, 859; **Corbis:** Yann Arthus-Betrand 780, Ron Boardman 838;
Corbis Royalty Free: 843; **Digital Vision:** 840; **Jennie Dooge:** 730, 768,
798, 817, 825; **Frank Lane Picture Agency:** 725, 728t, 731, 732, 733, 746,
747, 749, 752, 755, 756, 759, 766, 769, 770, 774, 776, 777, 778, 781, 782, 787,
791, 792, 796, 832, 833, 834, 837, 849, 850, 852, 854, 855, 858, 862; **Dax
Fullbrook:** 728b, 805, 807, 808, 810, 811; **Martha C. Hawes:** University of
Arizona 809; **Imagingbody.com:** 804; **Marshall Cavendish, London,
U.K.:** 860; **Mary Evans Picture Library:** 740, 751, 754, 764, 857; **NHPA:**
Eric Soder 776; **Pacific Northwest National Laboratory:** 772; **Photodisc:**
Georgette Douwma 729; **Rex Features:** Rick Colls 771, Sipa Press 779;
Science Photo Library: 773, 785, 801, 802, 812, 813, 815, 816, 818, 819,
820, 821, 827, 841, 842, 844b, 846, 856, 861; **Science & Society:** Science
Museum 741; **USDA:** Ron Nichols 851, Edwin W. Cole 853.

CONTENTS

USEFUL INFORMATION

Use this table to convert the English system (or the imperial system), the system of units common in the United States (e.g., inches, miles, quarts), to the metric system (e.g., meters, kilometers, liters) or to convert the metric system to the English system. You can convert one measurement into another by multiplying. For example, to convert centimeters into inches, multiply the number of centimeters by 0.3937. To convert inches into centimeters, multiply the number of inches by 2.54.

To convert	into	multiply by
Acres	Square feet	43,560
	Square yards	4840
	Square miles	0.00156
	Square meters	4046.856
	Hectares	0.40468
Celsius	Fahrenheit	First multiply by 1.8 then add 32
Centimeters	Inches	0.3937
	Feet	0.0328
Cubic cm	Cubic inches	0.06102
Cubic feet	Cubic inches	1728
	Cubic yards	0.037037
	Gallons	7.48
	Cubic meters	0.028317
	Liters	28.32
Cubic inches	Fluid ounces	0.554113
	Cups	0.069264
	Quarts	0.017316
	Gallons	0.004329
	Liters	0.016387
	Milliliters	16.387064
Cubic meters	Cubic feet	35.3145
	Cubic yards	1.30795
Cubic yards	Cubic feet	27
	Cubic meters	0.76456
Cups, fluid	Quarts	0.25
	Pints	0.5
	Ounces	8
	Milliliters	237
	Tablespoons	16
	Teaspoons	48
Fahrenheit	Celsius	First subtract 32 then divide by 1.8
Feet	Centimeters	30.48
	Meters	0.3048
	Kilometers	0.0003
	Inches	12
	Yards	0.3333
	Miles	0.00019
Gallons	Quarts	4
	Pints	8
	Cups	16
	Ounces	128
	Liters	3.785
	Milliliters	3785
	Cubic inches	231
	Cubic feet	0.1337
	Cubic yards	0.00495
	Cubic meters	0.00379
	British gallons	0.8327
Grams	Ounces	0.03527
	Pounds	0.0022
Hectares	Square meters	10,000
	Acres	2.471
Horsepower	Foot-pounds per minute	33,000
	British thermal units (Btu) per minute	42.42
	British thermal units (Btu) per hour	2546
	Kilowatts	0.7457
	Metric horsepower	1.014
Inches	Feet	0.08333

To convert	into	multiply by
Inches (continued)	Yards	0.02778
	Centimeters	2.54
	Meters	0.0254
Kilograms	Grams	1000
	Ounces	35.274
	Pounds	2.2046
	Short tons	0.0011
	Long tons	0.00098
	Metric tons (tonnes)	0.001
Kilometers	Meters	1000
	Miles	0.62137
	Yards	1093.6
	Feet	3280.8
Kilowatts	British thermal units (Btu) per minute	56.9
	Horsepower	1.341
	Metric horsepower	1.397
Kilowatt-hours	British thermal units (Btu)	3413
Knots	Statute miles per hour	1.1508
Leagues	Miles	3
Liters	Milliliters	1000
	Fluid ounces	33.814
	Quarts	1.05669
	British gallons	0.21998
	Cubic inches	61.02374
	Cubic feet	0.13531
Meters	Inches	39.37
	Feet	3.28083
	Yards	1.09361
	Miles	0.000621
	Kilometers	0.001
	Centimeters	100
	Millimeters	1000
Miles	Inches	63,360
	Feet	5280
	Yards	1760
	Meters	1609.34
	Kilometers	1.60934
	Nautical miles	0.8684
Miles nautical, U.S. and International	Statute miles	1.1508
	Feet	6076.115
	Meters	1852
Miles per minute	Feet per second	88
	Knots	52.104
Milliliters	Fluid ounces	0.0338
	Cubic inches	0.061
	Liters	0.001
Millimeters	Centimeters	0.1
	Meters	0.001
	Inches	0.03937
Ounces, avoirdupois	Pounds	0.0625
	Grams	28.34952
	Kilograms	0.0283495
Ounces, fluid	Pints	0.0625
	Quarts	0.03125
	Cubic inches	1.80469
	Cubic feet	0.00104
	Milliliters	29.57353
	Liters	0.02957
Pints, fluid	Ounces, fluid	16
	Quarts, fluid	0.5

To convert	into	multiply by
Pints, fluid (continued)	Cubic inches	28.8745
	Cubic feet	0.01671
	Milliliters	473.17647
	Liters	0.473176
Pounds	Ounces	16
	Grams	453.59237
	Kilograms	0.45359
	Tons	0.0005
	Tons, long	0.000446
	Metric tons (tonnes)	0.0004536
Quarts, fluid	Ounces, fluid	32
	Pints, fluid	2
	Gallons	0.25
	Cubic inches	57.749
	Cubic feet	0.033421
	Liters	0.946358
	Milliliters	946.358
Square centimeters	Square inches	0.155
Square feet	Square inches	144
	Square meters	0.093
	Square yards	0.111
Square inches	Square centimeters	6.452
	Square feet	0.0069
Square kilometers	Hectares	100
	Square meters	1,000,000
	Square miles	0.3861
Square meters	Square feet	10.758
	Square yards	1.196
Square miles	Acres	640
	Square kilometers	2.59
Square yards	Square feet	9
	Square inches	1296
	Square meters	0.836
Tablespoons	Ounces, fluid	0.5
	Teaspoons	3
	Milliliters	14.7868
Teaspoons	Ounces, fluid	0.16667
	Tablespoons	0.3333
	Milliliters	4.9289
Tons, long	Pounds	2240
	Kilograms	1016.047
	Short tons	1.12
	Metric tons (tonnes)	1.016
Tons, short	Pounds	2000
	Kilograms	907.185
	Long tons	0.89286
	Metric tonnes	0.907
Tons, metric (tonnes)	Pounds	2204.62
	Kilograms	1000
	Long tons	0.984206
	Short tons	1.10231
Watts	British thermal units (Btu) per hour	3.415
	Horsepower	0.00134
Yards	Inches	36
	Feet	3
	Miles	0.0005681
	Centimeters	91.44
	Meters	0.9144

FIBERS

Fibers are everywhere. They are long, hairlike strands present naturally in and on the bodies of animals as well as the stems, leaves, and fruits of plants. Animal fibers are made of protein and include hairs and feather barbules. Fibers also combine to make up nails, claws, horns, muscles, skin, cartilage, bones, tendons, and blood clots. Another animal fiber is silk, used in spider webs and silkworm moth cocoons. Although silk is produced by these animals, it is not part of their body. Plant fibers are made of cellulose and may be in the roots, stems, leaves, or fruits. Wood is largely made up of cellulose fibers, as are the parachute-like hairs on certain seeds.

Fibers are organic (carbon-containing) structures. Their constituent molecules, called monomers, are arranged in long chains called polymers. Some chains lie neatly side by side; others are bent and twisted. The spaces between the individual polymer chains of wool provide it with its insulation.

Plant fibers

Plant fibers consist mainly of cellulose, a carbohydrate made up of hundreds of molecules of glucose manufactured during photosynthesis from water and carbon dioxide. The fibers in roots, stems, and leaves strengthen the tissue. They also make the foliage difficult to bite off, unpleasant to chew, and hard to digest; thus, they offer some protection from herbivores. Wood provides trees and shrubs with a strong, persistent material to form their stems, which last for many years without decaying and during that time bear great weights and stresses.

Fruit fibers usually aid seed dispersal. Many plants have seeds with tufts of hairs (called a pappus). The pappus of dandelions (*Taraxacum* spp.) is shaped rather like an umbrella and allows the seed to be carried on the wind. Other wind-dispersed seeds with a pappus are found in thistles (especially *Cirsium* and *Carduus* spp.) and cottonwood trees (*Populus* spp.). The pappus of modern cotton varieties, which has been bred to be very large, is the source of the cotton fiber used by people. Another fruit fiber is coir, from the coconut palm (*Cocos nucifera*). Coir is the middle coat (mesocarp) of the coconut fruit. Its purpose is to provide buoyancy so that the seed will float away on the ocean (its natural habitat is tropical shorelines). It also protects the seed from saltwater damage.

Silk fibers are produced naturally by silkworm moths (Bombyx mori) to form their cocoons. The silk fibers are very fine threads of protein; the length of these threads is determined by the size of the cocoon.

Kapok fiber comes from the inner wall of the fruit of the tropical tree *Ceiba pentandra*.

Scientists have succeeded in getting bacteria to produce cellulose through genetic engineering (see GENETIC ENGINEERING). A genetically engineered fiber called Cellulon has a netlike arrangement to its structure that is only 0.1 µm thick and has unique thickening and coating properties.

Animal fibers

Animal fibers are made of protein polymers, which include keratin in hair, wool, horn, claws, and feathers; myosin and actin in muscle; fibrin, a plasma protein that enables blood clots to form (see BLOOD); collagen in tendons, cartilage, and skin; and elastin, the structural element of elastic fibers. Protein fibers also make up silk, which is obtained from the cocoon lining of silkworm moths (*Bombyx mori*). The cocoon protects the vulnerable insect in its immobile phase.

Keratin is noted for its ability to extend and contract reversibly. Wool mostly comes from the hair of sheep (*Ovis aries*) but may be obtained from several other mammals: goats, camels, cows, and horses. Animal domestication has led to the breeding of animals, such as merino sheep, that produce fibers in great quantity for human use. Fur in mammals such as cats is made up of coarse outer guard hairs and softer underfur, which provides insulation. Some hairs, called vibrissae (whiskers), have a sensory function. A mammal's coat provides insulation from cold, heat, water, and the ultraviolet (UV) rays of the sun. A coat can also act as a dispersal organ for scents, as hairs are porous and provide a large surface area. Birds' feathers, which have a lightweight, aerodynamic surface and shape, allow birds to fly. They also provide insulation in the same way that hairs do.

CORE FACTS
- Fibers are hairlike strands of a substance that are at least 100 times longer than they are wide.
- Natural sources of fibers are plants (consisting mainly of cellulose), animals (consisting of protein), and minerals.
- Except for certain minerals, such as asbestos, fibers are composed of organic (carbon-containing) compounds.

CONNECTIONS

- The fibers in some **SPIDER** silk are ten times better at resisting breakage than Kevlar, the material used in bulletproof vests. Whereas Kevlar is made in vats of hot, toxic chemicals, spiders produce their silk at room temperature using harmless substances, such as water.

SPIDERS IN A SPIN

When a fly lands on a spider's web, it is caught in silk fibers stronger than steel. Spiders produce a silk protein with amazing properties, using glands within their spinnerets. Most spiders produce both dry and sticky silk for their webs. The sticky parts trap prey, and the dry parts allow the spider to move across the web without getting caught. The sticky silk is replaced every few days, as it dries out. Spider silk has a tensile strength 16 times greater than that of nylon and an ability to supercontract to less than 60 percent of its original length when wet. Scientists collect the silk from spiders by wrapping the end of the silk around a motorized spindle. As much as 1,000 feet (300 m) can be collected from one such "silking." Genetic engineers are researching a spider gene that can be placed in a simple organism (such as a bacterium) to produce large amounts of silk, which could then be used to make strong fabrics and cables.

Horns, claws, hooves, and nails are made of densely matted keratin. This hard and often sharp material is used by animals in fighting and defense and also in catching, killing, and dismembering prey.

Bones, cartilage, and tendons are made with collagen fibers. Collagen fibers also form the body's connective tissue and make up about 30 percent of body protein. The collagen fibers in tendons are arranged parallel to one another to give the tensile strength of a light steel wire. In bone they provide a matrix for mineral crystals. Bone and cartilage are the basic framework (skeleton) supporting vertebrate bodies. Body movement is powered by muscles, which are made up of myosin and actin fibers, attached to the skeleton by the collagen-containing tendons. Muscles also power the cardiovascular and respiratory systems.

The collagen fibers of skin are randomly arranged to give strength and flexibility. Skin provides a protective, flexible, breathable case for animal bodies.

Other important fibers in the animal world are made from chitin, a polysaccharide that forms the exoskeleton of arachnids, crustaceans, and insects.

Properties of fibers

Fibers vary widely in their structure, depending on their function in the plant or animal that produces them. Function in turn determines their properties and their use in industry. Manufacturers need to know whether particular fibers will burn, melt, absorb water, be weakened by sunlight or chemicals, and resist mildew, rotting, or moths. They also need to know whether those fibers can be dyed easily. Other important properties of fibers include thickness, strength, elasticity, and flexibility.

The thickness of a fiber is measured in micrometers, symbol μm ($\frac{1}{25,000}$ inch). Fine fibers, such as silk, are about 5 μm thick, while some coarse vegetable and animal fibers measure from 75 to 125 μm. Strength (the ability to withstand pulling without breaking) is a fiber's most important quality. Elasticity is the fiber's ability to stretch when pulled and to return to its original length. Flexibility determines whether the fiber can bend without breaking.

Microscopic examination reveals why fibers have such versatile properties. For example, wool fibers have scales that make them stick together during spinning, whereas synthetic nylon fibers are round and smooth and do not stick together. Cotton, the world's most important nonfood agricultural product, is easy to spin because of the natural twist of the fiber and does not lose strength when exposed to moisture, sunlight, or mildew.

It is the fiber's chemical structure that determines many of these properties. Different proteins, for example, vary in the precise sequence of amino acids in their chains (see AMINO ACIDS; PROTEINS). Thus, hair and skin, composed of different types and arrangements of fibers, look and feel so different from each other. In plant fibers, the ratio of cellulose to water seems to contribute significantly to the character of the fiber. For example, hemp has more cellulose and less water than flax does. As a result, hemp has long, coarse, inflexible fibers, whereas flax is much softer.

E. KELLY

See also: AMINO ACIDS; BLOOD, CARTILAGE; CELLULOSE; CONNECTIVE TISSUE; GENETIC ENGINEERING; HAIR; PROTEINS; SKIN.

Further reading:

Chawla, K. K. 1998. *Fibrous Materials.* Cambridge and New York: Cambridge University Press.
Feughelman, M. 1996. *Mechanical Properties and Structure of Alpha Keratin Fibers: Wool, Human Hair, and Related Fibers.* Sydney: New South Wales University Press.

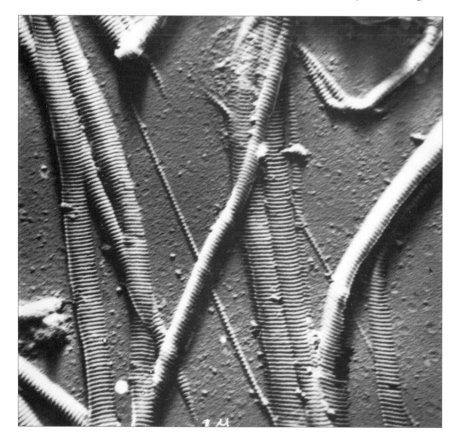

Collagen fibers in a tendon, magnified x 75,000. Collagen is the most abundant protein in the animal kingdom.

FISH

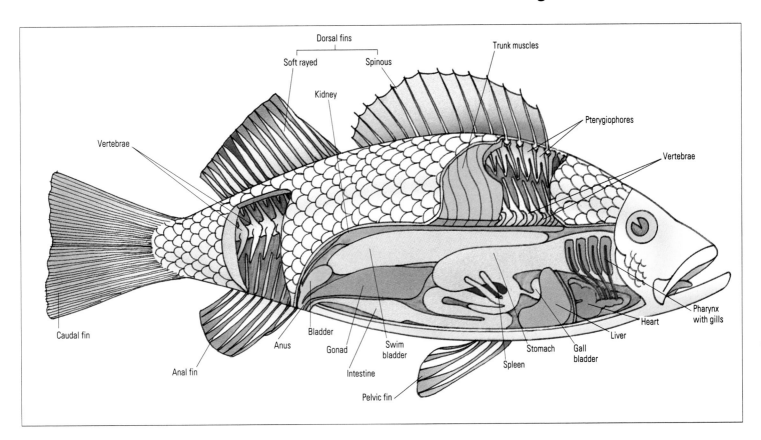

This diagram illustrates the basic structure of a bony fish from the large and diverse order Perciformes.

Some scientists think fish are the most successful vertebrates, with good reason. In terms of species, fish outnumber birds by more than two to one and mammals by seven to one. There are more than 24,000 known species of fish in the world, living in such diverse habitats as stagnant ponds, flowing rivers, ocean depths, subzero polar water, and thermal springs that heat up to 120 ºF (49 ºC).

Fish live in water and obtain oxygen from it using gills. Most fish have a streamlined body, are covered with scales, and use fins for movement and balance. There are three main types of fish: bony fish, cartilaginous fish, and jawless fish. Bony fish, as their name suggests, have a skeleton made of bone. They have a protective cover, the operculum, over their gills to protect them, and usually have thin, overlapping scales. Cartilaginous fish, sharks and rays, have a skeleton made of cartilage. Like bony fish, they usually have five pairs of gills, but no gill covers, and are covered with

small scales (denticles) that are half buried in their skin. The jawless fish, lampreys and hagfish, have no jaws, but instead have a sucker ringed with horny teeth for rasping food. They have a series of gill openings and smooth skin with no scales. Some are parasitic.

Basic body shape

Most fish have a streamlined body. Water flows over the body easily during swimming, and thus, they move through the water with little resistance. Many predatory fish, such as tuna, mackerel, and swordfish, have tapering bodies and powerful tails adapted for fast swimming. Predators such as freshwater pikes, which lie in wait for their prey rather than chasing them, are often shaped like torpedoes; this shape helps them move quickly over a short distance to ambush prey.

Some fish have developed body shapes that allow them to adapt to different ways of life. Flounders, for example, have flattened bodies that allow them to lie on the seabed and feed while hidden from predators. Other fish, such as angelfish, have upright, narrow bodies that allow them to maneuver through coral, dense vegetation, or other areas where there is limited space. Long, thin fish such as eels are adapted to living in cracks and crevices or wriggling into the mud to hide.

Respiration

All vertebrates need oxygen to survive. Most fish have to get their oxygen from the water. They obtain oxygen through their gills, which lie behind and to the

CORE FACTS

- There are three main types of modern fish: bony fish (Osteichthyes); cartilaginous fish (Chondrichthyes); and jawless fish (Agnatha).
- There are more than 22,000 species of bony fish, which include most of the commercial species.
- Most fish have a streamlined body covered with scales and gills through which they breathe.
- Fish have adapted to virtually all types of water environments.

CONNECTIONS

- **WHALES AND DOLPHINS** are aquatic **MAMMALS**, not fish. They do not have **GILLS** but breathe with **LUNGS**. They also produce live young, which they rear on milk, while most fish produce **EGGS** that develop outside the body.

- Fish are among the major **VERTEBRATE** groups, together with mammals, amphibians, birds, and reptiles.

The mudskipper (Periophthalmus barbarus), pictured on wet ground, is frequently seen out of the water and sometimes well away from it. The mudskipper's swim bladder has evolved as an accessory breathing organ, and out of water, the mudskipper is able to maintain its oxygen intake by actively gulping air.

oxygen, bony fish open and close their mouths to pump oxygen-depleted water out of the gills.

Some fish have adapted to living in water that contains very little oxygen. Walking catfish, native to Africa and Asia, have modified gills that are also used to breathe air. Normal gills tend to stick together when they are exposed to the air; the surface area available for gas exchange thus being reduced. Some eels can migrate short distances across land while taking oxygen in through their skin.

Electric eels have to breathe air. They have an area for gas exchange in their mouth and will drown if they cannot come to the surface to breathe. North American mud suckers also use their mouth to breathe, with oxygen uptake occuring in their specially evolved swim bladders. Some tropical catfish can exchange gas in their guts and so must swallow air to get adequate oxygen. Lungfish can obtain oxygen with the use of true lungs. During a drought, some lungfish burrow down into the mud and breathe air through a small tunnel leading up to the surface. Even when water is plentiful, they may still have to come to the surface to breathe air, though carbon dioxide continuously diffuses out from the blood into the water through their vestigial gills.

side of the mouth (see GILLS AND SPIRACLES). The gills are made up of bony or cartilaginous arches that support many pairs of filaments. Attached to both sides of the filaments are the gill lamellae, projections of thin permeable tissue that provide a large surface area for gas exchange.

In bony fish water is taken in through the mouth. Sharks, skates, and rays usually take in water through a pair of spiracles (modified gills) but also have moveable flaps of skin bordering the gill openings that move to increase the flow of water over their gills. Water passes over the outside of the lamellae in one direction, while the blood inside the lamellae flows in the opposite direction. This countercurrent arrangement allows oxygen in the water to diffuse easily through the lamellae into the blood and carbon dioxide to diffuse out. As the water passing over the gills loses its

Buoyancy

Fish are able to stay at a particular depth in the water without using much energy, because their bodies are the same density as the surrounding water. Some fish have large quantities of low-density compounds in their body. Many sharks, for example, have a large amount of lipids and a fatty hydrocarbon (a carbon- and hydrogen-containing compound) called squalene in their liver to give them buoyancy in sea water. Some bony fish have low-density oil in their bones to minimize their weight. Another way of avoiding sinking is to have a tail and fins shaped and angled in such a way as to give lift in the water during normal swimming, as sharks do, for example.

The swim bladder, an organ present in most bony fish, contains air and is used to control buoyancy.

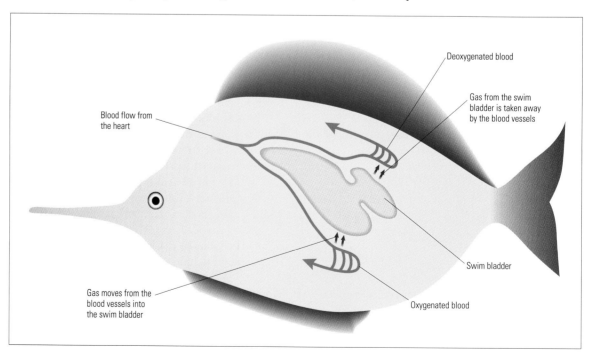

Deoxygenated blood

Gas from the swim bladder is taken away by the blood vessels

Blood flow from the heart

Gas moves from the blood vessels into the swim bladder

Swim bladder

Oxygenated blood

Most bony fish achieve buoyancy by using their swim bladders. The swim bladder is an organ containing gas, which originally developed from a pocket in the digestive system. Swim bladders are either connected to the gut and inflated by gulping air or are filled with gas during the juvenile stages of the fish's life before the swim bladder becomes isolated. The concentration and pressure of the air can be controlled by gas diffusing into or out of the swim bladder from the blood. As a fish swims downward, the surrounding water increases in pressure, and the swim bladder is compressed and deflated; as a fish swims upward, the surrounding water decreases in pressure, and the swim bladder inflates.

Movement

Fish can move in a variety of ways or drift passively in the water. Most swim efficiently by contracting the muscles on each side of their body in turn so that the contractions move backward along the body in a wavelike fashion and the tail whips from side to side and thus pushes them forward. In this way some fish, such as the the tuna, for example, can reach 50 miles per hour (80 km/h) in short bursts.

Most fish have unpaired and paired fins. The unpaired fins are the dorsal (back), anal, and caudal (tail) fins. The paired fins are the pectoral and pelvic fins; these correspond to the fore- and hind limbs, respectively, of other vertebrates. Movement of the

LIFE IN THE DEEP SEA

The deep sea is dark and cold. As fewer animals and plants live in the deep water, one of the main problems for deep-sea fish is finding food. Some, like the gulper eel, have a very large mouth and a stomach capable of stretching, so they can catch and eat large prey. Others attract prey with bioluminescent lights on their body (see BIOLUMINESCENCE). Angler fish, for example, have a modified fin spine on their head with a small luminescent lump at the end that acts much as bait on a fishing rod does. Small fish are attracted to the "bait" and are caught. Most deep-sea fish have large eyes to help them see in the gloom. For buoyancy, many deep-sea fish have swim bladders (gas-filled elastic sacs), which allow them to move up to shallower water, possibly to feed, and down again. Because the water pressure at depth is up to 15 times that at the surface, the bones and muscles of many deep-sea fish are very thin, light, and flexible.

A CLOSER LOOK

paired fins allows fish to maneuver and helps to stabilize them when they are swimming or hovering. During swimming, the vertical fins are used for stabilization and to produce thrust. The dorsal fin of the shark, for example, is used to stabilize the animal while it swims by using the tail to generate thrust.

Most fish swim forward, although some eels can swim backward by wriggling their whole body, and knife fish reverse their fin movements to move as quickly backward as they do forward. The sea horse

A school of lined sweetlip fish (Gaterin lineatus) hovering above a coral reef.

FISH EVOLUTION

The oldest known fishlike vertebrates are ostracoderms. They were small creatures with bony-plated armor covering their bodies and a bony protective shield that grew over their heads, covering a row of gills. They first appeared in the Cambrian period, over 510 million years ago, and are the first known members of the superclass Agnatha (jawless fish), which includes the cyclostomes. At the front of the head, a small mouth opened into a gill-lined chamber, but ostracoderms lacked a jaw or paired fins. They lived mainly in salt water. About 400 million years ago, jawless lampreys and hagfish appeared. They still exist, and their bodies have remained basically unchanged.

The very first fish with jaws appeared before the ostracoderms became extinct; they were acanthodians (spiny sharks) and placoderms. They, too, bore armor plates. Although their relationship to each other and to other early fish is still uncertain, some experts believe that placoderms eventually lost their bony armor and endoskeleton and gave rise to cartilaginous fish. Both acanthodians and placoderms had paired fins. Acanthodians had a skeleton of cartilage and bone, and their paired fins were supported by hollow spines. The bodies of placoderms were covered with two protective

shields, one over the head and the other over the anterior part of the trunk. The rest of the body was covered with scales.

Ostracoderms disappeared in the Devonian period (about 395 million years ago) and were replaced by two classes of jawed fish (gnathostomes): cartilaginous fish (Chondrichthyes) and bony fish (Osteichthyes). Why did most of the agnathans die out, while the gnathostomes went on to flourish? The answer might be the feature that distinguishes one group from the other: the hinged jaw. As the hinged jaw developed, so did a streamlined body shape and the fins that allow quick, accurate movement (important for catching prey). At the same time, gnathostomes developed stronger muscles, a stronger skeleton, larger brains, and in some cases, swim bladders.

The very first bony fish probably appeared at about the same time as cartilaginous fish. By the end of the Devonian period, they were abundant. Almost directly after they evolved, bony fish branched into two separate groups, ray-finned fish (Actinopterygii) and lobe-finned fish (Sarcopterygii). Ray-finned fish developed further to give rise to most modern fish. The lobe-finned fish, which include the coelacanth, eventually gave rise to all land vertebrates.

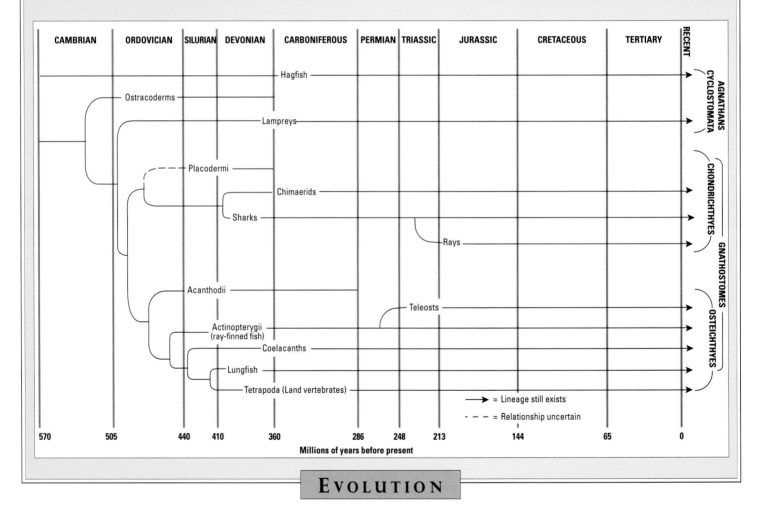

EVOLUTION

is one of the few fish that swims in an upright position by rapid vibration of the dorsal fin.

Other fish have developed ways of moving through air and even on land. Flying fish can burst out of the water and glide through the air by spreading out their long side fins. Frog fish have fins at the end of a small arm. They use these fins to crawl among seaweed searching for food. Mudskippers can jump through the

air by curling their tails around and then jerking their bodies straight, a movement that propels them forward.

Schooling

Many fish spend a good part of their life in large groups called schools. Forming large groups helps to protect individual fish from predators, makes it easier for a fish to swim, and increases the fish's chances of finding food and reproducing. Fish schools move in different patterns. When traveling, the school may have a long, skinny shape, or it may resemble a blob. If the fish in a school want to move at speed, the school takes on a wedge shape. By staying diagonally rather than directly behind the fish in front of it, each fish increases its swimming efficiency because the slipstream current from the fish ahead makes it easier for the fish behind to move. When the members of a school are feeding, they may not remain aligned, unless they are all circling a potential prey. In a fish school, each fish moves in close synchrony with the other fish and maintains a specific distance (half its body length) from each of its neighbors at all times.

One of the biggest drawbacks to schooling is that it appears to make the fish group more vulnerable to predation. What could be easier to catch than hundreds of fish, all swimming together? However, when under attack, the fish in a school may swim farther apart and form a long ribbon, a shape that makes it harder for a predator to catch one of them. Also, because small schooling fish are usually silvery in color a predator may be confused by the flash caused by light reflecting off the bodies of the fish when the school turns or moves. A school may also divide in two, each part swimming in different directions to avoid an attack. To counteract this behavior some predatory fish hunt in groups.

Schooling behavior seems to depend on vision. Each fish can fix on the sides of its neighbors and in this way keep its distance and swimming speed closely attuned. The lateral line system, which runs along the body of many bony fish, may also help the fish to remain in a school formation. The sensory organs in the lateral line can detect differences in the water pressure around the fish and therefore sense how close they are to other fish.

Temperature control

Most fish are cold blooded, which means that their body temperature varies with the temperature of the environment. Many have developed behavioral adaptations to cope with this trait, for example, by staying in areas of constant temperature or moving as it suits them. Canadian sockeye salmon remain in warm waters while feeding during the relatively short summer nights and then move to cooler water during the long days to slow their metabolism and conserve energy.

There are a few warm-bodied fish, such as the skipjack tuna, that utilize the heat from their own metabolism rather than the environment (they are described as endothermic homeotherms). These fish have an elaborate network of capillaries and nerve cells called the rete mirabile (which is Latin for "wonderful net"). The rete mirabile transfers the metabolic heat generated in the core of the body to the body surface. Heat exchange occurs between the veins carrying warm blood leaving the area of heat generation to the arteries, which are intertwined with these veins as they carry cold blood into the area of heat

generation. These fish have large veins and arteries to transport blood between the heart and gills and the rete mirabile. This system enables the fish's core temperature to remain higher than the temperature of the environment. Another advantage of this system is that it enables the fish to keep their muscles warm so that they can react quickly to chase after their prey or escape from potential predators.

Light perception and sight

Sight is very important in many fish. Most bony fish have a spherical lens in the eye and move the lens within the eyeball to focus. Most bony fish can see well, and many can see in color. Some fish have good binocular vision, which helps them to judge distance.

Sharks and rays have a slightly flattened lens. Some sharks can focus by changing the shape of the lens in the same way that land animals do. They can also greatly alter the shape of the pupil to change the level of light coming in through the eyes, especially in those species adapted to dark conditions. Sawfish and rays also have a sort of eyelid that descends over the eye to restrict levels of incoming light. Sharks and rays probably do not see in color.

The four-eyed fish, *Anableps*, has unusual eyes adapted to spending much of its time at the surface of the water. Its eyes are divided by a dark horizontal band into an upper and lower part. The upper part is adapted for vision in air, while the lower part is adapted for vision in water. The fish can therefore see what is going on above and below the water at the same time.

The pineal gland in the brain is also light sensitive. It is thought to influence the circadian rhythms (daily activity cycles; see BIORHYTHMS) of the fish by affecting their internal clock. Thus, fish adapt their behavior to the time of day or the season; this ability is especially important in fish that migrate or gather in large numbers to breed.

The upright, narrow body shape of the angelfish shows how this family of fishes has adapted to swimming through the coral reefs in its habitat.

COLORATION

Many fish are adapted to blend with their surroundings (see CAMOUFLAGE AND MIMICRY). Mackerels (*Scomber*), for example, have a dark blue, wavy pattern on their backs so that, seen from above, they merge into the water. They also have a white stomach so that, seen from below, they appear to merge with the sky. Pike have blotchy markings on their sides to help them hide among underwater plants without being seen. Many reef fish are highly colored and they blend into their colorful surroundings. Flounders (see below) have markings that help them to lie unseen on the seabed. The sea dragon (*Phycodurus eques*), found off Australia, is colored and shaped like a piece of seaweed. Like groupers (*Epinephelus* spp.) of tropical waters, many flatfish can change color to match their surroundings (see below). Lionfish are brightly colored to warn others that they are poisonous.

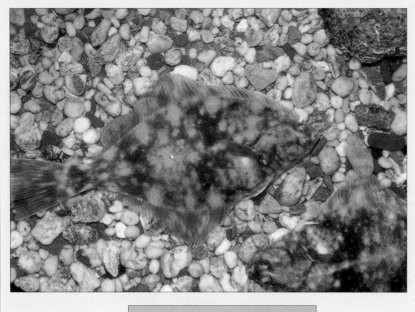

A CLOSER LOOK

Excretion

Fish have a problem that land vertebrates do not have to cope with: that of maintaining the concentration of their body fluids. Through the process of osmosis, water tends to move from an area of a weaker solution to a stronger one until they are both of equal concentration. Therefore, sea fish are in danger of losing body water to the more salty environment outside their bodies, and freshwater fish are in danger of taking in large amounts of water from their more dilute surroundings. Both situations are potentially fatal.

Fish solve this problem in different ways. In hagfish, the blood salt concentration is maintained at the same concentration as sea water, so there is no tendency for water to move in or out of the fish. Sharks and rays reabsorb their urea as it passes along the renal tube, making their body fluids the same concentration as the sea water. They then secrete any excess salt in a solution from the rectal glands.

Bony sea fish, however, which have a blood salt concentration about a third that of sea water, drink plenty of water to replace the amount they lose through the skin and gills. In contrast, freshwater bony fish have well-developed kidneys that excrete dilute urine to maintain their body fluids. Most fish excrete the nitrogen-containing wastes, that are left after digesting protein as ammonia, which diffuses out through the gills into the surrounding water. The African lungfish generally excretes ammonia into the surrounding water, but if the water dries up, it surrounds itself in a mucous cocoon in the bottom mud and excretes less-toxic urea instead.

Feeding and digestion

Most fish feed on small invertebrates or other fish. Simple teeth on the jaws are used to hold the prey, which is then swallowed whole. Sharks and piranhas have strong biting teeth. Sharks continually replace lost teeth. The new teeth develop behind the functional teeth. Minnows have no teeth in the jaw but instead have throat "teeth" on gill arch structures in front of the throat that are used to maneuver food down the throat into the gullet.

Fish that feed on small invertebrates have an O-shaped mouth with movable lips, while fish that eat larger animals usually have a wide, inflexible mouth. The position of the mouth gives a clue to the eating habits. Most fish have a mouth at the front of their head, which opens forward. However, bottom feeders have mouths that point downward, and surface feeders have mouths that point upward. Butterfly fish living in coral reefs, have the mouth at the end of an elongated snout, which can be used for poking into crevices in search of food. Lampreys do not have a jaw; instead they have a rounded mouth that acts as a sucker. The saltwater species is parasitic. It attaches itself to other animals and feeds off them by rasping their flesh with teeth located in this sucker.

Some fish, such as the basking shark, filter feed on plankton collected by straining water through their gills. The largest fish in the world, the whale shark, also feeds by this method. Many bony fish have a set of pharyngeal teeth in the throat region that are used to break down food before it enters the gut.

The digestive tract in different fish species is adapted to the feeding style and diet of the fish. Herbivorous fish and fish that take in mud and other inedible debris when feeding have longer intestines than carnivorous fish, as their food takes longer to digest. Herbivorous and omnivorous fish may not have stomachs. Fish such as mullets and shads have a muscular gizzardlike stomach in the intestine for grinding ingested matter. Carnivorous fish usually have well-developed stomachs that secrete enzymes and acids to break down the proteins in the meat they ingest. In sharks a spiral structure (spiral valve) within the intestine greatly increases the surface area for absorption of nutrients.

Reproduction

Most female fish produce a large number of eggs, which are fertilized and develop outside the body. The male sperm is usually produced as a milky white substance called milt, which is released over the eggs to fertilize them. Many fish leave their eggs once they have been fertilized. They invest no energy in brooding the eggs or rearing the young. Pelagic spawners, like tuna and sardines, spawn in open waters where there is a good current, which helps to disperse the fertilized eggs. Their eggs contain globules of oil or water, which help them to stay afloat. Salmon undertake a long migration from the ocean upriver to lay their eggs in the gravel beds where they once hatched.

Other fish, such as cichlids, look after their eggs. They remain at the spawning site as long as the embryos are developing, and many then tend the fry (young fish) until they are independent. Among many of these cichlids, the males clean the nesting area before spawning with the females. Many forms of nesting behavior are seen by males wanting to breed. For example, the male fathead minnow cleans algae off the bottom of logs and other suitable nest-building surfaces by rubbing his head on the surface. Stickleback males build a nest and entice females to lay eggs inside. After chasing the female away, the male keeps watch over the nest and cares for the young when they hatch.

Some fish carry their embryos around with them. South American catfish attach the fertilized eggs to their bodies. The female sea horse (in an unusual role reversal in the animal kingdom) drops the fertilized eggs into a pouch on the belly of the male, where they remain until they hatch. Certain cichlids and sea catfishes carry fertilized eggs in their mouth. The hatched young stay close to the parents and may go back into the mouth if they are threatened.

In some fish, the eggs are fertilized internally. They may then be released to develop in the water or may remain in the female until the young have hatched. The eggs are usually released soon after fertilization or in a larval stage. In fish that bear live young, nourishment may come from unusual sources. The fins of developing surfperches, for example, stay in contact with the walls of the ovary in which they develop and so absorb nutrients from the female. In sharks that bear live young, the developing fetuses may be nourished by yolk reserves or receive nourishment directly from the mother. In some species the embryos absorb uterine milk secreted from the mother's oviducts. In hammerhead sharks for example, the yolk sac is modified into a placenta-like structure that attaches to the uterus. Nutrients and oxygen pass to the fetus across the placenta and waste products are removed. Very rarely, parent fish provide their young with food after they have hatched. South American discus fish parents secrete a nutritious jelly on the sides of their bodies, which the young larvae feed off.

CLASSIFICATION

Fish classification is quite complex owing to the ancient lineage of the group and the enormous diversity of species evolved. Three main classes are defined: Agnatha (jawless fish), Chondrichthyes (cartilaginous fish), and Osteichthyes (bony fish).

Jawless fish

Jawless fish, which include lampreys and hagfish, have many primitive characteristics. The fish do not have a true jaw. They feed using suckers or by filter feeding. Lampreys breed in fresh water, although some spend most of their adult life at sea. Parasitic lampreys suck the blood and juices of live fish. Hagfish live on the seafloor and rasp the flesh off dead and dying fish using their horny teeth. Agnatha lack an internal skeleton but have a cartilage rod (the notochord) to support the spinal cord. They do not have pelvic fins or fin rays on the pectoral fin structures. Agnatha range in length from 6 to 40 inches (15 cm to 1 m).

Cartilaginous fish

Sharks, chimaerids, rays, skates, and their relatives are the only living cartilaginous fish. Cartilaginous fish were once numerous, but many types have become extinct and only about 600 species remain.

Except for their teeth and scales, cartilaginous fish have no bony material, and their skeleton is made of cartilage. The scales are made of dentine and enamel and are found over the entire body. They are enlarged to form teeth in the jaw. Scales and teeth are replaced when they are worn out. Sharks have several rows of teeth; the front, functional ones are eventually replaced

A male sea horse (Hippocampus guttulatus). The brood pouch, visible on his belly, is not yet fully developed.

by the row behind. Rays and dogfish use several rows of teeth at once. Almost all cartilaginous fish have a mouth on the underside of the head. Males have fins that function as pelvic claspers to transfer sperm internally to the females. Some species of cartilaginous fish have leathery-shelled eggs with trailing tendrils that anchor the eggs on underwater plants until the young hatch. They are called mermaid's purses.

Sharks, skates, and rays usually have five pairs of uncovered gills. Directly behind the first gill slit lies a spiracle (a gill-lined opening) used to take in water. They do not have a swim bladder. Rays and skates appear to have been flattened from the top (dorsoventrally) and have extended sides called wings, which move up and down to propel them through the water. The wingspan of the manta ray (*Manta birostris*) can reach almost 20 feet (6 m). The ratfish (*Chimaera*) has covered gill slits. Instead of teeth, it has bony plates to crush mollusks.

The Elasmobranch subclass, with species characterized by separate gill slits for each gill pouch (sharks, skates, and rays), has an impressive arsenal of weapons for protection and to catch prey. For example, all rays have weak electric organs in their tails, some of which can stun prey with an electric shock to make them easier to catch.

Bony fish

Osteichthyes (bony fish) constitute the great majority of fish and are split into two main subclasses: Sarcopterygii (lobe-finned fish) and Actinopterygii (ray-finned fish). Most have largely or wholly bony skeletons and thin scales over the surface of their skins.

Most lobe-finned fish are now long extinct. The only two living groups are the lungfish and coelacanths. Lungfish live in fresh water and have lungs for breathing air. Their scales grow throughout life, and they have fused teeth, which are modified for crushing and eating mollusks. Coelacanths can grow to a length of 6½ feet (2 m). They were thought to be extinct until a live specimen was caught off South Africa in the Indian Ocean in 1938. Although they are rare and live in very deep water, other examples have been found since. In the 1990s, a new species was discovered in Indonesian waters.

There are three infraclasses of ray-finned fish: Chondrostei (cartilaginous ganoids), Holostei (bony ganoids), and the Teleostei (higher bony fish). The term *ganoid* comes from ganoin, an enamel that covered the scales of all ray-finned fish during the Palaeozoic era and remains on some of the cartilaginous and bony ganoids.

• **Chondrostei:** This small group contains many species known only from fossils, as well as present-day sturgeons and paddlefish. Both sturgeons and paddlefish have a skeleton made mostly of cartilage, while their relative the African bichir is a true ganoid, with a bony skeleton and enamel-covered scales. Marine sturgeons ascend rivers in spring or summer to deposit their spawn. Their eggs (roe) are harvested by humans and eaten as caviar. The adults have barbels (whiskers) projecting from their head,

---

ELECTRICITY

About 250 species of fish can produce electricity. Fish are the only vertebrates that can do so. Some fish use their electric organs to stun prey, while others use electricity as a defense to ward off attackers. Torpedo and electric rays catch prey using electricity. In fact, using electricity, torpedo rays can catch fish that would otherwise be too large and quick for them. The South American mormyrid fish create a low-power electric field around themselves and can detect anything that breaks the field. As they live in murky, dark water, this mechanism is used to find their way around and warn them of any approaching danger.

A CLOSER LOOK

---

and they trail these over the seabed to find small invertebrates and fish to eat. Paddlefish have a paddle-shaped snout made of cartilage, which forms a third of their body length. They are found in the Mississippi River and its tributaries.

• **Holostei:** The two existing bony ganoids, gars and bowfins, are found in fresh water. Gars occur in North and Central America, bowfins in eastern North America. Gars have hard scales formed of ganoin, can grow to 10 feet (3 m) in length, and feed on other fish. Bowfins have a dorsal fin that runs the length of their body and eat fish and crayfish.

• **Teleostei:** This group includes all modern bony fish. They are called modern because they evolved most recently; nevertheless, they have existed for some 65 million years. Teleosts have lost many of the ganoid traits of other ray-finned fish. For example, their scales are flexible, their jaw and palate are more movable, their skull bones are thinner, and their bodies have taken on a vast array of shapes. Perches, eels, sea horses, flounders, and puffer fish, for example, are all teleosts. Teleosts have a skeleton made entirely or mostly of bone. They have a bony operculum, which covers the gill slits. They also have a homocercal tail, that is, the upper and lower halves of the tail are of about equal size. Teleost scales are thin, overlapping plates of bone that continue to grow throughout the life of the fish. They are layered like roof tiles to form a smooth protective surface.

Teleosts have adapted to almost every aquatic habitat. They make up 95 percent of all living fish (over 22,000 species). They vary from tiny gobies less than 1 inch (2.5 cm) long to large marlins of 11 feet (3.4 m) or more. Nearly all of the important sport and commercial fish species are teleosts.

J. SCHULHOF

See also: BIOLUMINESCENCE; BIOMES; BIORHYTHMS; CAMOUFLAGE AND MIMICRY; COLD-BLOODED ANIMALS; CORAL REEF BIOMES; GILLS AND SPIRACLES; LAKES AND PONDS; OCEAN HABITATS; SHARKS; SWIMMING.

Further reading:
Buttfield, H. 2000. *The Secret Life of Fishes*. New York: Harry N. Abrams.
Helfman, G. S, et al. 1997. *The Diversity of Fishes*. Oxford: Blackwell Science.

FLATWORMS

Flatworms are free-living or parasitic invertebrates in the phylum Platyhelminthes

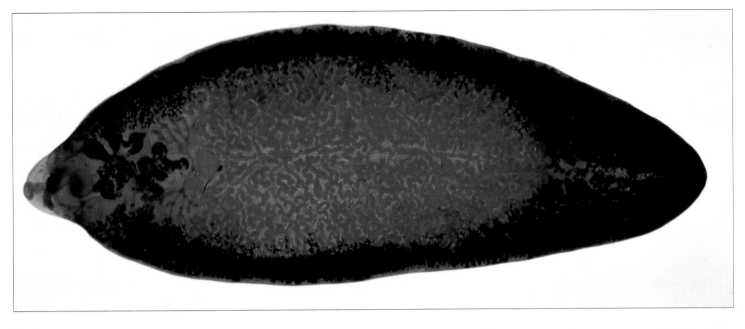

There are about 25,000 species of flatworms, but many are rarely seen because they make their homes inside the bodies of other animals. Flatworms are invertebrates in the phylum Platyhelminthes. The phylum is divided into four classes: Turbellaria (flatworms) are mainly free-living animals; however, Monogenea and Digenea (flukes), and Cestoda (tapeworms) are all parasitic. Some people group Monogenea and Digenea together in the class Trematoda. Monogeneans have a single host and mostly live on the outside of their host's body, while digeneans have two or more hosts and, like cestodes, live inside their hosts.

An evolutionary milestone

Although they look very simple, flatworms represent an evolutionary milestone. In flatworms, the right- and left-hand sides of the body are mirror images of each other. This characteristic is called bilateral symmetry. This body shape is an advance over the radial symmetry (symmetry around a central axis) of animals such as corals, jellyfish, and sea anemones. Flatworms are the simplest animals to show bilateral symmetry. This body shape allows animals to have a much more active lifestyle and to develop specialized

---

CORE FACTS

- Flatworms are invertebrates in the phylum Platyhelminthes.
- Many flatworms are parasites in humans and domestic and other animals.
- Flatworms have soft but solid bodies. They do not contain many specialized body organs.
- Flatworms are the simplest animals with bilaterally symmetrical bodies.
- Many flatworms can regenerate large parts of their bodies.

---

body areas and is seen in most of the more complex organisms, including humans.

Flatworms show other complex features that probably developed at the same time as bilateral symmetry. These features are the formation of a third cell layer (the mesoderm for the nerve net between the internal endoderm and the external ectoderm) and the development of a well-defined head.

Reproduction

Most flatworms are hermaphrodites, that is, each animal contains both male and female reproductive organs. Thus, these animals can self-fertilize their eggs or cross-fertilize if they find a partner. Many flatworms also reproduce asexually by breaking off parts of their body.

Turbellarians reproduce asexually by fission—splitting their body into two halves. The common planarian, *Dugesia*, for example, remains anchored by its rear end to a hard surface. The front end of the animal then pulls forward until the body breaks in two. Each section regenerates and grows the missing parts to form an entire animal (see box on page 737).

Turbellaria

Most turbellarians live on seabeds or riverbeds or in ponds and lakes, particularly on plant surfaces. A few smaller ones live inside the liver and intestine of live hosts. Their bodies are covered with hairlike cilia, and smaller turbellarians use these cilia to swim. In larger species, the cilia move in combination with muscles to cause a creeping movement. The animal may also secrete slime, which helps it glide along.

Turbellarians are mainly carnivorous. They have a powerful muscular pharynx (throat area), which is tubular and free within the pharyngeal cavity, except for the end attached to the intestinal sac; thus it can

A common fluke (Fasciola spp.), a member of the class Trematoda. It lives in the liver and gallbladder and is a common pest of grazing animals.

CONNECTIONS

- Some flatworms are **PARASITES**, living on the outside of the host's body or within the host's **DIGESTIVE SYSTEM**.

- Flatworms are **HERMAPHRODITES**, and their **FERTILIZATION** is internal.

- Free-living flatworms are **CARNIVORES** or scavengers.

- Flatworms possess no specialized **RESPIRATORY SYSTEMS**; gas exchange takes place across the body surface.

FLATWORMS AND DISEASE

Flatworms cause many diseases. Pork, beef, and fish tapeworms and the three species of blood fluke (*Schistosoma* spp., below) are the most common.

A person infected with a tapeworm may suffer pain and may lose weight even though his or her appetite has increased. (In fact, very unwisely, people used to swallow tapeworm eggs in order to lose weight.) Usually, however, the symptoms are not obvious, and the human host is completely unaware of the existence of a tapeworm.

Blood flukes are widespread in China, Japan, the Middle East, and much of Africa. They cause a serious illness called schistoso-miasis. Flukes alternate between human hosts and a type of freshwater snail, and so people who bathe and wash in infested rivers are likely to become infected. The first signs of an infection are an itchy rash and a tingling where the fluke has penetrated the skin. Later, flulike symptoms develop, including fever, chills, and aches. The condition can lead to bladder tumors and kidney failure.

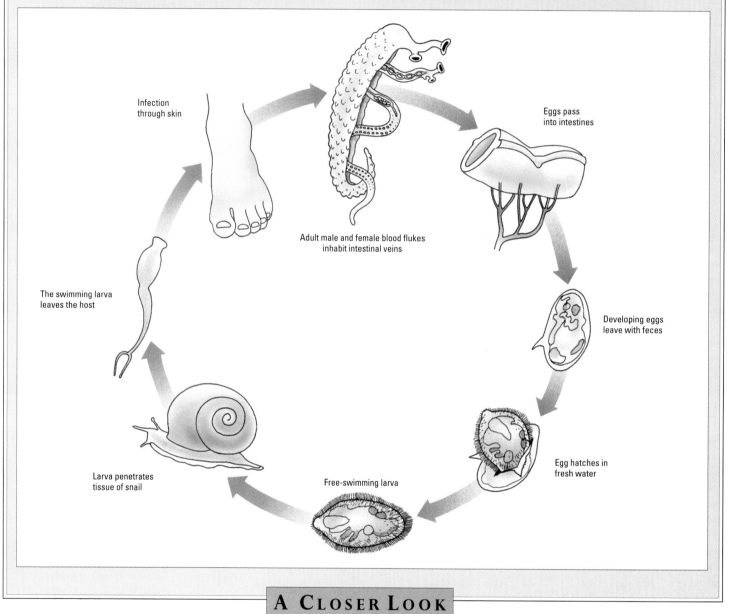

Infection through skin

Eggs pass into intestines

Adult male and female blood flukes inhabit intestinal veins

The swimming larva leaves the host

Developing eggs leave with feces

Larva penetrates tissue of snail

Free-swimming larva

Egg hatches in fresh water

A CLOSER LOOK

be projected out of the mouth during feeding. Free-living turbellarians have sensory organs that guide their movement. They have light-sensitive spots called ocelli on their head. Their body surface also contains tactile cells, which respond to touch, and chemoreceptors, which sense the presence of food.

Monogenea
Monogeneans are mainly external parasites of fish. They are adapted to living on the gills and external surfaces of fish, where they are exposed to strongly

flowing water currents. The larval stage is free living and attaches itself to a host fish, where it matures. A structure called the opishaptor allows these flatworms to keep a firm grip on their host.

Digenea
Digeneans, also known as flukes, have many adaptations that help them live inside another animal's body. Adults in this class are long and thin, a shape that allows them to travel through their host's blood vessels. They lack cilia but have hooks and suckers

to attach themselves to the host's tissues, and they have a protective outer covering that prevents them from being damaged by the host's enzymes or immune system.

Flukes feed on and damage vertebrate tissue (human and animal), including the liver, lungs, and muscle. The consequences can be serious. Blood flukes (*Schistosoma*) infect about 300 million people worldwide, causing a serious illness called schistosomiasis.

Cestoda

The class Cestoda contains tapeworms, which live inside the gut of vertebrates and include pork and beef tapeworms that can be passed onto humans through eating undercooked meat. They attach themselves to the gut wall of their host by an organ called a holdfast, or scolex. The exact structure of the holdfast varies with the species, but it generally consists of hooks, suckers, and spiny tentacles.

The tapeworm has no need for a mouth or for its own digestive system: instead it allows its host to do the work of digestion. The tapeworm is bathed by a "soup" of digested food, which it selectively absorbs through its body surface. The body is covered with small projections to increase the surface area. The tapeworm's cuticle also produces enzymes to enhance the absorption of nutrients.

The main problem for a parasite living in some animal's digestive tract is to avoid being digested itself, and a tapeworm's body is covered in an outer layer that resists the host's digestive enzymes. Cestodes also secrete enzyme inhibitors and acid to reduce their chances of being digested.

Tapeworms are made up of segments. New segments, called proglottids, are continually produced from behind the head. Each segment carries both male and female reproductive organs, and since the chance of two worms meeting is low, self-fertilization is common. The last segments at the tail end of the animal produce eggs. The eggs are shed and pass out of the host's body with its feces. Eventually they may be inadvertently eaten by another animal, and if the conditions are right, the eggs rapidly hatch into larvae.

Tapeworms can live only in a particular host or group of hosts, as they need a specific physical and chemical environment within the gut. Particular protein-digesting enzymes are needed before the eggs can hatch, and a specific type of bile and acidity are required to activate the embryos. The most common human tapeworm in the United States is the dwarf tapeworm (*Hymenolepsis nana*), which infects mainly children in the southeastern United States.

J. STIRLING

See also: ANIMAL KINGDOM; INVERTEBRATES; PARASITES.

Further reading:

Anderson, D. T. 2002. *Invertebrate Zoology.* Oxford: Oxford University Press.
Gittleman, A. M., and O. M. Amin. 2001. *Guess What Came To Dinner?: Parasites and Your Health.* New York: Avery Penguin Putnam.

REGENERATION

When humans cut themselves, the damaged skin and tissue respond and heal the wound. However, a human cannot regrow lost fingers or limbs. Nonparasitic flatworms can regenerate to a much greater extent. Regeneration depends on the ability of the remaining cells to grow the type of cells destroyed by an injury. The more complex an animal becomes, the less likely it is that all the cells can regenerate all parts of the body. Whole planarians, however, can be regenerated from any part of the worm. However, most parasitic flatworms cannot replace missing parts. The ability of a planarian to regenerate is greater the closer the damaged section is to the head end. A piece of planarian from near the tail takes a long time to regenerate a small head, while a piece taken from just below the head will quickly regenerate a new large head. If the planarian's head is cut down the middle, both sides will regenerate the missing piece of head, and the animal will then have two heads.

A CLOSER LOOK

*The tapeworm (*Taenia spp.*) has a knoblike scolex (headlike part), with suckers and hooks, which is used to anchor the worm to its host. Hosts include rodents, dogs, cattle, and humans.*

LIFE CYCLE OF THE BEEF TAPEWORM

Some tapeworms have a complicated life cycle involving more than one type of host. The beef tapeworm (*Taenia saginata*) alternates between humans and cattle. The microscopic larva lives inside a cyst within the muscle tissue of cattle. When beef from the cattle is eaten, human digestive juices break open the cyst and release the larva.

The larva matures into an adult in just a few weeks. It attaches itself to the gut wall using four suckers on its head. Just behind the head is a growing region, which produces body segments continually. The different segments are at various stages of development along the tapeworm's body, with those nearest the head being the youngest, and those farthest away the most mature.

Once the sections at the end of the body are ripe and full of eggs, they detach from the end of the tapeworm and are expelled with the host's feces. If a cow eats grass that is soiled by infected feces, the cycle begins again.

A CLOSER LOOK

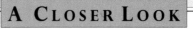

FLEAS

Fleas are wingless, parasitic insects that infest the skin, fur, or feathers of many mammals and some birds

Fleas are near-perfect parasites whose extraordinary jumping ability allows them to leap from host to host in search of blood. As they move, they carry diseases with them that have been a source of grief among humans for hundreds of years; millions have died in plague and typhus epidemics.

Fleas belong to a small order of insects called Siphonaptera (which means "sucking-tube without wings") that includes over 2,000 species and subspecies. All fleas are ectoparasites (living externally on a host); 96 percent of flea species live on mammals, and 4 percent live on birds.

Fleas can be separated into three distinctive (although nontaxonomic) groups based on their life history and habits. The first group, stick-tight fleas, which includes the chigoe (also called the jigger, *Tunga penetrans*), are species that feed at one site (actually living inside host tissues with an opening to the outside world) for a long time before seeking a new host. The second group, sedentary fleas, devote their whole life to one host, moving only when the grooming habits or death of their host forces them to do so. Those in the third and most common group, free-living (mobile) fleas, have a more varied lifestyle. The cat flea (*Ctenocephalides felis*), for example, usually roams from host to host. Free-living fleas carry most diseases.

Fleas are found nearly everywhere on Earth. Some have adapted to the freezing climate of the Poles, nourishing themselves on the blood of polar bears, Antarctic petrels (*Pelecanoides* spp.), and Arctic snowshoe hares (*Lepus americanus*). The chigoe flea lives only in the tropical climates of South and Central America and Africa.

Adaptations to a parasitic life

The entire biology of the flea is geared toward life as a blood parasite living in a constricting environment. With a body flattened like that of a fish and a helmet-shaped head that serves as a sort of plow, a flea easily maneuvers across the hairy terrain of its host. Retractable antennae and the absence of wings aid the flea's movement, while the sharp claws of its six legs allow it to cling tightly to hair, fur, feathers, or skin. Additional combs and bristles along the tough body further brace the flea when the host scratches in an attempt to dislodge this irritating pest.

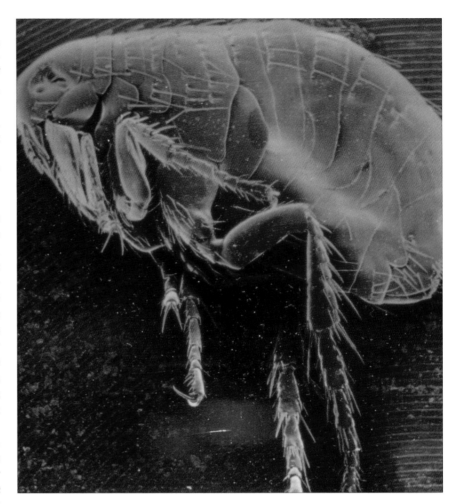

Fleas can jump up to 150 times their own length, with an acceleration at least 50 times that of a space shuttle at liftoff.

The flea draws blood through a long, piercing snout (a proboscis). An extended upper lip (stylet) pierces the host's skin, allowing the proboscis to enter. Inside the flea's head is a membrane made of resilin, the same elastic protein that gives the flea its jumping power (see the box on page 739). When the flea finds a particularly appetizing patch of host skin, the stylet muscles press a hammerlike bar against the resilin; when the muscles relax, the resilin plunges the bar down, and thus drives the stylet into the skin. The flea then injects its own saliva through the proboscis; the saliva contains enzymes that prevent the host's blood from clotting so that the flea can feed freely for several hours at a time.

Although their names suggest otherwise, some fleas feed on several hosts. The cat flea (*Ctenocephalides felis*) competes with the dog flea (*Ctenocephalides canis*) and has also found suitable living conditions on humans and livestock. Both dogs and cats can serve as temporary hosts for the human flea (*Pulex irritans*) and the bird flea (*Echidnophaga gallinacea*).

Other fleas are more particular about what kind of animal they can feed on and have adapted to life on a specific host. The bat flea (family Ischnopsyllidae), for example, which lives its entire life cycle on its flying host, has lost the ability to jump. The European

CORE FACTS

- Fleas are ectoparasites, living on their hosts as opposed to inside them, and are found on a variety of animals, including rats, dogs, humans, horses, and some birds.
- These tiny creatures have astonishing jumping power, some reaching distances 150 times their own length.
- Fleas are important vectors (carriers) of serious diseases, such as the bubonic and pneumonic plagues.

CONNECTIONS

- The bubonic plague (the black death) is one of the best-known examples of **INFECTIOUS DISEASES**. Others include malaria (spread by mosquitoes) and sleeping sickness (carried by tsetse flies).

- Unlike fleas, some **PARASITES**, such as tapeworms, live inside their host; they are called endoparasites.

rabbit flea (*Spilopsylla cuniculi*) has such an intimate relationship with its host that the hormone fluctuations of the rabbit's reproductive cycle dictate the flea's own breeding cycle.

Finding a host

Fleas have become masters of their environment. Changes in temperature, atmospheric conditions, and air currents can all warn the flea that a host is present. Some species can distinguish dark and light; a flea will thus jump toward a shadow, suspecting it is a potential host. Other cues from the host include body heat, exhalation of carbon dioxide, and smell. Fleas are also believed to be capable of orienting themselves in the direction of a vibration and have been known to pursue that cue over relatively long distances.

Life cycle

Like other insects, the flea goes through a complete cycle of metamorphosis. Eggs are sometimes deposited onto a host, but they eventually fall off and hatch into larvae somewhere within the host's habitat, often in or near a nest. The larvae feed off dirt, feces,

EVOLUTION OF FLEAS

Little is known about flea evolution. The oldest fossils belong to the family Hystrichopsyllidae (parasites of insectivores such as moles and shrews) and are found in Baltic amber, dating back some 50 million years. Scientists think fleas may have been around for a longer time, possibly 160 million years. Fleas probably evolved from winged nest scavengers. The idea that fleas may have once been able to fly is supported by traces of wings on flea pupae. From this scavenging lifestyle, fleas eventually developed the ability to feed directly on the blood of the animals they lived with. With such a nutritious and widely available food supply, fleas lost the wings, which would have hindered their progress through fur and feathers. Over time, fleas developed instead specialized legs and a body form that allowed them to leap and grapple and to become highly specialized and successful parasites.

EVOLUTION

HOW A FLEA JUMPS

Fleas have three pairs of jointed legs that are supported by powerful muscles, allowing them to spring freely forward or sideways on the host or to another host. The distance of the jump varies with the species; some can reach distances of 150 times their own length. The human flea, for example, measuring $\frac{2}{25}$ to $\frac{1}{10}$ inch (2 to 3 mm) in length, has been recorded as having jumped distances of 1 foot (30 cm).

Fleas' remarkable jumps are achieved by the contraction and expansion of a superelastic protein, resilin, in the helmet-shaped pleural arch—the part of the flea's thorax just above its long hind legs. As a flea gathers itself to jump, certain muscles in the rear leg (trochanter depressor muscles) distort the cuticle (the outer cover of the flea), and other muscles compress the pleural arch. A series of

plates in the flea's outer skeleton interlock, clamping the three segments of the thorax together. The rear legs are now raised, and the flea, resting on its trochanters (the bases of the legs), is poised for takeoff. When the flea is stimulated by the host, the muscles relax, and a sudden burst of energy down the cuticular ridge into the trochanters accelerates the flea away rapidly.

The recoil of this force is heard as a click. The leap is usually accompanied by a series of aerial acrobatics in which the flea flips end over end. To ensure a successful leap, the flea rotates either its second or third set of legs upward so that the dual claw at the end of each leg faces forward. In this way, no matter how it lands, the flea has a set of hooks ready to grab hold of its victim.

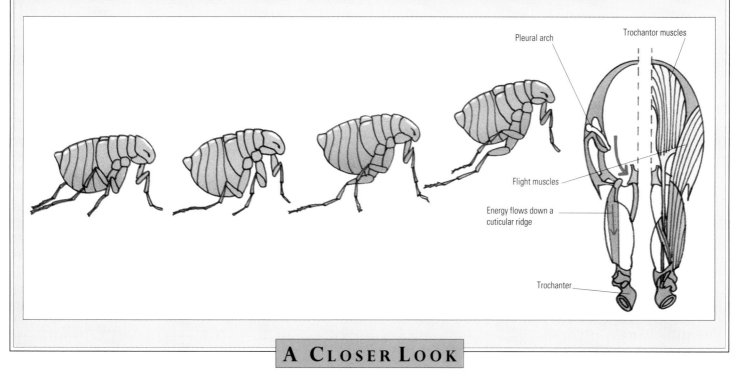

Pleural arch

Trochantor muscles

Flight muscles

Energy flows down a cuticular ridge

Trochanter

A CLOSER LOOK

FLEAS AS COMIC RELIEF

People have long endured the unpleasant company of fleas, but a number of ingenious pastimes make the best of that relationship. The art of clothing fleas may have been started by Mexican nuns. They created miniature images of the world around them, crafting delicate costumes in which to dress dead fleas. This practice continued into the early part of the 20th century, with a particular fascination for fleas dressed as brides and grooms.

The attraction of fleas as performers in the flea circus was recognized as early as the 16th century, although they did not reach the height of their popularity until the 1830s, under the Italian showman Signor Bertoletto. By harnessing their powerful hind legs, crafty entrepreneurs "trained" their fleas to pull miniature carriages, juggle balls with their feet, and dance under the skirts of tinfoil ballerinas. No training was really necessary, as the fleas labored instinctively as they attempted to escape. Human fleas were the usual performers, fed on the arm of their owner. The female was preferred over the male for her superior strength. Flea circuses are now rare, because modern hygiene has gradually reduced the human flea population and human interest has moved on to other pastimes.

and droplets of blood passed from the adult flea's anus. When mature, the individual larva constructs a cocoon of silk and organic debris, where it develops into a pupa. Pupation may last from five days to several months, depending on the species and stimuli such as temperature and physical pressure.

Once the adult flea has emerged from its cocoon, it attempts to find a host to feed on. Sometimes a suitable host may be nearby, but often none are to be found. The flea then has two options: to wait for a host to pass by or to venture out in search of a host. In both cases, the flea will limit its activity to habitats in which the hosts occur, thus increasing the chances of an encounter. The flea's survival rate is linked to its environment; it can live for a long time in moisture-saturated air, so it usually prefers to stay in humid conditions such as a burrow or a nest. In the right conditions, a cat flea can live without feeding for three to four weeks, while some flea species associated with rodents can survive for nearly a year.

Once they find a host, fleas begin to mate shortly after their first feed. In male cat fleas, sperm production increases progressively within the first 24 hours. Females can mate eight hours after they start feeding. The adult female produces eggs daily, an average of 10 a day in many species. The cat flea boasts the highest reproductive rate, producing over 50 eggs a day at its peak level, and has been reported to produce an average of 27 eggs a day over a period of 50 days.

Fleas and disease

As blood-feeding insects, fleas are ideally suited to carry diseases and to pass them to their hosts. In historic times, fleas have long been connected to the spread of bubonic plague and its related forms, pneumonic and septicemic plagues. The rat flea (*Xenopsylla cheopis*) carried the black death (named for the black patches that formed on the skin) that killed nearly 25 million Europeans during the 14th century. It introduced the plague into its human hosts after feeding off infected black rats.

When a flea feeds on a diseased host, *Yersenia pestis*, the bacteria that cause plague, stick to spines in the blood-filter chamber that leads to the flea's stomach and multiply rapidly until the chamber becomes blocked. When the hungry flea attempts to feed on a new host, it is unable to suck blood into its stomach, so the blood flows back into the host, carrying some bacteria with it.

Despite current knowledge of how this disease is spread and the development of pesticides and antibiotics, fleas continue to carry plague among rodents such as prairie dogs (*Cynomys* spp.), common rats (*Rattus rattus*), and rock squirrels (*Spermoophilus* spp.). If they move into human dwellings, these rodents expose bacteria-carrying fleas to people. People in areas without modern medical facilities are at particular risk, as without treatment, the mortality rate from bubonic plague can be more than 90 percent. About 3,000 cases of the plague are reported annually to the World Health Organization, which has described the disease as "an enemy in ambush."

J. SPIRRIZZI

CLASSIFICATION

There are three superfamilies of fleas: Pulicoidea (which contains most domestic fleas), Malacopsylloidea, and by far the largest, Ceratophylloidea.

The Pulicoidea comprises a single family of nearly 200 species, which include the best-known fleas, such as the Arctic hare flea (*Euhoplopsyllus glacialis*), the cat flea (*Ctenocephalides felis*), the hedgehog flea (*Archaeopsylla* spp.), the human flea (*Pulex irritans*), the plague flea (*Xenopsylla cheopis*), the rabbit flea (*Spilopsylla cuniculi*), and the chigoe (*Tunga penetrans*).

Malacopsylloidea, also comprising nearly 200 species, but in three families, include the alakurt (*Vermipsylla alakurt*), which parasitizes deer, yaks, goats, and horses in Central Asia, and penguin fleas (*Parapsyllus* spp.)

Ceratophylloidea number over 1,500 species, in 12 families, including the beaver flea (*Hystrichopsylla schefferi*), bird fleas (*Ceratophyllus, Callopsylla,* and *Frontopsylla* spp.), and the European rat flea (*Nosopsyllus fasciatus*).

See also: INSECTS; INVERTEBRATES; PARASITES.

Further reading:
Burgess, N. R. H. 1993. *A Color Atlas of Medical Entomology*. New York: Chapman & Hall Medical.
Stevens, K. 2000. *Fleas*. Naturebooks. Chanhassen, Minn.: Child's World.

FLEMING, ALEXANDER

Alexander Fleming discovered the so-called miracle drug penicillin

Alexander Fleming (1881–1955) dedicated his entire professional career to investigating the defenses of the human body to bacterial infections, but he is best remembered for his discovery of penicillin. In 1945 he was awarded the Nobel Prize in physiology or medicine along with Howard Florey (1898–1968) and Ernst Chain (1906–1979), who developed the enormous therapeutic power of penicillin.

Early life

Alexander Fleming was born in Lochfield, Ayrshire, Scotland on August 6, 1881. He was only seven when his father died, leaving his mother and an older brother to bring him up and manage the family farm. At 13 he was sent to London to live with his elder brother, Tom, who was a physician. Fleming completed his education at the Polytechnic School in Regent Street and then worked for a few years in a shipping office, but he did not enjoy it. When an uncle died leaving him a small legacy, he used it to study medicine, training at St Mary's Hospital Medical School in London. He remained there, except during World War I (1914–1918), for the rest of his career. Fleming became a doctor of medicine in 1908 and started work as junior assistant to Almroth Edward Wright, a prominent pathologist and well-known advocate of inoculation. They collaborated for over 40 years, during which time Fleming was appointed lecturer in bacteriology and later professor (in 1928). Fleming became one of the very few physicians in London able to administer salvarsan, a chemical treatment for syphilis developed by Paul Ehrlich (see EHRLICH, PAUL).

When war broke out in 1914, Fleming, along with most of his colleagues, joined the Royal Army Medical Corps. He was sent to a battlefield hospital laboratory in Boulogne, France, where he identified bacteria taken from soldiers' wounds before, during, and after surgery. Fleming quickly realized that chemical antiseptics could not sterilize wounds effectively. The infections were often so severe that soldiers quickly died from them. The impact of these deaths on Fleming was such that, after the war, he decided to focus his research on antibacterial substances (later called antibiotics). He was convinced that the ideal antiseptic should attack the microorganisms causing infection but leave natural body defenses unharmed.

Alexander Fleming examining a culture of penicillin in his laboratory at St Mary's Hospital, London, in 1943.

He condemned the use of ordinary germicides because they damaged white blood cells. Over the next ten years, Fleming discovered two natural antibacterial agents, lysozome and penicillin.

The discovery of penicillin

In 1922 Fleming discovered the antibacterial agent lysozome, an enzyme found in many body fluids. Although it neutralizes some bacteria, lysozome is not successful against other infectious organisms. Nevertheless, it proved to Fleming that substances harmless to body cells, but lethal to bacteria, did exist. In September 1928 Fleming noticed a mold growing in a petri dish containing strains of the *Staphylococcus* bacteria. More important, he observed that the bacteria surrounding the mold were being destroyed. He preserved the original culture plate and made a subculture of the mold in a tub of broth. The mold was later identified as *Penicillium notatum*. Because the substance was nontoxic to humans and did not interfere with the action of white blood cells, Fleming realized that penicillin could be of great human significance. He described his findings in a paper published in the *British Journal of Experimental Pathology* in 1929; it is now generally regarded as one of the most important medical papers ever written.

CORE FACTS

■ The discovery of penicillin happened by chance when a fungus contaminated one of Fleming's experiments.

■ Fleming was unable to stabilize penicillin, and so the intended clinical trials were abandoned.

■ Florey and Chain succeeded in isolating penicillin using an aqueous solvent, paving the way for mass production.

CONNECTIONS

● The discovery that pencillin inhibited the growth of **BACTERIA** was a major landmark in the history of medicine (see **MEDICINE, HISTORY OF**). Penicillin is still a front-line **ANTIBIOTIC** for treatment of infections.

Fleming continued to investigate the antibiotic properties of penicillin, collecting data that clearly established its chemotherapeutic potential. However, he was unable to purify and concentrate penicillin, and so the intended clinical trials were abandoned. Fleming's discovery therefore passed almost unnoticed until Florey and Chain succeeded in stabilizing pencillin so that it could be produced in volume. Fleming subsequently received many honors and awards for his work, including the 1945 Nobel Prize in physiologoy or medicine (with Florey and Chain) for the discovery of penicillin and its curative effect in various infectious diseases. He was knighted in 1944 and made commander of the French Legion of Honor in 1945. Fleming died in London on March 11, 1955. He is buried in St Paul's Cathedral.

Florey, Chain, and clinical development

Howard Walter Florey was born in Adelaide, Australia on September 24, 1898. From an early age he wanted to be a doctor, and in 1917 he attended medical school at the University of Adelaide, qualifying in 1921. In 1922 he received a scholarship to study at the Honours Physiology School in Oxford, England, and it was here that he first became interested in pathology (the study of diseases). He then spent a year in Cambridge, England, and another in the United States as a Rockefeller Foundation traveling fellow. On his return to England, he worked in London, Cambridge, and Sheffield before being elected professor of the Sir William Dunn School of Pathology at Oxford in 1935. He held this post for 27 years until 1962.

Enrst Chain was born in Berlin, Germany, on June 19, 1906. Chain was always interested in chemistry, probably because his father, a chemist and industrialist, frequently took him to his laboratory and factory. Chain studied biochemistry at Freidrich Wilhelm University in Berlin, graduating in 1930. For the next three years he carried out enzyme research at the Charité Hospital in Berlin. However, when Adolf Hitler became chancellor in 1933, Chain left Germany and went to England. For two years he worked in Cambridge on a variety of subjects, including snake venoms and tumor metabolism. He moved to Oxford in 1935, and it was there that Chain met Florey.

Florey and Chain discussed the possibility of working together on a systematic study of the antibacterial products of microorganisms. They obtained financial support for this research in 1939 from the Medical Research Council and the Rockefeller Foundation. Chain had already discovered Fleming's earlier work on penicillin, so they knew penicillin was active against *Staphylococcus* bacteria, but there was still the biochemical challenge of stabilizing it. They decided to reinvestigate.

In 1940, working with their colleague Norman Heatley, they discovered one of the key steps in isolating penicillin. Instead of extracting it into an organic solvent, they simply used a neutral aqueous (water-based) solution. Florey had also experimented with impure penicillin by treating mice infected with *Streptococcus pyogenes*. The untreated mice died within 15 hours, whereas those that had been given penicillin remained healthy. The next step was a clinical trial on humans. In February 1941 they gave penicillin to a patient with severe streptococcal and staphylococcal infections. Although his condition improved dramatically, he eventually died because the supply of penicillin was inadequate. Florey and Chain realized that a large continual supply of penicillin was essential. As England was now heavily involved in World War II (1939–1945), Florey and Heatley went to the United States and, with the help of the U.S. government, persuaded American pharmaceutical companies to mass-produce penicillin. By 1944 there was enough of it to treat all Allied troop casualties in Europe. Soon penicillin was being used against a range of different diseases, and after 1944 the number of people dying from infection plummeted.

Like Fleming, both Florey and Chain were honored for their work. Besides recognition by various scientific bodies, Florey was awarded a knighthood in 1944 and membership of Britain's Order of Merit in 1965. Florey died on February 21, 1968; Chain died in 1979.

P. NEUSHUL/K. DENNIS-BRYAN

See also: ANTIBIOTICS AND ANTIMICROBIALS; ANTIBODIES; ANTISEPSIS; ERHLICH, PAUL.

Further reading

Bickel, L. 1996. *Florey: The Man Who Made Penicillin.* Melbourne: Melbourne University Press. Tocci, S. 2002. *Alexander Fleming: The Man Who Discovered Penicillin.* Berkeley Heights, N.J.: Enslow.

WHAT IS PENICILLIN?

Originally penicillin was the name used to describe the antibiotic derived from the fungus *Penicillium*. It became medically important because it killed many of the bacteria that cause human diseases and was particularly effective in treating wound infections during World War II. Penicillin prevents the peptide chains of peptidoglycan, one of the main constituents of bacterial cell walls, from cross-linking and thus reduces cell wall rigidity. New cells grow but cannot divide and so do not multiply. The weakened cell walls eventually collapse, and the bacteria die. Most antibiotics target peptidoglycan because it is unique to bacteria, while others inhibit protein synthesis. Although penicillin has a devastating effect on bacteria, it is not toxic to humans, so there are few if any side effects.

The use of penicillin increased when the natural forms were chemically modified. The new variants, such as ampicillin, could be taken by mouth and were effective against an even wider range of bacteria. The success of penicillin encouraged scientists to look for other microorganisms that produce a similar antibacterial action. Among fungi they found antibiotics such as griseofulvin and cephalosporins. They also discovered streptomycin, which is produced by soil actinobacteria of the genus *Streptomyces*. These organisms, which have stringy threads similar to fungal hyphae, are responsible for most of the antibiotics now used in medicine. Some bacteria, such as *Staphylococcus*, have developed resistance to antibiotics, but penicillin is still regularly prescribed to combat common infections.

FLIES

Flies are winged insects in the order Diptera

This closeup of a housefly's head shows its large compound eyes and proboscis.

CONNECTIONS

● Flies have been the scourge of humankind for centuries as carriers of **INFECTIOUS DISEASES.**

● Many flies play a vital role in the **POLLINATION** of **FLOWERS.** In this role, they function much like **WASPS AND BEES,** and **ANTS.**

● Flies have keen senses. They have large compound **EYES** and **ANTENNAE** to detect changes in their environment.

From houseflies to horse flies and midges to mosquitoes, flies are among the most familiar of all the insects. There are between 85,000 and 150,000 different species (scientists are still not certain), of which about 17,000 live in North America. Some flies have a bad reputation for carrying diseases, damaging crops, soiling our food, and being household pests, but flies are also important pollinators, and by feeding on decomposing plant and animal matter, flies recycle valuable nutrients through ecosystems.

Flies belong to the order Diptera (from the Latin for "two wings"). They are often called true flies to distinguish them from other insects with the word *fly* in their name, such as dragonflies and stoneflies. Diptera are divided into three groups (suborders). Midges, gnats, mosquitoes, and crane flies belong to the suborder Nematocera. Horseflies, bee flies, and robber flies are placed in the Brachycera. Houseflies, fruit flies, and blowflies are in the suborder Cyclorrhapha. Flies range in size from tiny midges only $\frac{1}{20}$ inch (1.3 mm) long to mydas flies that measure 2 inches (5 cm) in length.

Most flies live in temperate and tropical climates. They are the most commonly found insects in temperate regions and are second only to beetles in the tropics. Flies can also survive in the harsh environments of deserts and polar fringes.

Many flies resemble other insects, particularly bees and wasps. This mimicry may protect them from predators who usually avoid insects that sting (see CAMOUFLAGE AND MIMICRY).

Distinguishing features

True flies have one pair of wings, unlike most other insects, which have two pairs. The ancestors of flies had a second pair of wings, but over time, these evolved into two small club-shaped rods called halteres. Halteres are balancing organs that monitor how the body moves during flight and allow the fly to maneuver while flying. Many flies are brown or black and covered with a fine coating of hairs called tomentum. Flies in desert regions are often pale colored. The body is covered by an outer covering of chitin, called the integument. The feet (tarsi) are divided into five segments. All flies have mouthparts that are adapted for lapping, sucking, or piercing. Flies also undergo complete metamorphosis during their life cycle, that is, they change form throughout their life. They begin as eggs, which hatch into larvae. The larvae develop into pupae, and the pupae finally develop into adults.

Senses

Most adult flies have two sets of eyes. A set of single, simple eyes (ocelli) and a pair of large compound eyes. The fly's set of single ocelli are found on top of the head. These eyes usually sense light intensity and are not used for vision. The fly's compound eyes are made up of many ocelli side by side, each with its own nerve and a six-sided lens (known as a facet). There can be many thousands of facets in each eye. Compound eyes enable flies to see movement in many directions.

Flies have two antennae on the front of the head between the eyes. Hairs arising from antennae joints are stimulated by touch and are sensitive to pheromones and odors carried on air currents. The size and shape of the antennae vary among different species and can even vary between males and females of the same species.

Mouthparts

All adult flies feed on liquids from animal or vegetable matter, which they suck or lap. A strawlike tube (the proboscis) extends down from the head. The major sucking organ, the labium, has a central groove to direct liquid into the mouth. The tip of the labium expands to form two spongelike lobes (labellae), each of which absorbs and carries liquids to the groove.

Even though the popular names of several fly species include the word *biting*, flies do not bite or chew because they cannot open their jaws. In some flies, biting midges, mosquitoes, and black flies, for

---

CORE FACTS

■ Although many insects can fly, true flies, the Diptera, have only one pair of wings.

■ The Diptera include gnats, mosquitoes, horseflies, houseflies, frit flies, and fruit flies.

■ All flies have mouthparts that are adapted to suck or lap liquid food. Some have piercing mouthparts to feed on the blood of other animals.

■ Flies are responsible for transmitting many human diseases, including malaria and yellow fever.

example, the females have mouthparts (mandible and maxilla) that are shaped like blades inside the proboscis. The bladelike mouthparts are called stylets. The females of these species feed on blood. The stylets pierce the skin and blood vessels of the host, and the female fly sucks the host animal's blood. The males do not have a mandible; they feed on flower nectar instead. Some flies without stylets can still pierce the skin of an animal host. The males and females of the tsetse fly and stable fly use their hardened labium and labella for piercing. Robber flies use their hypopharynx to pierce flying insects and suck them dry. After piercing the skin of their victim, blood-sucking flies inject saliva into the wound. It contains substances that cause the victim's blood vessels to dilate and prevent the blood from clotting, making feeding easier.

Movement

Flies have one pair of wings and three pairs of jointed legs. The wings of flies are generally transparent and are efficient and powerful: some midges can beat their wings 1,000 times a second. The wings have veins, and sometimes crossveins, that act as supports. Strong muscles attached to the inside wall of the thorax move the fly's wings and legs. A fly becomes airborne as soon as it beats its wings. The wings continue to beat until the fly's feet touch something the fly can land on. The strong, well-developed legs of predatory flies, such as the robber flies, are used for grasping their prey, usually other insects.

The halteres that lie behind the wings each consist of a narrow stalk with a clubbed head. During flight, they vibrate and act as tiny gyroscopes, making it easy for the fly to dart in any direction.

Life cycle

The life cycle of all Diptera consists of four stages: egg, larva, pupa, and adult. The larvae looks quite different from the adults and often live in a different habitat. For example, mosquito larvae live in water, while the adults do not. The two separate lifestyles benefit the flies and allow them to adapt to environmental changes. In fact, some flies such as midges, spend most of their life as larvae and live as adults for only a short time.

All adult female flies produce eggs. A few species, including the tsetse fly, hatch their eggs internally and keep the larvae inside a kind of uterus until they are fully grown. Many females have an extendable structure at the end of the abdomen for laying eggs, called an ovipositor, which allows the female to deposit her eggs in out-of-the-way places where food will be available for the larvae and where they will be less susceptible to predation or parasitism. Deposits may be on the ground, in plant crevices or dead wood, or buried in garbage or dung. Eggs of mosquitoes and other flies that have aquatic larvae are laid on the surface of water.

The larvae spend most of their time feeding, and the larval stage may last for days or months. As the larvae grow, they molt (shed their outer covering) periodically. Those in primitive fly families have four to nine molts, while more highly evolved families usually have three. Larvae do not have jointed legs or any wings. The larvae of primitive fly families have pseudopods (false legs), like those of caterpillars, and

MOSQUITOES AND MALARIA

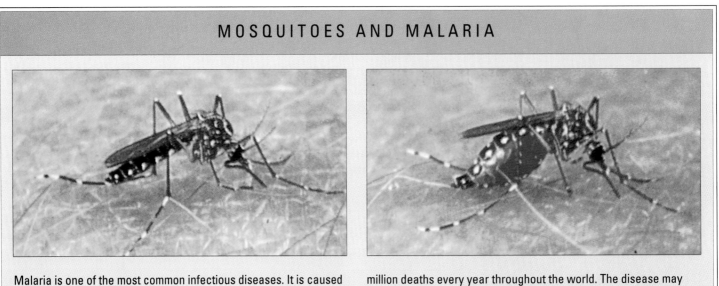

Malaria is one of the most common infectious diseases. It is caused by a protozoan called *Plasmodium*. The protozoan is injected directly into the human bloodstream by a female *Anopheles* mosquito as she feeds. The mosquito pierces the host's skin, and then injects saliva into the wound that dilates the blood vessels and ensures a constant flow of blood. The mosquito's saliva may contain the malarial protozoans if it has previously fed off the blood of an infected person. Malarial symptoms include periods of chills, sweating and fever, anemia, and enlargement of the spleen. It causes about a million deaths every year throughout the world. The disease may have been introduced to the United States by the early visits of Europeans. Malaria can also be transmitted by contaminated hypodermic syringes or via a transfusion of contaminated blood. Effective treatment is based on quinine, a substance taken from the bark of the cinchona tree. Programs to eradicate mosquitoes have been introduced in tropical areas where the disease is common. Adults are killed with insecticide sprays, and the water where the larvae breed is covered with a film of oil to prevent them from breathing.

A CLOSER LOOK

well-formed heads. Most fly larvae, like adult flies, breath through small openings known as spiracles.

When the larva is fully grown, it enters pupation, during which the characteristics of the larva disappear and are replaced by the adult features. The pupae of more primitive families are sometimes enclosed in a cocoon of silk, which may be covered with sand or soil. The shape of the head, wings, legs, and other features can often be seen through the covering.

In some fly species, pupation takes place in a puparium: a coat that forms when the larval skin hardens. The aquatic pupae of mosquitoes may swim about, but the pupae of most flies are more or less inactive. Some flies break out of the cocoon or puparium before moving to the surface of the soil or water; others, by wriggling back and forth, push the puparium to the surface and then emerge from it.

When the adult leaves its puparium, its body and wings are soft and crumpled. The body expands and hardens as the body fluids flow through the veins. If males and females emerge from the pupal stage at the same time, they mate as soon as body hardening is completed. In species where the males and females emerge at different times, the two sexes must search for one another in order to mate. For some species, such as nonbiting midges, adulthood lasts only long enough to mate and lay eggs.

The most familiar fly

The most familiar fly is the housefly (*Musca domestica*). Housefly larvae grow in almost any damp, decaying organic matter, such as carrion, garbage, manure, and even wet newspapers. This versatility has enabled the housefly to accompany humans to almost all parts of the world. Houseflies are responsible for transmitting many of the world's most miserable diseases, including typhoid and dysentery.

Houseflies do not have piercing mouthparts. They have two soft, oval-shaped labellae, which they use like sponges to mop up liquids. When the housefly feeds, it changes solid food into a liquid form by depositing saliva on it. Most of the drop is sucked back in through a long proboscis, but some remains on the food. This liquid may contain disease-causing organisms from previous feedings, possibly from excrement or other infected fly saliva.

When a housefly lands on a piece of food, it walks around it, carefully testing whether it is edible or a suitable site for laying eggs. The hairs on the fly's feet react to the chemicals present in the food in much the same way that taste buds in humans react to flavors. The fly can also sense the moisture content and texture of the material. If the material is judged suitable for eating, the fly will taste it with its palpi (small, antenna-like feelers around its mouth) before lowering its tubelike proboscis. Fine hairs around the lower edge of the labellae enable the fly to taste as it eats. The process during which saliva flows down the proboscis to dissolve the food does not turn everything into a liquid. The remaining tiny particles are sent through a separate tube to an inner sac, the crop, for storage. Solids repeatedly travel to and from the crop

until they are digested. This regurgitation process often takes place on new food sources, and if the solids contain harmful microorganisms, it also contributes to the spread of disease.

Houseflies are meticulous about their personal grooming. Using their leg bristles as combs, they clean their legs, head, proboscis, abdomen, and eyes. Grooming is essential to survival. Even the smallest particle on their ultrathin wings would interfere with their balance while flying.

Flies have a variety of senses. The fine hairs on a housefly's short, thick antennae respond to the chemicals in odors by twitching, sending signals to the central nervous system. Thick bristles on the housefly's legs and thorax respond to the movement of air. Bristles on the legs vibrate to sound waves at different speeds and rhythms, providing a type of hearing. In addition to their compound eyes, which have around 4,000 facets, houseflies have three simple eyes (ocelli) in a triangle between their compound eyes.

Attached to the last segment of a housefly's feet are two adhesive pads (pulvilli) and two claws. The claws enable houseflies to clutch rough surfaces. The pulvilli, like small suction cups, enable them to walk on smooth or slippery surfaces.

Compound eyes, an ability to walk on almost any surface, and a sensitive sense of smell, touch, and hearing give houseflies an advantage over their predators, even humans armed with a fly swatter.

Houseflies can live from two weeks to three months, depending on the temperature, humidity, and availability of water. Houseflies die if the temperature falls below 32 °F (0 °C) or rises above 115 °F (46.5 °C). Under certain conditions, a housefly's body can shut down temporarily (a state called diapause) and revive when conditions return to normal. Flies can enter diapause at any stage of their life cycle. Most of the eggs laid in late summer and early fall go into diapause until spring.

Many fly larvae (center) feed on decaying plant or animal matter. The female fly lays her eggs on material, such as this rotting flesh, that will provide the larvae with a good supply of food.

THE FRUIT FLY AND SCIENTIFIC RESEARCH

Leave a bowl of fruit out in the summer, and you will soon see tiny, red-eyed flies attracted by the odor. These are fruit flies (also known as vinegar flies) belonging to the genus *Drosophila*. Fruit flies have played a very important role in helping geneticists discover the rules of inheritance.

In 1910 a U.S. scientist named Thomas Hunt Morgan (1866–1945) discovered a fruit fly that had white eyes instead of the usual red. After carefully mating this fly and its offspring for many generations, he concluded that some traits are sex linked: that is, the genetic information needed to make white eyes is on one of the chromosomes that help determine sex (although white eyes are found in both males and females). The work by Morgan and his students also helped establish the chromosome theory of inheritance—that genetic information is carried by specific chromosomes. He was awarded the Nobel prize in physiology or medicine for his work in 1933. Fruit flies have contributed to science in other ways. Using fruit flies, another U.S. scientist, Hermann Joseph Müller (1890–1967), proved that X rays can cause changes in genetic material. Called mutations, these changes can cause harmful defects in the body. Müller found that X rays increased the mutation rate 150 times. He drew attention to the danger of X-ray radiation to humans. Müller was awarded the Nobel prize in physiology or medicine in 1946.

More recently, fruit flies have been used to study the way genes control development and evolution. Some mutations, called homeotic mutations, change one body part of a fruit fly into another part, mimicking the body plan of more primitive insects. For example, one mutation partially changes the halteres of a fly into wings. Another mutation changes the antennae of the fly into legs.

A CLOSER LOOK

Economic importance

Among the various insects that plague humans or act as carriers of disease, none equals Diptera. Flies feed and lay their eggs on rotting material that may contain germs. The fly's mouthparts and feet become contaminated with germs. If the fly then walks over food or kitchen utensils, they will also become contaminated. Cholera and salmonella can be transmitted in this way. Many types of flies also feed on blood and during this process transmit disease-causing microorganisms from host to host. A large number of bacterial, viral, and protozoan infections are transmitted to humans in this way. Among the diseases that Diptera transmit to humans are malaria, cholera, yellow fever, and African sleeping sickness.

In developing countries, millions of children die each year from dehydration caused by severe diarrhea transmitted by flies.

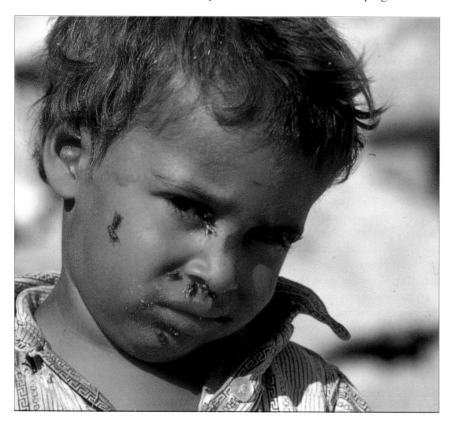

The larvae of certain species can also parasitize humans and other animals directly. Warble flies and botflies lay their eggs on a mammalian host. When the eggs hatch, the larvae burrow through the skin into the flesh or enter the host's body through openings such as the nostrils. The maggots live within the host animal's tissues, emerging when they are ready to pupate. The sores caused by the feeding larvae are open to infections. Cattle grubs, ox warble flies, and sheep botflies infect agricultural animals, irritating their skin and ruining their hides for the leather trade.

Frit flies damage agricultural crops by feeding on young crop plants, such as oats. Other species can affect the appearance of fruit, such as apples, so that, although the tree is not damaged, the fruit is not fit for sale. Those species injurious to crops belong to about a half dozen families.

On the positive side, flies are important recyclers of organic material. The larvae of blowflies (green- and bluebottle flies) and other related families provide an ecological cleaning service by feeding on carcasses and other organic debris. Some flies are very helpful to humans. The larvae of tachina flies feed on insects that attack crops, and the adults pollinate flowers.

More recently, flies such as blowflies and flesh flies are proving valuable in forensic science. The rate at which some species of flies develop on corpses and the species of flies present can offer clues as to time of death and method of death, and can help tell if the body has been moved from one place to another.

M. DICANIO

See also: ARTHROPODS; CAMOUFLAGE AND MIMICRY; FORENSIC SCIENCE; GILLS AND SPIRACLES; INSECTS; INVERTEBRATES; LARVAE AND PUPAE; METAMORPHOSIS.

Further reading:

Brookes, M. 2002. *Fly: The Unsung Hero of Twentieth-Century Science*. New York: Ecco Press.
Miller, S. S. 1998. *From Flower Flies to Mosquitoes*. New York: Franklin Watts, Inc.

FLIGHT

Many animals are able to fly through the air. Some, such as flying squirrels and flying lizards, glide through their forest habitats, but the only animals that truly power their flight by flapping their wings are birds, bats, and insects. In order to fly, an animal such as a bird must generate enough forward and upward force to counter the effects of two resisting forces. The first of these resisting forces, weight, is caused by Earth's gravity which pulls objects toward Earth. The second, drag, is caused by the resistance of air to objects moving through it.

Flight basics

In cross section, the wings of all flying animals form a teardrop shape called an airfoil, with the bulge at the front (called the leading edge) and the point at the back. The shape of an airfoil has an important influence on air moving over it. Air traveling over the top of an airfoil has farther to travel and therefore moves more quickly than the air traveling underneath. This situation causes a pressure difference that creates an upward-acting force on the wing. This force is called lift, and it counteracts the weight of the bird. For the bird to counter the effects of drag, however, another force is required. This force is called thrust. Flying animals generate thrust by flapping their wings.

CORE FACTS

- Only insects, birds, bats, and the extinct pterosaurs have evolved the capability for true powered flight, although many other animals are able to glide or parachute.
- Flight allows animals to escape from predators, to search out food in other areas, and to hide their young in inaccessible places.
- The main disadvantage of flight is that it requires relatively large amounts of energy.

How wings work

To move forward, flying animals alter the shape and angle of their wings during the wing stroke. There must be differences in thrust between the downstroke and upstroke. Different birds flap their wings in different ways to achieve thrust. The wings of small birds, such as starlings, and those with relatively small wings, such as ducks, are held out flat during the downstroke, but during the upstroke, the wing is held in close to the body to minimize drag.

When taking off from the ground, larger birds use a similar stroke, but once airborne, they flap their wings in a different manner. During the upstroke, the wingtip is withdrawn just a little, but the rest of the wing is not drawn in tight. These different wing strokes have major effects on the aerodynamics of

Bats evolved after birds but exploited a new niche by foraging for food at night. One species, the Azorean bat (Nyctalus azoreum), lives on the Azores—islands free of avian predators. This species is unique in that it forages for food in the day.

CONNECTIONS

- Flight allows animals to find food. **BIRDS OF PREY** possess acute **VISION** so that they can spy their food from the sky. **BATS** use **ECHOLOCATION** to locate their food in the dark. They emit high-pitched sounds and can detect the echoes with astonishing accuracy.

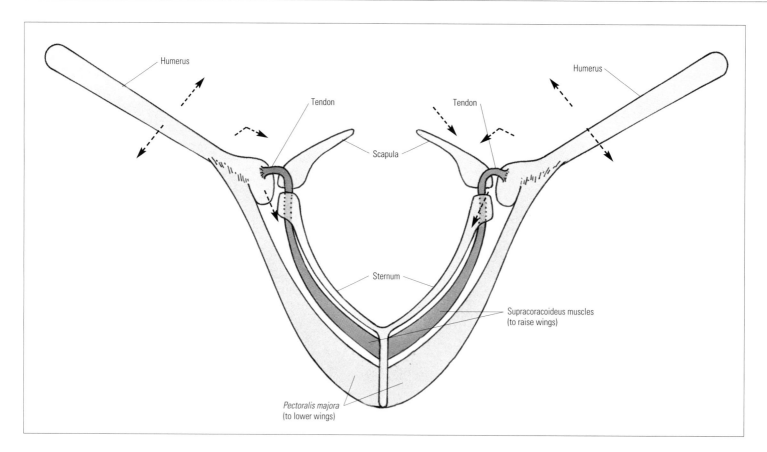

Humerus

Tendon

Tendon

Humerus

Scapula

Sternum

Supracoracoideus muscles
(to raise wings)

Pectoralis majora
(to lower wings)

The pectoralis majora *are the largest muscles in the body of flying birds. Powering the downstroke, they provide thrust to the bird in flight.*

the animal. Owing to the pressure differences over the wing, air moves around it to form a rotating swirl of air called a bound vortex. As the bird moves forward, the vortex is shed behind the bird—the strength of the vortex is closely linked to the lift and is related to the mass and speed of the bird.

Since air is transparent, studying these swirls of air may seem challenging, but scientists have used a novel technique to observe them. Air in a tunnel is seeded with tiny soap bubbles filled with helium; the bird flies through the bubble cloud, and the movement of the air translates into movements of the bubbles. Scientists found that the vortices produced by large birds with pointed wings, such as kestrels, form a pair of tubes called a continuous vortex, which follows the path of the bird's wingtips as it flies. Vortices of smaller birds with more rounded wings are very different. They form doughnut-shaped rings in the air, with each downstroke producing a separate doughnut. Experiments with insects and bats have shown that these animals also produce vortex rings in flight.

Bats have few problems taking off: they drop into the air from their perches. For birds on the ground, however, takeoff is more problematic since gravity must be overcome. Birds coincide a leap into the air with a downstroke from the wings to get them going. All birds use the vortex-ring stroke during takeoff; it is only at higher speeds that some birds switch to the continuous stroke instead.

The story of flight

Soon after their ancestors invaded the land, around 400 million years ago, insects developed wings and took to the skies. Of modern-day insects, all but a couple of wingless groups are descended from these ancient animals. Insect wings may have evolved from outgrowths of the thorax or perhaps the gills; they may first have been modified into flaps to help the insect warm up in the sun. Later, the flaps developed into gliding surfaces and then functional wings.

During the Permian, around 250 million years ago, some winged insects grew to tremendous sizes. *Meganeura*, for example, was a dragonfly with a wingspan of more than 30 inches (75 cm). Above a certain size, the tracheal (breathing) system of insects becomes rather inefficient, but paleontologists think the oxygen content of the air was much higher in the Permian. The high oxygen concentration permitted these insects to oxygenate their tissues well enough to allow them to fly.

Around 245 million years ago, Earth suffered a cataclysmic mass extinction—around 90 percent of all life disappeared. In the aftermath, the survivors quickly radiated into new niches, and several groups of reptiles took to the air. *Longisquama* glided on long featherlike shafts on its back, while *Sharovipteryx* glided with a membrane shaped just like the delta wing of a Concorde airplane. However, only one group—the pterosaurs—truly flew. Over the next 160 million years, these reptiles diversified into a wide range of sizes and lifestyles. *Pterodactylus* were small, sparrow-sized pterosaurs, while *Quetzalcoatlus* was the largest flying animal ever known. This pterosaur, which soared above Earth 70 million years ago, had a wingspan of around 50 feet (15 m). Like birds, pterosaurs were probably warm blooded—exceptional fossils of one species, *Sordes pilosus*, have shown that these pterosaurs bore a pelt of fine hair over their bodies.

Around 150 million years ago, pterosaurs were joined in the sky by birds. Birds evolved from small therapod dinosaurs—a fact conclusively proved by scientists in the late 1990s, following almost a century of vehement debate, with the discovery of a suite of feathered dinosaurs in Liaoning, China. Ancient birds looked different from those of today. Many, such as archaeopteryx, bore teeth, for example, a characteristic retained by some groups long after the appearance of beaked species, such as *Confuciusornis*.

Following the extinction of the dinosaurs around 65 million years ago, bats took to the wing. Their evolution remains enigmatic, since the earliest bat fossils, such as *Icaronycteris* from the Eocene (55 million years ago) of what is now Wyoming, are morphologically almost identical to modern species. Some scientists think that fruit bats are more closely related to primates than other bats, so flight may have evolved independently in this group.

Advantages and disadvantages

Being able to fly can be very useful. It enables animals to escape from predators, especially predators that cannot fly. It also allows them to keep their young safe in places above ground, such as in trees, on cliffs, or on mountainsides. Flighted species can spread out and colonize new areas quickly. Some can migrate to other areas in search of food; birds and some bats and insects (such as locusts), travel over large distances. Being able to fly allows these animals to cross oceans, mountain ranges, and deserts. The Arctic tern (*Sterna paradisea*) migrates between the Arctic and Antarctic throughout the year, enjoying perpetual summer weather as it travels. The direct journey covers 9,000 miles (14,484 km), although many terns do not follow the direct

PARACHUTING AND GLIDING

The only true fliers living now are bats, birds, and insects. However, animals from a wide variety of other groups transport themselves through the air by parachuting and gliding. Parachuting is controlled falling, and it uses the forces of gravity and drag. A number of frog species are well adapted for parachuting. Wallace's flying frog (*Rhacophorus nigropalmatus*) has webbing between its fingers and toes. It splays out its limbs as it leaps from the canopy of the rain forest and thus increases drag and slowing its fall.

Gliding involves both horizontal and vertical movements. There is an extraordinarily diverse range of gliders, including flying fish (family Exocoetidae), flying lizards (*Draco* spp.) from southern Asia, the North American flying squirrels (*Glaucomys* spp.), flying lemurs (order Dermoptera), and even flying snakes (*Chrysopelea* spp.) and squid (*Onychoteuthis* spp.). All gliders have surfaces on their bodies that provide lift; for example, flying squirrels have flaps of skin between the fore- and hind limbs, while flying lizards can flip out their modified, skin-covered ribs to form a wing. Many gliders live in trees, so they can easily glide downward. However gliders that live under water, such as flying fish, have no such luxury and must build up speed beneath the surface before takeoff.

Although these amazing animals can launch themselves into the air, they are passive fliers. The gliding surface produces lift to counter the weight of the animal, but it does not produce thrust, and so drag causes the animal to gradually lose altitude until it lands.

*A North American flying squirrel (*Glaucomys volans*) takes to the air. These creatures look like flying lemurs and sugar gliders but are not closely related. This resemblance is an example of convergent evolution.*

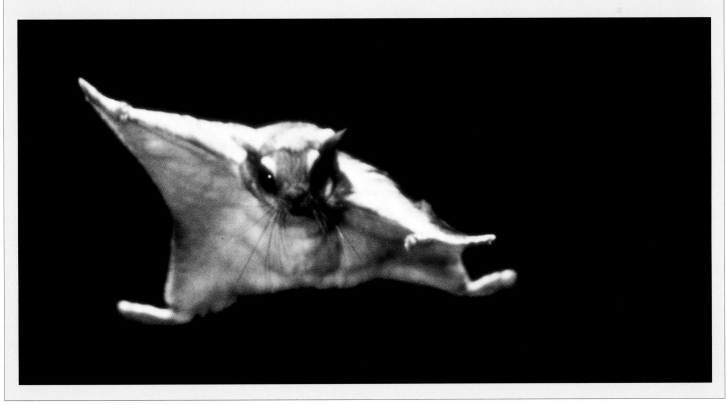

Scientists often use multiflash photography—the exposure of several flashes of flight on a single photographic film plate—to track the speed of an animal and the changes in the orientation of the wings and body.

route and cover even longer distances. This is the longest-known migration of any animal species.

The main disadvantage of flight is the large amount of energy it requires. To provide this energy, the animal must be able to find a large amount of food. Birds that eat while they fly have to carry extra weight around in the form of food. A small bird like the spotted flycatcher (*Muscicapa striata*) can generate enough energy to carry a quantity of food equal to its own weight. Larger birds, such as vultures, may pay a high price for gorging themselves. Feeding for these birds can be infrequent, so when they find a carcass, they gorge themselves, storing some of the food in the crop. The increase in mass can cause problems during

takeoff, and if confronted by a predator, they may need to discard some of the stored food.

Adaptations for flight

To be able to fly, an animal needs wings that can provide a surface large enough to produce adequate lift. Wings must also be relatively light and flexible. Insect wings, which are located on the thorax, are made of a thin membrane that is stiffened by tiny veins. Flies have one functional pair of wings, with the hind pair modified into balance organs called halteres. Stylopids have a similar system, although their halteres are formed from the forewings. Beetle forewings are also modified; they form tough cases called elytra that protect the delicate hind wings at rest. Other insects have two pairs of wings, and since the first pair creates air turbulence, most four-winged insects avoid a problem by linking their fore- and hind wings with hooks or other coupling systems. The insects can then function as a two-winged insect. Butterflies, for example, bear an elaborate ratchet system on their wings to hold them together. Two groups, dragonflies and grasshoppers, have no wing-coupling system; instead, their wings beat completely out of phase to minimize turbulence.

The wings of insects developed from gills or outgrowths of exoskeleton from the thorax. By contrast, the wings of bats, birds, and pterosaurs are modified forelimbs. In each of these groups, the development of a suitable wing came about in a different way. Bat wings were formed from elongated bones of the hand, while bird wings consist of the arm bones

---

DO FISH REALLY FLY?

About 50 species of fish in the family Exocetidae can be seen sweeping over the sea. Are they actually flying? The fish have greatly enlarged pectoral fins that resemble the wings of birds. However, unlike birds' wings, the fins are held out at a fixed angle and do not move up and down, so they cannot propel the fish through the air. To take off, the fish accelerate before leaping up out of the water, sometimes taxiing on the surface for a short distance. However, they remain airborne solely through lift—they do not flap their wings, and there is no thrust. Flying fish do not fly—they glide.

Most flying fish reach a height of no more than about 3 feet (99 cm) above the waves, but they can travel impressive distances; some four-winged flying fish can cover more than 650 feet (200 m). Gliding in flying fish has evolved as a defense against predators such as tuna and dolphins.

HUMAN ATTEMPTS AT FLIGHT

People have been fascinated with the idea of flight since ancient times. Many myths and legends focused on people or gods taking to the skies. The first documented attempt to emulate birds took place in 875 CE. A Moorish scientist, Ibn Firnas, built a machine that allowed him to glide from the top of a mountain near Cordoba, Spain. A monk named Eilmer performed a similar feat in 1000 CE. Eilmer strapped wooden boards to his arms before leaping from the top of Malmesbury Abbey, England. He glided for several hundred feet before crashing and breaking both legs. The intrepid Eilmer survived, but it would be hundreds of years before further advances in human flight would take place. Many thinkers devoted their time to dreaming up flying machines based on the shapes of the wings of animals. Leonardo da Vinci (1452–1519) drew more than 150 aircraft designs in the late 15th and early 16th centuries, but it was not until 1738 that a Swiss mathematician, Daniel Bernoulli (1700–1782), described how lift acts on a wing as air passes across it.

In 18th century Britain, Sir George Cayley (1773–1857) summed up the goal for flight researchers. It was to devise a machine that possessed a wing for lift, had its own propulsion system, and could be controlled in flight. By 1799 Cayley had built a glider that satisfied the first condition, but it did not have its own propulsion system and could not be controlled. Almost 100 years passed before a German engineer, Otto Lilienthal (1848–1896), found a way to control the flight of a glider by shifting his weight about during flight. He made about 2,000 experimental glider flights, the last of which was fatal.

Other experimenters followed. Wilbur (1867–1912) and Orville (1871–1948) Wright expanded on Lilienthal's work and designs. They built an aircraft that had a vertical rudder to control the motion from side to side and a horizontal rudder, called an elevator, that kept the nose of the aircraft from dipping or rising. They also devised a method by which the pilot could control the rolling from right to left or left to right. The Wright brothers provided the machine with a source of propulsion by using an internal combustion engine fitted with a propeller. On the morning of December 17, 1903, at Kitty Hawk, North Carolina, the first aircraft, *Flyer 1*, rose from the sand dunes, droned ahead for about 35 yards (32 m), and landed safely. This first flight lasted for 12 seconds. The air age had begun.

In the 1890s Otto Lilienthal found a way to control a glider by shifting his weight about during flight. The Wright brothers expanded upon his work to build the first airplane, named Flyer 1, *in 1903.*

themselves. Pterosaur wings were stretched across the elongated little finger bone.

Bat wings consist of a thin membranous skin, while bird wings are feathered. Different types of feathers have different functions. The long primary feathers are used to generate lift and thus are light and stiff. The contour feathers near the wing base are smaller and lie close together to provide a smooth surface area. The primaries allow air to pass between them on the upstroke, but they close together on the downstroke to provide a large surface for lift production. Animals that fly must have lightweight bodies to minimize the energy needed to get them off the ground and to maintain prolonged flight. Modern birds have hollow bones, which have a honeycomb-like structure inside to provide strength and lightness.

Birds also need powerful pectoral muscles to flap their wings, and they have an enlarged chest bone (the sternum) to which the flight muscles are attached. Birds have also developed an efficient breathing system to ensure that plenty of oxygen is carried to the body tissues to provide energy for the flight muscles. Their lungs are connected to a series of air sacs that extend throughout the body, and thus, birds can store large amounts of air at one time. This specialized breathing system allows birds to fly for long distances without tiring.

Not all birds can fly. Birds become flightless for many reasons. Species that evolved on islands free of predators, such as the kiwi from New Zealand, are often flightless, as are groups that became too large to fly, such as ostriches and emus (see FLIGHTLESS BIRDS). Penguins use their modified wings as flippers for swimming. Two groups—diving petrels and auks—both swim and fly with their wings. Auks, such as puffins, have relatively small wings and thus, flight is energetically expensive and maneuverability poor. However, smaller wings help them power through water.

Saving energy

Flight is an energetically demanding mode of transport. Small animals such as insects often use wind currents to help them get about. Small birds, such

By catching the right air currents, the black-browed albatross (Diomedea melanophris) can soar for many miles without flapping its wings.

as sparrows and buntings, save energy by using flap-bounding flight: short, powerful bursts of flapping carry the bird upward, and the bird then tucks its wings in and arcs down toward the ground before flapping again. Larger birds save energy by flap-gliding: periods of flapping are interspersed with periods of gliding gently downward.

Many birds make use of an aerodynamic phenomenon called ground effect. When a wing comes close to a flat surface, such as the surface of a lake, the circulation of the vortex around the wing changes. A cushion of air is created beneath that causes lift to increase and leads to a corresponding fall in drag, and thus the energetic efficiency of flight is increased. For birds, ground effect has an influence only during very low-altitude flight—no more than around two wing lengths above the ground. At that height, birds stand a greater risk of predation by ground predators or enemies from above. Nonetheless, many birds exploit ground effect, from swallows swooping low over pastures to pelicans returning across the sea to their nests. Aerodynamics also explains why migrating geese fly in a shallow V-shape. The goose at the front of the V must work much harder to fly; geese behind benefit from the lifting action of vortices produced by the flapping wings of the goose in front. The position of leader changes regularly during the journey, so one goose does not end up doing all the hard work.

Many large birds, such as vultures, condors, and storks, use the movement of columns of air to help them stay aloft—a phenomenon called soaring. The heat of the sun warms the air at ground level, and this air rises to create an upward current, or thermal. By flying in a circle around the thermal, a vulture can gain height from which it can search for carrion below. Once high enough, it can glide gently down-ward to another thermal. By moving from thermal to thermal in this way, vultures can travel long distances without needing to flap their wings.

Other soarers

The master soarers, however, are albatrosses (Diomedeidae). These birds come to land only to breed; the rest of the time they travel over the southern oceans, stopping only to feed on floating carrion or small animals, such as krill. Albatrosses save energy through a process called dynamic soaring. Close to the ocean surface, friction between the air and the water reduces the speed of the wind almost to zero, but the speed increases quickly with height above the waves. From a height, the albatross glides with the wind. As it closes on the water surface, it turns, alters the shape of its wings to maximize lift, and is carried back upward, and thus, the bird can repeat the cycle. Albatrosses use dynamic soaring to travel for thousands of miles without flapping.

Albatrosses and some other birds, such as petrels, also fly without flapping by slope soaring. Wind speeds up when it encounters an object, such as a wave. Birds can use these gusts to power themselves upward. Similarly, fulmars and other coastal birds use gusts of wind passing up cliff faces to remain aloft for long periods.

J. MARTIN

See also: BIRDS; CONVERGENT EVOLUTION; FLIGHTLESS BIRDS; INSECTS.

Further reading:

Bishop, N. 1997. *The Secrets of Animal Flight*. Boston, Mass.: Houghton Mifflin Co.
Feduccia, A. 1999. *The Origin and Evolution of Birds*. New Haven, Conn.: Yale University Press.

FLIGHTLESS BIRDS

Flightless birds have lost the power of flight as they have adapted to an aquatic or terrestrial lifestyle

Penguins are flightless birds that are adapted to swim and dive. Their flipper-shaped wings propel the birds through the water, while the tail and legs are used as rudders.

The eagle soars, hummingbirds hover, swifts twist and turn—the very idea of birds losing the ability to fly may seem absurd. Yet the phenomenon of flightlessness is more widespread than it first appears and for a very practical reason. In terms of the amount of energy it requires, flight is an expensive skill to have, and if there is no reason to maintain it—an absence of natural predators, an ability to defend itself on land, or possession of supreme swimming skills—a bird's flight apparatus may all but disappear.

CORE FACTS

- Flying uses up a great deal of energy, and if there is no reason to fly, flightlessness can evolve.
- Flightlessness has evolved several times since birds first appeared on Earth.
- Flightless birds evolved in three directions: swimmers powered by their feet, wing-powered swimmers, and terrestrial birds.
- The greatest diversity of flightless birds developed in New Zealand and Australia, countries protected by a sea barrier where no large mammals evolved to compete with birds.
- Flightlessness often evolved on islands, where birds can become vulnerable if predators are introduced after the power of flight has been lost.
- Many flightless birds have been driven to extinction by the activities of humans.

Flightlessness is a trait that has occurred many times in the history of birds. Some of the early flightless birds became extinct, while others have survived, but in each case flightless forms have developed from flying ancestors over a very short evolutionary time. The loss of flight seems to have evolved as a result of arrested development (neoteny; when part of an animal fails to develop to the mature form with the rest of the body). Usually such an individual will not be as well equipped to survive as its fully developed counterpart and will die young. Occasionally, though, such a defect may prove to be a strength rather than a weakness: the animal survives, reproduces, and passes on the characteristics to its offspring. In flightless birds, the wings fail to develop properly, but flightlessness has become an advantage. Flightless birds are unusual but represent some of the most intriguing life-forms on Earth.

Origins of flightless birds

Scientists believe that modern birds may have originated from the genus *Archaeopteryx*, a crow-sized bird with limited powers of flight that lived at the time of the dinosaurs. From these origins, birds that lost the ability to fly evolved in three directions: swimmers powered by their feet (the most ancient group), swimmers powered by their wings, and terrestrial birds. Each group has particular adaptations to its body form and its behavior, that is, in natural

CONNECTIONS

- Many flightless birds live in **ISLAND HABITATS,** where the lack of natural **PREDATORS** has allowed flightlessness to evolve.

- True **FLIGHT** is found only in **BIRDS, BATS,** and **INSECTS**.

- Penguins are supreme swimmers. Like seals, sea lions, and other aquatic **CARNIVORES,** they have a streamlined body to move through the water and a layer of insulating **FAT** to keep them warm in the freezing Antarctic water.

- A famous flightless bird, the dodo, was once found on the island of Mauritius. It was driven to **EXTINCTION** by the end of the 17th century.

conditions they have been able to survive and flourish without the power of flight.

AQUATIC FLIGHTLESS BIRDS
Foot-propelled swimmers

Palaeontologists (scientists who study fossils) have traced the origins of the foot-propelled swimmers back 135 million years to *Enaliornis*, the first ancient bird known to have lost the ability to fly. Fossils show the wing structure reduced to a few thin bones, while the legs were well developed for swimming.

Although on land the foot-propelled swimmers must waddle or shuffle along, often tripping over their own feet, they are supreme swimmers. The Magellan flightless steamer duck is the world's fastest surface-swimming duck: it has been recorded at speeds up to 25 miles per hour (40 km/h). Its huge feet have webs measuring 6 inches (15 cm) across when spread, and the bird also strikes its wings on the water for additional thrust. The Galápagos cormorant, which lives on islands off the coast of Ecuador, uses its powerful webbed feet for swimming. It does not use its wings for swimming or flying, a trait reflected in the fact that its breastbone has lost the keel to which flight muscles are attached in flying birds. It has small wings, which it holds out to dry after each swim.

The great auk (Pinguinus impennis) measured 2½ feet (75 cm). The last recorded individual was killed in 1844.

Wing-propelled swimmers

Originally represented by flightless auks in the Northern Hemisphere and penguins in the Southern Hemisphere, wing-propelled swimmers have evolved to spend most of their lives in the sea. Flightless birds of this type are represented solely by penguins (order Sphenisciformes); the last two flightless great auks (*Pinguinus impennis*) were killed on Eldey Island, Iceland, in 1844.

Penguin fossils have been traced back over 45 million years. The change from a largely aerial to a largely marine way of life is a radical one, which probably occurred over a period of one to two million years, although it may have happened relatively quickly. Their exact evolutionary development is a mystery, but scientists believe penguins are distantly related to albatrosses and petrels.

The 18 living species of penguins fall into six genera and are widely distributed in the cooler waters of the Southern Hemisphere. Most are found in subpolar and polar waters, but other breeding colonies occur in areas of Australia and nearby islands, southern Africa, and South America. Penguins are highly social animals, often breeding in vast colonies, defending only a small area around the nest (which may be on open ground or in a burrow), and huddling together in extreme cold to conserve heat.

Penguins are exceptional among flightless birds, because their wings are still used for propulsion, although through water, not air. The wings are paddlelike and are short enough not to be folded back. The swimming muscle systems look much like flying muscle systems, with a large breastbone and strong pectoral muscles (the same muscles used in flight) modified exclusively for swimming. These birds shoot through the water, reaching speeds of up to 20 knots in short bursts. Under water they are streamlined, and with a dense, sleek, furlike plumage, they plunge through waves, diving with a proficiency unmatched by any other bird.

The fat-insulated body is large in proportion to the wings, which are flattened, and the bones are widened to form a rigid, powerful flipper. The feet and toes are short, with the legs set well back on the body, and the tail is used as a rudder. The bones are more solid than those of flying birds; thus, penguins weigh only a little less than the water they displace. This fact is important in reducing the energy required for diving. The Humboldt penguin (*Spheniscus humboldti*) dives to depths of up to 320 feet (100 m) for up to 6 minutes at a time, while the emperor penguin (*Aptenodytes forsteri*) pursues fish to 900 feet (270 m) and can remain submerged for up to 20 minutes at a time.

Penguins have mastered the seas. They are as graceful and swift as any whale or dolphin under water. Some species, such as the Humboldt penguin, hunt cooperatively, diving simultaneously and driving their prey toward other members of the group. It is clear that any disadvantage caused by the loss of flying ability is more than compensated for by the penguin's superior swimming skills.

The ostrich (Struthio camelus) is the largest living bird. The males have jet-black plumage, while females are a duller brownish color, the color camouflaging them as they guard their nest.

TERRESTRIAL FLIGHTLESS BIRDS

Ostriches, rheas, cassowaries, emus, and kiwis are often grouped together as ratites. During evolution, these flightless birds lost the large keel (a bony extension) on the breastbone, to which the large flight muscles would normally attach. Thus, the breastbone is flat, like a raft (*ratis* is Latin for "raft"). Other characteristics include a covering of downy feathers that replace the normal flight feathers and a wing greatly reduced in size. With the exception of the little kiwis, these are the largest birds in the world.

The giant extinct ratites were some of the largest birds ever known. Scientists have identified over 40 species, including the elephant birds of Africa and Europe. The elephant bird (*Aepyornis titan*) that was found in Madagascar measured about 10 feet (3 m) tall and weighed around 1,000 pounds (450 kg).

Although ratites are not closely related, they seem to share a common ancestor, *Diatrymas*, which was 6½ feet (2 m) tall and had a skull the size of a horse's and a massive hooked beak. Found in South America, Africa, and Australasia 54 to 38 million years ago, it evolved into many diverse forms.

Over time, mammals became the dominant land animals, but flightless birds remained in some niches. They were able to establish themselves either in the absence of mammalian competitors or where they had become large enough to compete for food with other grazing animals and to protect themselves or were swift enough to escape.

Ostriches

The African ostrich (*Struthio camelus*) is the largest and fastest running bird alive on Earth, at over 8 feet (2.5 m) in height and weighing up to 350 pounds (156 kg). Its strong muscular legs can carry it at speeds of up to 40 miles per hour (65 km/h). Although capable of outrunning a lion or felling it with a single kick, the ostrich will avoid danger rather than confront it. The long legs and neck, coupled with keen eyesight and eyes larger than those of an elephant, give the ostrich an enormous field of vision.

In South Africa, ostriches are raised for their meat, feathers, and eggs. The striking jet-black body and white outer wing and tail plumage of the male ostrich is highly conspicuous and important in courtship displays. The female and chicks are gray or brown, an excellent camouflage color. The myth that ostriches bury their heads in the sand probably stems from the fact that at certain times, particularly during feeding and egg incubation, they will lay their necks on the ground. Camouflage is the key to this behavior; the dull plumage of the female looks like just another hillock on the open landscape.

Rheas

There are two species of South American rhea, the lesser or Darwin's rhea (*Pterocnemia pennata*) and the gray, or common, rhea (*Rhea americana*). They closely resemble the ostrich but are much rarer, because of overhunting by humans. Living in mixed herds for protection from predators, rheas make up in running skills for their inability to fly. Their long

THE KAKAPO

The kakapo (*Strigops habroptilus*), also called the owl parrot, is an almost extinct terrestrial flightless bird. It is nocturnal and ground living, sleeping in holes in the thick New Zealand vegetation. Not officially a ratite, it nevertheless shares the same characteristic flat breastbone—a result of evolving not to fly. Historically there were no predators for the kakapo in New Zealand, but after the introduction of predatory mammals by settlers, the population was all but wiped out. Kakapos follow complex paths through the undergrowth, the tracks of which are well defined and link curious bowl-shaped depressions in the ground. For years it was thought these depressions were used as dusting bowls by the birds to keep their feathers in good condition. They are now known to be booming bowls, which the males use for courting. Once in the bowl the male bird inflates his body with air and booms. Enhanced by the bowl, the calls carry far and wide to attract females.

*A brown kiwi (*Apteryx australis*) feeding among dead leaves. Nocturnal birds, kiwis find food mainly by smell, and probe the forest floor with their long, curved bills.*

muscular legs propel them in a swift weaving run—at full tilt the body is held horizontally to the ground with the neck stretched out in front and one wing out to the side as the bird swerves and dodges, as fast as a galloping horse. Hunted for sport, meat, and feathers, the numbers of the puna rhea (*Pterocnemia pennata tarapacensis*) in particular are declining rapidly. These birds are now classified as endangered (see ENDANGERED SPECIES).

Cassowaries

The outlook for the cassowary is more optimistic. This bird is a member of the family Casuariidae, order Casuariiformes, which also includes emus. There are three known species: the common cassowary (*Casaurius casaurius*), the largest, standing at 5 feet (1.5 m) tall; the one-wattled cassowary (*C. unappendiculatus*); and the dwarf cassowary (*C. bennetti*), measuring 3 feet 10 inches (1.1 m).

Cassowaries live in tropical rain forests in Australia and New Guinea. They move rapidly along narrow tracks in the forest, foraging for fruit and insects. Their heads are topped by a casque, a hornlike structure that gives the bird its name.

Cassowaries are good at defending themselves and have been known to kill humans with a slashing blow of the foot, which bears a long, daggerlike claw. Their large size and lethal kick have helped cassowaries survive without the power of flight.

Emus

The emu (*Dromaius novaehollandiae*) is the second largest living land bird, reaching heights of over 6 feet (1.9 m) and weighing in at 125 pounds (55 kg). Three living subspecies are found in Australia. Emus are more or less vegetarians, mainly eating fruit, and a few insects. They mate for life, defend a territory when they are breeding, and are capable of speeds up to 30 miles per hour (50 km/h), outrunning any natural enemy they encounter.

Kiwis

About the size of a domestic chicken but with a longer body and stouter, more powerful legs, kiwis, native to the New Zealand archipelago, have taken flightlessness to extremes. Tiny vestigial wings are buried under the shaggy brown plumage, and the tail has disappeared altogether. The long bill is curved, with openings for air passages located at the tip. It is used to probe for food in the dense undergrowth. Kiwis' eyes are small and, although vision is sharp enough to enable them to run fast through the dense undergrowth, the sense of smell rather than sight is used to investigate the surroundings. Named after its shrill call, these strange birds are shy and nocturnal, living with a lifelong mate in a small territory from which other kiwis are rigorously expelled.

Three species of kiwi exist: the common, or brown, kiwi (*Apteryx australis*), the little spotted kiwi (*A. oweni*), and the great spotted kiwi (*A. haasti*), each occupying distinct regions of the islands of New Zealand. The kiwi is small and unable to defend itself. These species probably evolved only because of the absence of mammals. They once thrived because they had no natural predators, but with the introduction of alien mammals, competition for resources (with elks and rabbits, for example) and predation (by cats and rats, for example) have become serious problems.

Flightless birds at risk

Flightless birds have often evolved or simply survived on islands, where there were few natural competitors or predators and therefore no need to fly. However, living on an island can also threaten the birds' survival: once flightlessness is lost, it is gone forever. If predators are later introduced to the island, the birds are highly vulnerable. Already, humans have been responsible, directly or indirectly, for the extinction of many species, including the dodo, the great auk, and the flightless wren (*Xenicus lyalli*). The flightless wren, which lived only on Stephen Island off the New Zealand coast, was exterminated in 1894 by a single domestic cat imported by the keeper of a lighthouse that had just been built there.

The brightly colored takahe (*Notomis mantelli*) of New Zealand's South Island has twice been resurrected, having been thought extinct in the late 1800s and again in 1948. Takahes are selective vegetarians, and the arrival of humans, predators, deer, and sheep destroyed the birds' habitat and food sources. The number of takahes declined. The survival of the few remaining individuals now depends on careful management of the birds' habitat.

I. HOLMES

See also: ENDANGERED SPECIES; FLIGHT.

Further reading:

Arnold, C. 1990. *Ostriches and Other Flightless Birds*. Minneapolis: Carolrhoda Books.
Brennan, P. 2002. *Penguins and Other Flightless Birds*. Animals of the World. New York: World Book.

FLOWERS AND FLOWER STRUCTURE

Flowers are the reproductive organs of flowering plants

From the most fragrant rose to blooms that produce a stench similar to rotting meat, flowers are a plant's reproductive organs. Special structures within the flower produce the reproductive cells (gametes) that form the next plant generation, and the flower protects them as they pass through the process of fertilization.

Flowering plants are also known as angiosperms (from the Greek words *angion*, which means "vessel," and *sperma*, "seed"; see ANGIOSPERMS). The developing seeds of angiosperms are enclosed in structures within the flower and are therefore able to develop in greater safety than seeds of gymnosperms ("naked seeds"), such as conifer trees. Angiosperms include most garden plants, farm crops, and flowers grown for cutting. They range in size from tiny floating duckweeds to trees such as maples (*Acer* spp.) and oaks (*Quercus* spp.).

CORE FACTS

- Flowers are the reproductive organs of flowering plants, which belong to the plant group Angiospermae.
- Flowers have four main sets of organs: sepals, petals, stamens, and a pistil or pistils.
- Some flowers are unisexual, with either male or female organs, while some are bisexual, with both.
- Plants may be self-pollinated or cross-pollinated. Many cross-pollinators use color, scent, and stores of nectar or pollen in their flowers to attract pollinating insects, birds, or other animals.

Flowering plants display their flowers on a seasonal basis. Unless they are wind pollinated, the flowers develop their full range of colors and scents at exactly the right time to attract insects or other animals that will visit them and spread their pollen. Transfer of the pollen from the male part of a flower (the anther) to the female part (the stigma), a process known as pollination starts the reproductive cycle.

GENERAL STRUCTURE

Although an enormous variety of flowers exists, all flowers have the same basic design. There are four key sets of organs, each derived from modified leaves: sepals, petals, stamens, and a pistil or pistils.

Sepals are the outermost parts of the flower. Collectively, they are called the calyx. In most cases, sepals are similar to their leafy ancestors and are green and leaf-like in appearance. In some plants, the sepals look like flower petals. The main function of sepals is to protect the developing flower bud, although they can also photosynthesize and contribute to the plant's food supply. The sepals are attached to the receptacle, an enlargement at the top of the stem that bears the various parts of the flower.

Clematis is a woody climbing plant in the buttercup family. On clematis species, unlike most other plants, the sepals rather than the petals are brightly colored.

Petals are usually the brightly colored or heavily scented part of the flower that make up the second layer. In primitive plants, petals may also be leaf shaped. Generally, petals are not able to photosynthesize. The main role of the petals is to advertise the plant to potential pollinators. Flowers seem to have evolved alongside insects and other pollinating animals, such as bats and hummingbirds, in a process known as coevolution (see box on page 760). The animal needs nectar or pollen grains for food, and the

CONNECTIONS

● Housing the **REPRODUCTIVE SYSTEMS** of plants, flowers are often brightly colored or heavily scented to attract **INSECTS**, **BIRDS**, and other animals for **POLLINATION**.

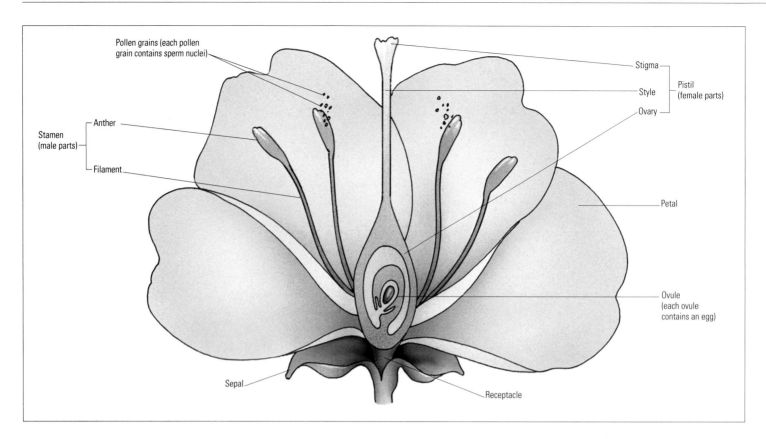

Pollen grains (each pollen grain contains sperm nuclei)

Stigma

Style — Pistil (female parts)

Ovary

Stamen (male parts)

Anther

Filament

Petal

Ovule (each ovule contains an egg)

Sepal

Receptacle

The structure of a flower, showing the sepals, petals, stamens, and a pistil.

flower needs the animal to aid pollination. When pollination is passive, by the wind, for example, petals are reduced in size or even absent. Collectively, the petals are known as the corolla.

The stamens lie inside the petals. Each consists of a pollen-producing "head," the anther, held aloft by an often long and slender stalk called a filament. Collectively, these structures are referred to as the androecium, the male part of the flower, because it produces the gamete that travels in the pollen.

The pistil (gynoecium) is the female part of the flower because it produces the gamete that stays in the flower (in the ovule) and it houses the developing seeds after fertilization. Pistils are composed of one or more structures called carpels, each of which evolved originally from a leaf folded inward along its length. The fold has become a protected internal cavity, and the whole structure has thickened and modified over time. The individual carpels are fused lengthwise in a multicarpellate pistil. A flower can also have more than one unicarpellate pistil. The pistil is made up of three parts, (from the top) a stigma, a style, and an ovary. The stigma makes a sticky site for the deposition and initial growth of the pollen grains. It is held up to catch pollen by the style, an often long structure down which the pollen tube grows after pollination to reach the ovary beneath. The ovary contains one or more ovules. It is the ovule that develops into the seed after fertilization. The ovary itself becomes the fruit.

Variations in flower design

Flowers vary in design because they have evolved to take advantage of particular habitats and of specific methods of pollination and species of pollinator. For example, many flowers can be grouped together to form what is known as an inflorescence, which concentrates the effects of the color and fragrance. A special example is the daisy family (the Compositae or Asteraceae), in which usually numerous tiny individual flowers called florets make up a composite head. The flower head of a daisy (*Bellis perennis*) acts as a single flower to attract insects. The sunflower (*Helianthus annuus*), also in the family, shows the same design on a much larger scale.

Over time, flowers have also evolved to increase the efficiency of their pollination. Many flowers, such as monkshood (*Aconitum* spp.), can be opened only by the powerful force of a large insect such as a bee, suggesting that these flowers and the large insect pollinators evolved together. In some flowers, the petals are joined together, often fused into a tube, a design that encourages specific visitors and discourages others. The advantage to a plant in becoming partly or totally involved with one type of pollinator is the increased likelihood that its pollen will be carried to a flower of the same species.

Flowers can be unisexual (with either male or female organs) or bisexual (with both). Plants with bisexual flowers are hermaphrodites. In unisexual flowers, either an androecium or a gynoecium is present, and the flowers are referred to as staminate (male) or pistillate (female), respectively. Staminate and pistillate flowers may be present on the same plant, as is the case with corn (*Zea mays*); such plants are called monoecious. The tassels at the top of a corn plant are the pollen-producing staminate flowers, while the threads of silk emerging from the ear of corn represent a combination of stigma and style. In a plant such as the date palm (*Phoenix dactylifera*), staminate and pistillate flowers are on separate plants; such plants are called dioecious.

Variation of flower organs

Some flowers, such as daisies and buttercups (*Ranunculus* spp.), have several planes of symmetry running through the center of the flower; such flowers are termed actinomorphic, or "perfect." Other flowers, such as violets and pansies (*Viola* spp.) and members of the pea family (Leguminosae or Fabaceae), have only one plane of symmetry bisecting the flower and are termed zygomorphic, or "imperfect." Flowers that have no planes of symmetry are extremely rare.

The individual floral organs are also extremely variable. The sepals in some species may be brightly colored, for example, in the fuchsias (*Fuchsia* spp.). In some cases, petals and sepals are indistinguishable from each other and are referred to as perianth segments. Examples are crocuses (*Crocus* spp.), tulips (*Tulipa* spp.), daffodils (*Narcissus* spp.), and the cactus family (Cactaceae). Daffodils have an additional, tubular structure, a corona, attached to the perianth segments. In other species, including campions (*Silene* spp.), the petals and sepals are separate, and the sepals are fused to form a calyx tube.

The number and size of stamens also vary considerably among different flowers. Water lilies (*Nymphaea* spp.) have several hundred stamens. At the other extreme, orchids (the Orchidaceae) have only a single stamen (see ORCHIDS). In most flowers, the carpels are fused into one structure, the pistil, but they can also be separate, each with a tiny ovary attached, as in the buttercup family. The position of the ovary also varies. It may be in the superior position, as in the tomato (*Lycopersicon esculentum*), where it is attached to the receptacle and above the calyx and the corolla, or it may be in the inferior position, below

the calyx and the corolla and visible as a bump at the top of the stem, as in roses (*Rosa* spp.).

Life cycle

At first sight, the life cycle of flowering plants seems extremely complicated. In most animals, a male sperm and a female egg fuse directly to produce the next generation, but plants take a less direct route, which involves alternating generations.

THE ONSET OF FLOWERING

The timing of flowering is critical, as plants may need to flower and form fruits and seeds before the start of the cold or dry season. Two main mechanisms promote flowering: a response to changes in day length (photoperiodism) and response to a change in temperature, usually to a spell of cold weather.

Photoperiodism is the response of plants to relative lengths of daylight and darkness (see BIORHYTHMS). Plants have pigments that can absorb different wavelengths of light and initiate chemical reactions. The pigments that are involved in detecting different day lengths are two forms of phytochrome: phytochrome red (P_r), which by absorbing red light is converted to phytochrome far red (P_{fr}), which by absorbing more light in the far-red region of the spectrum converts back to P_r.

Daylight has more red than far-red light, so phytochrome exposed to it will develop a higher proportion of P_{fr}. At night, the proportion of P_r increases as P_{fr} is converted back to P_r. Some plants are short-day plants: P_{fr} inhibits flowering, and a long, uninterrupted period of darkness is required to permit flowering. These plants flower in late summer or fall. They include chrysanthemums (*Chrysanthemum* spp.) and poinsettia (*Euphorbia pulcherrima*). In long-day plants, P_{fr} induces flowering, and the day length must be long enough to convert sufficient P_r to P_{fr}. Such plants flower in late spring and early summer. They include clover (*Trifolium* spp.). Some plants are day neutral—their flowering is not affected by changing periods of light and dark. Tomatoes and dandelions (*Taraxacum* spp.) are in this group.

The flowers of tropical **Rafflesia** *species, such as the one shown below, are the largest in the world. Some measure up to 3 feet (1 m) in diameter.* **Rafflesia** *flowers also have an extremely bad smell— they stink of rotting meat.*

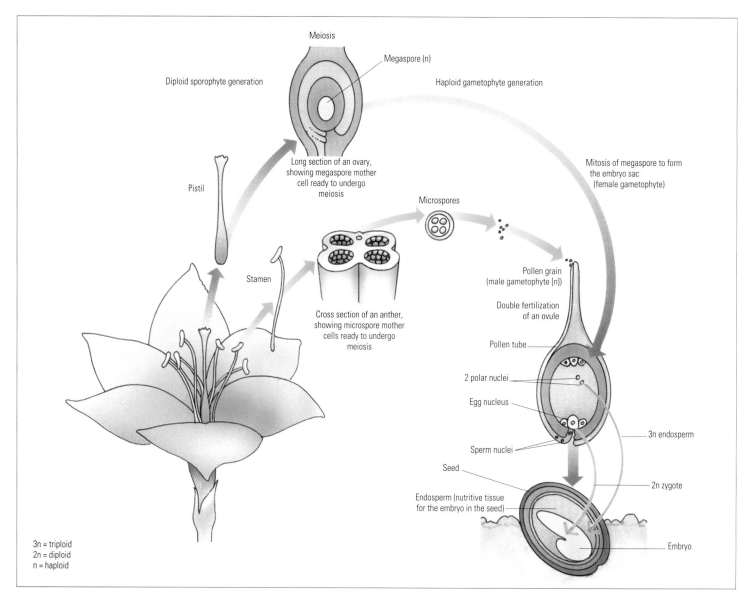

Double fertilization in the life cycle of a typical flowering plant.

The spore-producing (sporophyte) generation alternates with the gamete-producing (gametophyte) generation. The sporophyte is diploid: that is, it contains a double set ($2n$) of chromosomes. By contrast, the gametophyte is haploid: it contains half the $2n$ number of chromosomes, thus, it has a single set of chromosomes (n). In angiosperms, the gametophyte generation is enclosed within and dependent upon the sporophyte plant. This arrangement protects the gametophyte from drying out and allows flowering land plants to colonize even the driest areas.

The male gametophyte develops within the pollen grain, forming two nuclei, the generative nucleus and the tube nucleus. Before or after pollination, the generative nucleus divides to produce two sperm nuclei. The female gametophyte is the embryo sac within the ovule and usually consists of eight nuclei, one of which is the egg. During pollination, pollen is transferred from the anther to the stigma. On the stigma each pollen grain germinates, and the tube nucleus forms a microscopic tube that travels down the inside of the style and into the ovary to allow the sperm nuclei to reach an ovule. As the pollen tube enters the embryo sac of an ovule, it bursts open, and one sperm nucleus fuses with the egg. The fertilized egg (zygote) then develops into the embryo, the next sporophyte generation. The other sperm nucleus fuses with two other nuclei within the embryo sac, the polar nuclei, and becomes the triploid ($3n$) endosperm, which is a food store for the developing embryo once germination starts. This double fertilization is unique to flowering plants. However, in many ways sexual reproduction in flowering plants is similar to that of mammals. Both employ the production and union of

COEVOLUTION WITH ANIMALS

Many flowering plants rely on animals to collect their pollen and take it to another flower. The color, shape, and fragrance of flowers were all developed to entice pollinating animals. Many animals, including bats, bees, butterflies, moths, and hummingbirds, rely on nectar or pollen as a food source. Certain features of animals, such as the long proboscis of butterflies or the pollen sacs on bees' legs, are adaptations to obtaining nectar or pollen from flowers. Early in the evolution of flowers, in the absence of other insects, beetles probably acted as the first pollinators. Beetles still pollinate many types of plant, including the most ancient group of nonflowering seed plants, the cycads (see GYMNOSPERMS).

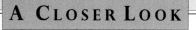

gametes, and both protect and nourish the developing embryo in enclosed structures (see FERTILIZATION).

POLLINATION

During pollination, pollen can be deposited on the stigma of the same plant (in a process called self-pollination), or it can be deposited on the stigma of a different individual of the same species (in a process called cross-pollination; see POLLINATION). Both methods have their advantages. Although self-pollination reduces genetic variability in the offspring, it does produce many similar plants that are already highly adapted to a specific habitat. Self-pollination is often employed in harsh environments, such as the tundra (see TUNDRA BIOMES), where insect pollinators may be rare or absent. In many plants self-pollination is used as a last resort when attempts to cross-pollinate have failed. In some members of the daisy family, the stigma of an aging and unfertilized flower will curl under, touch the stamens, and carry out self-pollination.

Cross-pollination reduces inbreeding and increases genetic variability in the plant population. As land plants are fixed and rooted to one location, they rely on wind, water, or animals to transfer the pollen from the anther of one flower to the stigma of another. The eelgrass plant (*Zostera marina*) is an example of a water-pollinated plant. Wind-pollinated plants include rushes (*Juncus* spp.) and grasses (family Graminae or Poaceae), as well as catkin-bearing trees such as willows (*Salix* spp.). Insect pollination is more precise than either water or wind pollination, so the plant can save energy by producing less pollen. However, it will often produce a large supply of nectar so that pollinators will visit the same type of flower again and again.

Flowering plants usually attract animal pollinators with colors, fragrances, and supplies of food such as nectar and pollen. However, some flowers have developed even more ingenious devices. Numerous orchids of the genus *Ophrys*, which grow throughout the Mediterranean basin, have flowers that actually look like insects. The plants use a subtle combination of colors, patterns, contrasts, textures, and pheromonal mimicry (fake insect hormonal scents) to simulate female insects and attract males—usually a species of solitary wasp or bee. The males attempt to mate with the flower and collect pollen sacs in the process. Then, when the insect "mates" with another flower, the pollen sacs are deposited on the sticky stigma, and thus pollination is accomplished.

Color

Flower color may vary with the type of pollinator. Bees, for example, like yellow flowers, birds prefer red, and moths are attracted to white. Many insect-pollinated flowers, such as evening primroses (*Oenothera* spp.) and poppies (*Papaver* spp.), have ultraviolet (UV) markings that are invisible to humans but easily seen by insects. The UV lines leading to the center of a flower are called honey guides. The color of petals may come from one of two different sources.

Some petals contain structures called chromoplasts in their cells. Chromoplasts contain many pigments, including the yellow, orange, and red carotenes and xanthophylls, collectively known as the carotenoid pigments (see CAROTENES). These compounds provide the bright yellow color of buttercup petals.

In bachelor's buttons (*Centaurea cyanus*) and larkspur (*Consolida* spp.), the brilliant blue coloration comes from pigments called anthocyanins. Anthocyanins can be pale pink, red, blue, or purple, according to the pH of the cell sap. The pink flowers of the hydrangea (*Hydrangea macrophylla*) become blue in acidic soils. Anthoxanthins, another type of pigment, give petals colors ranging from cream to deep yellow.

Coloration is not limited to the corolla. In anemones, the corolla is absent, and the calyx is

A bee pollinating a flower. Pollen grains are exploited as an important source of food by many species of bees. This source of food is so important that bees have evolved special baskets on their legs to carry large quantities of pollen back to their hive.

FLOWERS THAT TRAP INSECTS

Arum maculatum is commonly named jack-in-the-pulpit. Its inflorescence (the flowering part of the plant) consists of a central column (the spadix) that terminates in a colorful and bulbous swelling (the appendix; see picture below). This bulbous swelling produces a smell of decaying flesh, which attracts such insect visitors as the dung fly and carrion beetle. Because its cells have an unusually high rate of respiration, this tissue is warmer than the rest of the plant, an added attraction to carnivorous insects.

The spadix of the jack-in-the-pulpit bears pistillate (female) flowers at its base and staminate flowers (which ripen about 12 hours after the pistillate ones) above. Both sets of flowers are separated by a layer of downward-pointing sterile flowers, and the spadix is partly enclosed by a leaf-like structure called the spathe. Insects are attracted to the plant by its foul smell and tumble past the sterile flowers into the basal, flasklike part of the spathe. Here, while they walk around, they pollinate the pistillate flowers (with pollen from the previous plant visited) and feed on nectar, but they are prevented from leaving by the barrier or bristlelike sterile flowers farther up. After about 12 hours, however, when all the pistillate flowers are pollinated, the anthers mature and drop their pollen onto the insects. Only then do the sterile flowers wither, and the insects are free to go to another plant, where they fertilize the pistillate flowers and continue the process.

A CLOSER LOOK

colored instead. In acacias (*Acacia* spp.), the calyx and the corolla are greatly reduced, and the filaments, which are long and brightly colored, act as attractants.

Fragrance

Many insects have a keen sense of smell, and flowers produce an array of fragrances to attract specific visitors. These fragrances are usually provided by essential oils in the petals; they can be isolated and used in perfumes and in aromatherapy products.

Flower fragrances are grouped into five categories according to their chemical origin. Aminoids are fragrances in dogwoods (*Cornus* spp.). Benzoloids are the source of the fragrance of some of the best-scented flowers, such as jasmine (*Jasminum* spp.), heliotrope (*Heliotropum arborescens*), lily of the valley (*Convallaria majalis*), and hyacinth (*Hyacinthus orientalis*). Indoloids smell of decaying animal flesh or feces and attract flies. Members of the Araceae family, such as jack-in-the-pulpit (see box left) smell horrible to humans but attractive to flies. Paraffinoids give off a smell of goat and are produced by the lizard orchid (*Himantoglossum* spp.). Terpenoids are responsible for the lemon scent of certain thymes (*Thymus* spp.).

Nectar

Nectar is a clear, thick, sugary solution with no smell. The containers for the nectar, the nectaries, occur all over the plant but are concentrated in the flower to attract insects there. The quantity of nectar produced varies from species to species and depends on the type of visitor. Fuchsia (*Fuchsia* spp.) and hibiscus (*Hibiscus* spp.), which are bird pollinated, produce massive amounts of dilute nectar. At the other extreme, golden saxifrage (*Chrysosplenium* spp.), which has tiny flowers and is pollinated by small flies, produces small amounts of concentrated nectar.

Pollen

Pollen grains from plants that rely on pollination by animals have developed hooks that allow the pollen to become attached to an animal's body. In wind-pollinated flowers, the pollen grains have a smooth surface. Some water-pollinated flowers have thread-like pollen grains with the same density as sea water. They curl around the feathery stigmas of the female flowers upon contact, flowing with the current.

J. STIRLING

See also: ANGIOSPERMS; ANTIBODIES; BIORHYTHMS; CAROTENES; DICOTYLEDONS; FERTILIZATION; FRUITS AND FRUIT PLANTS; GERMINATION; GYMNOSPERMS; MONOCOTYLEDONS; ORCHIDS; TUNDRA BIOMES.

Further reading:
Bernhard, P. 2002. *The Rose's Kiss: A Natural History of Flowers*. Chicago and London: University of Chicago Press.
D'Arcy, W. G., and R. C. Keating. 1996. *The Anther: Form, Function, and Phylogeny*. Cambridge and New York: Cambridge University Press.

FOOD PRESERVATION

Food preservation is the use of chemical agents and other methods to delay food spoilage by microorganisms

Slimy salads, moldy bread, rotting vegetables, and stinking fish—these are all foods with living organisms feeding on them and leaving behind their excreted wastes. These unwanted microorganisms, mostly bacteria and fungi, cause food to spoil, changing its flavor and texture and making it unsafe to eat. Every year, millions of tons of food would be lost to microbial and enzyme action if nothing were done to stop it. Preservation of food has, therefore, been used over the centuries to kill or slow down the growth of microorganisms in foods or arrest the action of naturally occurring enzymes or oxygen on food.

Many different methods of food preservation have been developed. Methods can be divided into two kinds: those that kill microorganisms and those that merely inhibit their growth.

Cooking

The heat of cooking is sufficient to kill many of the microorganisms in or on food and to deactivate any enzymes present. The higher the temperature and the longer the duration of cooking, the more efficient it is, but overcooking can result in dry and tasteless food. Moist heat will kill bacteria better than dry heat. In a pressure cooker, for example, temperatures can rise above 212 °F (100 °C), which may well be necessary to kill certain species of heat-resistant bacteria.

However, once the food has cooled, it is again a rich source of nutrition for microorganisms: mold and bacterial spores carried in the air and live bacteria deposited by flies can rapidly reinfect it.

Drying and smoking

People discovered early on that raw food could be preserved longer by drying, since microorganisms cannot multiply well without water. Meat and fish can be hung up in warm winds, and fruit and vegetables can be spread on the ground in the heat of the sun. Dried foods, particularly meat and fish, are usually hard and have to be soaked in water before they are palatable. People tend to dry flesh over wood fires in cold and wet climates. The smoke of the fires gives the food an attractive flavor and, since it contains tarry substances that kill bacteria, the process can be stopped while there is still some moisture in the flesh.

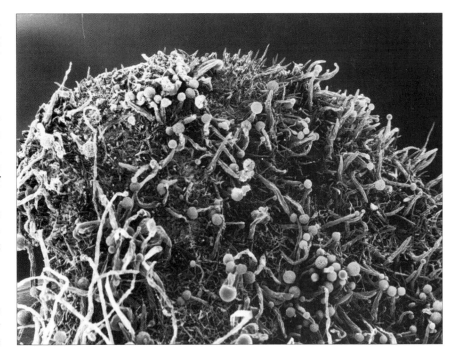

An electron micrograph of bread thickly covered with a growth of Mucor mold. This mold is not poisonous, but the products of its metabolism give the bread an unacceptable flavor.

Both drying and smoking are still widely used in food preservation. Many products, such as coffee and a variety of prepared foods, can be preserved by freeze drying, which involves rapid freezing of the food and then drying in vacuum under refrigeration.

Fermentation

Most food spoilage is caused by some kind of fermentation, but controlled fermentation can also be used to preserve foods or add to their flavor. Often, when the products of fermentation reach a concentration that inhibits further microbial growth, the process ceases naturally.

Some products of fermentation can be separated and stored, the best known being alcohol, produced by anaerobic (oxygen-free) yeast fermentation of sugar. The ancient Egyptians discovered that, when grapes are crushed and stored without access to air, the yeast on their skins acts on the sugar to produce wine, which can be strained off and kept in sealed containers for many months. Beer, which is made from roasted barley grains, water, and yeast, will not keep so well, although adding hops, which contain natural antibiotics, helps to prevent bacterial spoilage.

Milk also can be fermented. Yogurt, made by the action of *Streptococcus thermophilus* and *Lactobacillus bulgaricus*, will keep days longer than unrefrigerated raw milk. Lactococci bacteria will form cheese, and if molds are then allowed to grow on the cheese, the flavor and color are enhanced. Roquefort cheese, for example, gets its blue-green color from *Penicillium roqueforti* mold, found only in caves in southern France. Other common fermented foods include sauerkraut, soy sauce, and tofu.

CORE FACTS

■ If not for preservation, millions of tons of food would decompose because of microbial and enzyme action.

■ Many food preservation techniques (such as chilling, freezing, bottling, drying, smoking, salting, and pickling) have been used for centuries.

■ Food preservation can prevent bacterial production of toxins that cause food poisoning in humans; even so, millions of Americans suffer from food poisoning annually.

CONNECTIONS

● Animal feeds, such as hay, can be stored in silos for use when fresh **GRASS** is scarce during winter and early spring. In the silo, the hay undergoes a mild, controlled **FERMENTATION** to form silage.

● Early experiments in refrigeration were carried out by the English statesman and philosopher Francis Bacon (1561–1626), who was also the first to define and practice **SCIENTIFIC METHOD**.

CHEMICAL PRESERVATIVES

Many chemicals, such as salt, sodium nitrite, and sulfur dioxide, had been used for food preservation long before the Food and Drug Administration (FDA) was set up in 1906. These chemicals had proved to be safe and were classified as GRAS (generally recognized as safe). All chemical additives used since 1906 have had to be approved as GRAS by the FDA. Chemicals used include butylate hydroxyanisole (BHA) or butylated hydroxytoluene (BHT) to slow down oxidation (prevent rancidity). Sodium ferrocyanide and sodium silicoaluminate are used to stop mixtures from caking. A number of organic acids such as ascorbic, sorbic, propionic, or benzoic acids are added to bread, cheeses, and pickles to inhibit the growth of molds and yeasts. Sulfur dioxide and sulfites kill insects and microorganisms in dried fruits and wine; they also retard discoloration. Sodium nitrite is added to canned meat to prevent the growth of *Clostridium* (botulism bacteria) and to stabilize the color. However, recent research has shown that several of the GRAS food preservatives may be low-level carcinogens or have other health effects.

Adding preservatives

The earliest natural preservative was fruit sugar. Fleshy fruits are most in danger of spoiling from the yeasts present on their skins, which rapidly multiply and invade the flesh once they are picked. Drying the fruit concentrates the sugar to the point where the yeasts can no longer multiply. The discovery that these very sweet dried fruits would keep for many months led to the addition of naturally occurring sugar (usually honey) to freshly picked fruit. Cooking the mixture resulted in jams, jellies, and other sweet preserves.

Early people also discovered that salt was a good preservative for meat, because few bacteria can survive in a strong salt solution. Later saltpeter, natu-

Mammoths have been preserved whole in the permafrost of northern Siberia. Meat from a carcass was cooked and eaten at a great scientific banquet in Russia—it was at least 12,000 years old.

rally occurring potassium nitrate, was added. However, high concentrations of potassium in the diet can be poisonous, and with the development of the chemical industry in the 19th century, saltpeter was replaced by sodium nitrite, which is still used as a meat and fish preservative.

With the early discovery of yeast fermentation of sugar to alcohol and the subsequent bacterial fermentation of alcohol to vinegar, it was not long before vinegar was also found to be a good preservative and the pickling of fish and vegetables was developed.

Many herbs and spices help to preserve food because they contain natural antibiotics. Garlic, cinnamon, mustard, and oregano are examples. A range of chemical substances is also used to preserve food, but this practice has come under attack as consumers pay more attention to the possible health effects of ingredients and additives in the foods they eat.

Cooling and freezing

Lowering the temperature of food slows microbial reproduction (except in the case of certain fungi) and reduces the rate of enzymatic breakdown, although it does not stop it altogether. Root cellars were a standard feature of homes in colonial America. Holes dug beneath houses or in shady hillsides kept raw vegetables and fruits cool (but not frozen) and naturally humid (but not wet) and thus slowed their inevitable decomposition while preventing too much drying.

Ice, too, has been used for many centuries to preserve food, particularly meat. Large blocks were cut from frozen lakes and ponds in winter and stored in ice houses sunk into the ground and covered with grass or sawdust to insulate them as much as possible from the summer heat and prevent them from melting.

It was not until after the 1830s, when ice-making machines were invented, that freezing was widely applied in temperate climates. It was soon discovered that there were problems in freezing many foods. Water expands as it turns to ice. Large ice crystals inside the cells of the food bursts them so that, when the food thaws, the juices leak out, making the food mushy and flavorless. Freezing the food rapidly, however, forms smaller crystals that do not burst the cells.

Modern frozen foods were first introduced in the 1920s when an employee of the U.S. Fisheries Association, Clarence Birdseye (1886–1956), invented a technique for quickly freezing fish. His Bird's Eye process is still in use, and a line of frozen foods bears his name.

Bottling and canning

Food preservation took a big jump forward at the beginning of the nineteenth century when Napoleon Bonaparte (1769–1821) noted that his armies were susceptible to scurvy. This disease is caused by a lack of vitamin C (ascorbic acid) in the diet and results in gum problems and loose teeth and, if untreated, death. Napoleon knew his men's diet of dried beans, bread, and meat preserved in salt was not good enough. He offered a reward of 12,000 francs to anyone who could invent a reliable method for preserving foods.

Nicholas Appert (ca. 1750–1841), a French chemist, won the prize by putting meats, vegetables, and milk into glass bottles, using heat to drive out the air, and sealing them. Soon after, in 1812, England's Bryan Donkin (1768–1855) successfully sealed food inside metal cans for the first time.

Pasteurization

When Louis Pasteur (1822–1895), another French chemist, conducted his experiments with bacteria and fermentation, he discovered that it was the heat of the canning process, as well as the evacuation of air from the cans, that preserved foods by killing off the microorganisms. Pasteur's process (pasteurization) is a way of heating designed to kill as many microorganisms as possible without significantly affecting flavor. Depending upon the food, it may be exposed to a high temperature, just below 212 °F (100 °C), for a few seconds or to a lower temperature for a longer time. Pasteurization does not kill all the microorganisms present, and thus, pasteurized food still has to be refrigerated.

Freeze-drying and vacuum packing

Freeze-dried foods are made by passing them through a vacuum chamber as they are being frozen so that the ice is evaporated off as fast as it is formed. Foods can also be pasteurized and packed under vacuum, so organisms that need air cannot multiply. Care must be taken when using shrink-wrap materials, as some of these are permeable to oxygen and may allow the food they contain to become rancid by the chemical attack of oxygen on the food molecules.

Irradiation

A relatively recent addition to the list of food preservation methods is irradiation, the use of nuclear radiation to extend shelf life and destroy harmful organisms (see box below right).

Genetic engineering

Many attempts have been made by genetic engineers to develop foods, particularly fruits, that can be preserved for longer periods. One example is Flavr Savr tomatoes. Tomatoes develop most of their flavor while ripening on the plant, but in the past in order for them to arrive in good condition on market shelves, they were picked green. Now, varieties such as Flavr Savr are genetically engineered to have a longer shelf life so that they can be picked later, with a consequent improvement in flavor.

Another experiment in genetic engineering was intended to produce fruit (tomatoes, strawberries, and raspberries) that could be frozen or stored at sub-zero temperatures without losing their flavor or structure. Geneticists took a gene from the arctic flounder, a fish that can survive temperatures at which other fish are frozen, and copied it into tomato cells to give them the same property.

F. POWLEDGE

See also: BACTERIA; BIOTECHNOLOGY; FUNGI KINGDOM; MOLDS AND MILDEWS.

FOOD POISONING

Yeasts, molds, and bacteria in foods can sometimes produce substances that are poisonous. Food poisoning occurs when the sufferer becomes infected with live microorganisms that continue to multiply and produce toxins inside the body. One of the commonest kinds of food poisoning is gastroenteritis, caused by salmonella bacteria, particularly *S. typhimurium*. Humans usually become infected by eating contaminated meat, poultry, or eggs. Another common cause is *Campylobacter jejuni*, which occurs in cattle, chickens, and turkeys and can be transmitted in raw milk. Listeriosis, is caused by *Listeria monocytogenes*, sometimes found in unpasteurized milk and cheeses and in unwashed salads. Infection can bring about abortion of an unborn child and can be fatal to young children and the elderly.

Food intoxication—poisoning by products already present in the food—occurs more often than is suspected. The commonest toxins are produced by *Staphylococcus aureus*, bacteria that occur frequently in the nose or on the hands. If contaminated food has been left out for three to four hours at room temperature, enough bacteria will be present to cause poisoning. Another widespread food intoxication is caused by *Clostridium perfringens*, which occurs in soil, water, and the intestinal tract and multiplies in the absence of oxygen. When meat products are heated, much of the oxygen is driven out, and if they are then kept at room temperature for three or four hours, the toxin is rapidly formed. A related bacterium, *C. botulinum*, is the cause of a usually fatal disease of the nervous system called botulism, but fortunately cases are rare. *C. botulinum* thrives in moist conditions in the absence of air, as in a can of food that has not been heated properly during the canning process. A bulging can is usually a sign that the bacterium is present.

As well as bacteria, fungi can also cause food intoxication. Rye smut (*Claviceps purpurea*, known as ergot) is a fungus that grows on grains, such as rye, that are not properly stored. It produces LSD and other hallucinogens and causes psychotic delusions and convulsions (ergotism). Many instances of ergotism were reported in the Middle Ages in Europe, where bread was often made from contaminated rye.

Further reading:

Chadwick, J. B. 1995. *The Busy Person's Guide to Preserving Food*. Pownal, Vt.: Storey Books.
Shephard, S. 2001. *Pickled, Potted, and Canned: How the Art and Science of Food Preserving Changed the World*. New York: Simon & Schuster.

IRRADIATION OF FOOD

The U.S. FDA has permitted the use of irradiation on foods since 1963, starting with its use on wheat and wheat flour to kill insects. (Many countries do not permit its use.) The irradiation process involves exposing food to high-energy electrons or gamma rays. Irradiation raises the food's temperature only a few degrees, so it does not cook the food, nor does it make the food radioactive. The lowest dosages of radiation can be used to extend the storage life of onions and potatoes by restraining their ability to sprout. Higher dosages can be used to kill pathogens that harm humans, such as the worms that cause trichinosis, which are often left viable in undercooked pork. Insect eggs and larvae are destroyed by more intense radiation. At even higher levels, salmonella bacteria are killed as well as all other bacteria.

Opponents of irradiation argue that the process reduces the nutritional value of the food and that there are not enough data to show that people would not be harmed by this and other changes in the food. They say that the FDA has not adequately tested its effects and that its widespread use would amount to a huge scientific experiment on an unsuspecting population. Another argument against the widespread use of food irradiation is that it may be used as a quick fix for contamination problems in food preparation areas that are better kept clean by traditional methods. Thus, opponents are concerned that food irradiation may allow unsanitary food preparation to be "fixed" by irradiation of the finished product and thus be of benefit primarily to food producers rather than consumers. Nonetheless, irradiation of food is increasingly used in the United States.

FOOD WEBS

Food webs are networks of organisms connected by energy flowing among them in an ecosystem

The variety of life on Earth ranges from microscopic organisms, such as bacteria, to large organisms such as giant sequoias, elephants, and blue whales. Although they vary greatly in size, all organisms share a common factor: they all need nutrients to live and reproduce.

Interactions

A population is a group with members of a single species that live together in the same area at the same time, and can refer to any creatures, whether they are large—such as cats or humans—or small—such as mosquitoes or bacteria. A community consists of all the populations of all the different species that live and interact with one another within a certain area. The term *ecosystem* is used to described the interactions between the communities and their environment. A single ecosystem can be extremely large (the whole Earth), a medium size (a river and its tributaries), or quite small (a few drops of rainwater caught in the fold of a leaf).

Many processes occur within a single ecosystem. The most important of these processes is the exchange of energy and nutrients between different organisms. Without this exchange, none of the organisms in the ecosystem would be able to survive.

Food chains

The term *food chain* describes the feeding relationship between different populations in a particular ecosystem and shows how the energy from the food is transferred from one organism to another. Simple food chains are rare, as members of different chains will feed on one another. Predators feed on several types of prey, and many animals are hunted by more than one predator. A food web is a more complex and realistic model of the energy flow than the food chain, as it consists of the interconnected chains that exist within an ecosystem.

Green plants are the primary producers in most terrestrial food chains.

CORE FACTS

- Food webs describe the energy flow in an ecosystem.
- Energy, from food, flows from one organism to the next.
- Food webs consist of several interconnecting food chains.
- Primary producers (such as plants), detritivores (debris eaters), primary consumers (herbivores), secondary consumers (small carnivores), and sometimes, tertiary consumers (larger carnivores) make up a food web.
- Productivity is a measure of the efficiency of an ecosystem in terms of its energy flow.
- Human activities can alter the productivity of a whole ecosystem.

CONNECTIONS

- Some species in the same trophic level of a food web are in direct **COMPETITION** with one another for food. If one species increases in number, another one may have to find an alternative food source.

- One way in which human actions have increased the number of **ENDANGERED SPECIES** is by altering the balance within food webs.

Where does the energy to start the web come from? In most cases, the energy comes from the Sun. In the process of photosynthesis, the Sun's energy is absorbed by special pigments in the cells of plants, algae, and some bacteria and protists. This absorbed energy is converted to chemical energy, usually in the form of sugars or starches. Some organisms chemosynthesize their food using chemicals, instead of photosynthesizing it using energy from the Sun. A few bacteria, called lithotrophs (literally "rock eaters"), bypass the Sun and get their energy by breaking down inorganic compounds such as ammonium and hydrogen sulfide. These bacteria live in the soil and in hot, deep springs, where there is no sunlight.

Producers and consumers

The first link in a food chain (and web) is a group of organisms called primary producers. They use photosynthesis to obtain their energy. On land green plants are the primary producers. In aquatic communities, however, the primary producers are usually floating, microscopic organisms called plankton (from the Greek word *planktos*, meaning "wandering"). Some of these, including green algae, blue-green algae, and diatoms, can photosynthesize and are called phytoplankton.

Primary consumers eat the primary producers. In the water, animal-like zooplankton (the primary consumers) eat phytoplankton. On land primary consumers called herbivores (plant-eating animals, such as insects, rabbits, and cows) eat plants.

Secondary consumers—carnivores—eat the primary consumers. In one example of a food chain, grass (the primary producer) is eaten by a rabbit (the primary consumer), which is in turn eaten by a fox (the secondary consumer). Tertiary consumers also exist. They are usually large carnivores, such as bears and lions. Omnivores, such as pigs and humans, eat both plants and animals, so they are able to act as primary consumers, secondary consumers, and occasionally, tertiary consumers in several food chains.

Detritivores

Detritivores, which include bacteria, fungi, some protozoans, and many insects, obtain their energy from many trophic levels. Detritivores feed on non-living organic material that was once part of a living organism, such as dead plants, dead animals, and animal feces. Detritivores are key players in nature's great recycling plan: as they feed, they reduce all the dead organisms into nutrients that can be reused by other organisms in the food chain. Detritivores are nature's ultimate recyclers: they break down organic material and release inorganic products that can then be used by plants.

Detritus feeders are especially abundant in aquatic environments, where they burrow into the bottom soil and consume the organic matter that collects there. Earthworms are also detritus feeders. They are very useful to farmers and gardeners

UNDERSTANDING FOOD WEBS

Scientists use increasingly sophisticated tools to increase their knowledge of food chains and food webs. Radioactive isotopes are unstable forms of elements, such as carbon, phosphorus, or tritium, that emit a characteristic pattern of radiation as they decay. These radioactive isotopes may be used to "label" a particular area of soil or grass. In one such experiment, a researcher used nets to catch insects that fed on grasses that were labeled in this manner. The worker then measured the levels of radioactivity in the catch to find out which insects ate the grass and therefore where those insects fitted into the food web of the area.

The ability to understand food chains is hindered by the fact that relatively little is known about life in the oceans or about the part insects play in the overall food picture. Another problem is that nature is dynamic—always changing. Although people talk about a "balance of nature," there really is no such thing because the balance of an ecosystem is always being altered by variations in the climate and the environment and changes in the populations of the different organisms that live there. Mountains are constantly being eroded by winds and rain, some volcanoes erupt from time to time, and many of the narrow barrier islands along the oceans are losing their sandy coastlines and are getting smaller, while other islands are gaining that same sand and getting bigger. This balance or equilibrium is also going to be subject to disturbances such as earthquakes, fires, and storms.

because, while the earthworms tunnel through the ground digesting the organic matter, they aerate the soil and redistribute its mineral and organic matter so that the soil is more fertile.

Producers and detritivores are vital organisms in the maintenance of the food chain. The producers provide the initial food and oxygen, and the detritivores, by breaking down the dead organisms, recycle the organic materials locked up within them and thus prevent them from accumulating. Consumers are also important to most communities, but they are not indispensable to the long-term survival of either producers or detritivores.

Detritivores, such as this fungus, break down dead plant and animal matter; the nutrients are then released into the environment.

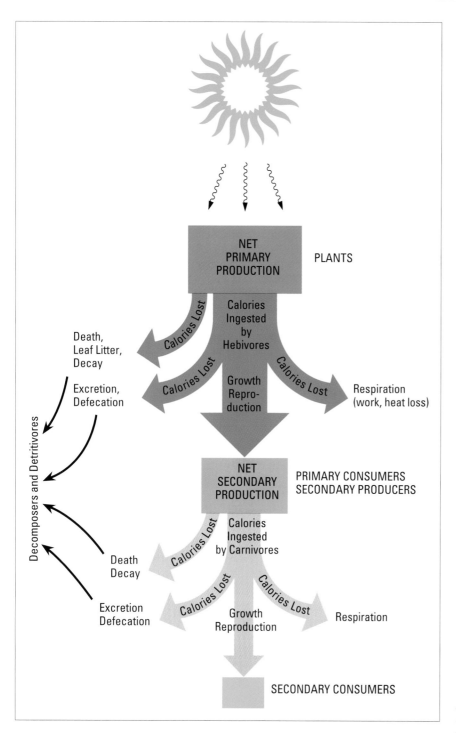

NET
PRIMARY
PRODUCTION   PLANTS

Calories
Ingested
by
Hebivores

Calories Lost
Calories Lost

Death,
Leaf Litter,
Decay

Excretion,
Defecation

Growth
Repro-
duction

Calories Lost

Respiration
(work, heat loss)

Decomposers and Detritivores

NET
SECONDARY
PRODUCTION   PRIMARY CONSUMERS
SECONDARY PRODUCERS

Calories
Ingested
by Carnivores

Calories Lost
Calories Lost

Death
Decay

Excretion
Defecation

Growth
Reproduction

Calories Lost

Respiration

SECONDARY CONSUMERS

Some of the potential energy flow from plants to secondary consumers is lost owing to respiration, death and decay, and heat loss by plants, primary consumers, and secondary consumers.

The energy pyramid

Each stage of the food chain is known as a trophic level (*trophic* means "nourishment"). These levels represent steps in the transfer of energy, in the form of food, through a community. Scientists such as the British zoologist Charles Elton (1900–1991), who coined the terms *food chain* and *food web*, devised the idea of an energy pyramid to describe what happens as the energy moves from a producer to a consumer. The energy pyramid shows the energy relationships in an ecosystem and indicates the rate of energy flow between trophic levels.

The passage of energy in an ecosystem flows in one direction only, but the amount of energy that is generated by the producers is by no means the same amount that reaches the top of the chain or even the primary consumer. As energy is transferred from one trophic level to the next, a large amount of the total energy is lost into the environment through the consumer's respiration. Photosynthesizing producers, such as green plants, trap the radiant energy of the sun and convert it to organic materials, such as glucose. These are then broken down by enzymes during the process of cellular respiration so that the energy is readily available for use in the plant. Some of the energy is lost to the environment in the form of heat, and it cannot be reused.

A scientific rule of thumb is that the amount of energy that is passed on to an occupant of the next (higher) trophic level is about 10 percent of the energy that the occupant of the lower level originally received. In other words, if the producer at the bottom of the trophic levels (and the energy pyramid) produces 100 percent of the total energy, the primary consumer is likely to receive only 10 percent. The secondary consumer gets 10 percent of the primary consumer's energy (which is 10 percent of the original output of energy from the producer), so the secondary consumer receives only 1 percent of the original total energy.

The consumer at the top of the chain is called the top carnivore. In a chain with three trophic levels, the top carnivore would get only 10 percent of the secondary consumer's energy, which is only 10 percent of the primary consumer's energy, which is only 10 percent of the producer's original energy. So the top carnivore gets 0.1 percent of the producer's original energy. It is easy to see that the producers at the bottom of the chain have a very important role to play. Without them, there would be no energy.

The ever declining amounts of energy that pass up a chain's pyramid place limits on the number of creatures that can participate in that food chain. While the lengths of the chains vary, they seldom contain more than six trophic levels. A three-level chain has producers, primary consumers, and carnivores (and, of course, the detritivores that feed off the dead organisms), as can be seen in areas where grass is eaten by rabbits, who are then eaten by foxes. In the sea, the chain may be longer, as phytoplankton are eaten by zooplankton, which are then engulfed by tiny anchovies, which are eaten by larger fish, such as herrings, which are eaten by even larger fish, such as tuna, which may then be caught and eaten by humans.

Depicting a food web

When a food web contains only a few components, a simple pyramid can be used for illustration. Using a corner of the southwestern U.S. desert as an example, a long rectangle at the bottom of the pyramid represents the plant life that supports the whole system. An arrow points to a shorter rectangle above the plants; this second rectangle might represent a small herbivore, such as a desert rat, that eat the plants. Another arrow points upward to another, shorter rectangle representing the desert snakes that eats the desert rats—and so on, ending in the large desert mammals that are the feeders at the top of the chain, such as bobcats.

A more complicated web contains several primary, secondary, and tertiary consumers and thus need a more complicated drawing. The producer may have arrows pointing to several primary consumers (rabbits and deer as well as rats may eat the grass), and each of these consumers will have several arrows pointing to one or more secondary consumers above them (perhaps owls, gopher snakes, and hawks). Bobcats may feed on gopher snakes, and even though bobcats do not eat owls and hawks, they would still be considered the top carnivore (and the tertiary consumer) in this food web.

Pyramid of numbers

A pyramid of numbers shows the number of organisms at each trophic level in a particular ecosystem. In most pyramids, each successive trophic level contains fewer organisms, although the organisms themselves may be much larger in size. In virtually all communities, there are more plants than herbivores, more herbivores than carnivores, and more small carnivores than large carnivores. It is also possible to have an inverted chain, in which the higher trophic levels contain more organisms than the lower levels, as often occurs where one tree provides food for thousands of herbivorous insects. However, the next level would have a smaller number of insect-eating organisms.

Ecosystem productivity

Attempts have been made to assess the amounts of energy that are produced or that move through a food

CHARLES ELTON

The work of British scientist Charles Elton forms the foundation of modern ecology and the study of food webs and food chains. Elton, a zoologist at the University of Cambridge in England, was born in 1900. He took part in four expeditions to the Arctic in the 1920s and paid particular attention to the records that trappers kept of their catches of fur-bearing animals. This study led to his 1927 book, *Animal Ecology*, in which he introduced the theories of food chains and food webs now in widespread use in the scientific community.

Before Elton, scientists spoke of the "Great Chain of Being" (a Christian concept relating to the Creation); this chain included all Earth's creatures. The "lesser" creatures were at one end, and humans (thought to be the most important creatures by the people who devised the idea) were at the top. Elton saw that there were many different chains, and that the bottom elements of those chains were far more important than those at the top. In some chains, humans do not appear at all.

Elton also introduced his colleagues to the notion of the food web— the interactions of all the food chains in any given ecological community. These webs can be extremely complex. The web and the design that came to be called the energy pyramid were important contributions to the understanding of ecosystems. Food webs are not uncluttered and simple, like the Christian Great Chain of Being, but are a valuable shorthand for understanding the complexity of the natural world.

DISCOVERERS

web. Researchers refer to the *gross primary productivity* of the producers at the bottom of the pyramid. This term refers to the total amount of organic matter that is synthesized by the producers (by photosynthesis or chemosynthesis). It is measured in terms of heat energy (usually in calories) per unit area (usually in

Salt marshes are highly productive ecosystems. They are very fertile areas, that can sustain a variety of animal and plant life.

Bears, which have no natural predators, are the top carnivores of their food chains.

square meters) in a given unit of time (usually in one year). The net primary productivity is the amount of food accumulated in plant tissues that is potentially available to the plant consumers—that is, all the primary productivity that is not used by the plants during respiration. The net primary productivity is calculated by subtracting from the gross primary productivity the energy that is used by the producers themselves.

Another term, *biomass*, is the total amount of organic matter that is produced within an ecosystem. Other measures include how much chlorophyll the producers contain, the amount of carbon dioxide they absorb, and how much oxygen they produce.

A number of factors influence the productivity of a particular ecosystem. They may include the amount of sunlight that reaches the primary producers, the availability of nutrients and water, and other climatic factors, such as wind and humidity. For example, the high productivity of intertidal communities is determined by the wave action of the tide. Many of the organisms in these communities feed on detritus, which is carried to them by the motion of the tides. If the wave action is rapid, the organisms use less energy in trying to obtain their food, so they have a higher net productivity.

Some ecosystems are much more productive than others. Those that convert the most energy include river estuaries, salt marshes, coral reefs, some forests, and some agricultural systems, such as rice paddies. Ecosystems with reduced productivity include grasslands, shrublands, and some open waters. Tundra regions (such as the Arctic) and deserts are the least productive, as few plants grow there owing to the extremely high or low temperatures of these areas (see DESERT BIOMES; TUNDRA BIOMES). As might be expected, there is more productivity in the tropical regions, which enjoy plentiful rainfall and warm temperatures.

The human effect

Humans now play important roles in virtually all food webs, even if they do not eat any of the animals involved. Human activity has profound effects on most producers and consumers. For example, if people drain a marshy area, a food web that is made up of dozens of chains may be disrupted because the aquatic environment is converted into a terrestrial one. If people hunt large carnivores to extinction, they may remove the top carnivore of a chain, so the organisms of the trophic levels below it are unchecked by their natural predator and are able to increase in number.

People can also upset the delicate balance of a food chain by introducing a new species into a habitat or by controlling pests or predators. In 1957 fishers brought goats to Abingdon Island, one of the Galápagos Islands off the coast of South America. A rare species of tortoise lived on the island, but within five years, it became extinct even though the goats were herbivores. A disruption occurred because the goats had no natural predators on the island, so they increased in number and ate the plants that the tortoises usually ate. The tortoises were unable to find another source of food, so the entire species died out.

F. POWLEDGE

See also: BIOMES AND HABITATS; CARNIVORES; DESERT BIOMES; ECOLOGY AND ECOSYSTEMS; ENERGY; FEEDING; GAIA HYPOTHESIS; NUTRITION; POPULATION; PREDATION; SAPROPHYTES; TUNDRA BIOMES.

Further reading:
Pimm, S. L. 2002. *Food Webs*. Chicago: University of Chicago Press.
Reagan, D. P., and R. B. Waide, eds. 1996. *The Food Web of a Tropical Rain Forest*. Chicago: University of Chicago Press.

FORENSIC SCIENCE

Forensic science is a scientific method of collecting clues from a crime scene and using those clues to reconstruct the events of a crime

When a crime is committed, there is always evidence at the crime scene. It is the job of the forensic scientist to collect and analyze that evidence. French scientist Edmond Locard (1877–1966), one of forensic science's founding fathers, stated the basic principle of forensic science: every contact leaves a trace. If a person wrestles with and wounds another, or puts a boot through a window, splashes of blood or a few hairs or minute glass fragments will attach themselves to the person responsible or will be left behind at the scene of the crime.

Forensic scientists must find these tiny traces of evidence to help police catch the criminal. Their work is wide ranging and includes identifying bloodstains or semen from an assault or rape victim; examining remains of burned-out buildings to determine whether arson or an accident was the cause; matching a footprint at the crime scene with the suspect's shoe print, and matching fragments of glass found in clothing with that of a broken window.

A number of specialists with a variety of skills are employed to investigate the evidence. Forensic scientists, therefore, include pathologists, biologists, chemists, dentists, poison experts, firearm experts, physicists, biochemists, and psychologists.

In many cases fingerprinting and the gathering of evidence are carried out by police officers. Forensic scientists later analyze the key evidence that was preserved and prepare reports for presentation at a court hearing. Forensic scientists are called in only for serious cases, such as homicide.

Crime scene investigation

A crime scene investigation is difficult and time consuming. Investigators must be thorough and not leap to conclusions in order to gather all possible

A police officer dusts for fingerprints at the scene of a crime.

CORE FACTS

- Forensic scientists rely on the fact that when one object touches another, evidence of that contact is left behind.
- Forensic scientists might be doctors, insect experts, dentists, or psychologists.
- DNA profiling is the most accurate way yet found of pinpointing who was involved in a crime.

CONNECTIONS

● Investigation of a crime, whether burglary, assault, or fraud, is often an example of the application of **SCIENTIFIC METHOD.**

● Forensic science makes use of the full range of laboratory **ANALYTICAL TECHNIQUES.**

evidence, and the crime scene must be kept safe from unnecessary intrusion until the gathering of evidence is complete. Several theories concerning the crime are generated and gradually eliminated with the incoming information. Reasonable inferences about what happened are produced from the appearance of the scene and witness statements. Many different experts may be at the scene: paramedics, crime scene investigators, forensic scientists, and photographers. Just as the criminal leaves a trace at the scene, so will the experts, and great care must therefore be taken to prevent contamination that could interfere with the evidence.

Literally any object can be physical evidence. Commonly collected evidence includes fingerprints, shoe prints, dead skin cells, body fluids and bloodstains, bullets, weapons, tool marks, poisons, traces of explosives, paint and glass fragments, hairs, and minute threads and fibers. Since weapons are easily recognized, the perpetrator usually destroys them. Often the only remaining evidence is the microscopic evidence that the assailant unknowingly left behind.

The appearance of the crime scene is carefully documented. Written notes, photographs, and sketches of the scene are made. Evidence such as shoe prints and gunshot residues are fragile and are collected immediately. Only when the crime scene has been properly recorded is evidence bagged separately in noncontaminating plastic and labeled before being taken back to a laboratory for analysis.

Forensic scientists make use of a full range of modern analytical techniques. Among them is the mass spectrometer, which identifies the chemical composition of a substance.

Suspicious deaths

When a dead body is discovered, the first task of the medical examiner is to establish the time of death. The most usual technique used is body temperature, which begins to fall as soon as the heart stops and usually reaches the temperature of the surroundings within 18 to 20 hours. However, the rate at which a body cools depends on many factors—the environmental temperature, the size of the body, and the amount of clothing worn.

The extent of rigor mortis is another clue. Rigor mortis is the temporary muscle stiffness that occurs after death because of a chemical reaction in the muscle fibers. Actin and myosin (proteins in the muscles) fuse to form a gel, which stiffens the muscle fibers. Stiffening normally occurs around 3 hours after death and can last for 36 hours, after which the body becomes flaccid again. The onset and disappearance of rigor mortis also vary, occurring faster at warm temperatures and slower at cold temperatures. Rigor mortis also occurs more quickly in those who have undergone physical exercise just before death and is extremely rapid if the victim was electrocuted.

A further indication of the time of death comes from hypostasis, a reddening of the skin. As soon as circulation stops, blood begins to settle in the lowest levels of the vascular system. As the red blood cells settle, pink-purple zones of hypostasis are formed on the skin. Victims who die on their back turn pink on the back, buttocks, thighs, calves, and

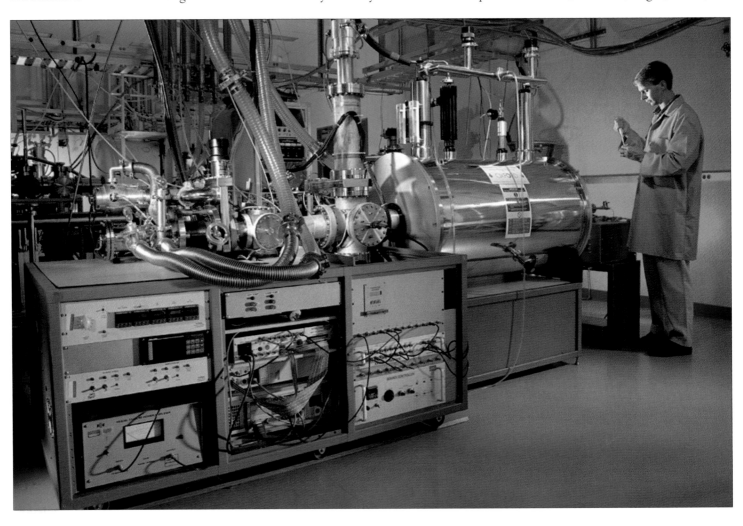

back of the neck. Where the body has been on a hard surface, the skin is pale because the pressure squeezes the blood out of the capillaries and veins. These marks first appear an hour after death and are fully developed after about three to four hours. Hypostasis may give other clues. If the body was moved a few hours after death, the position of the pink markings will show how the victim originally fell. The color of hypostasis may also indicate the cause of death. Cherry pink denotes carbon monoxide, while brick-red hypostasis may indicate cyanide.

Biological evidence

When bodies lie undiscovered for days or weeks, forensic entomologists (biologists who study insects) can work out the time of death from the presence and development of different species of insects in the decaying body. Various insects invade the body in succession. The first insects to arrive are blowflies and flesh flies, which lay their eggs in moist areas such as eyes, lips, or wounds. After a short time the eggs hatch into larvae, which live on the dead tissue and molt at regular intervals as they grow. After a time they pupate (a cocooned dormant stage), and winged adult insects soon emerge. Since the insect arrives at the body soon after death, estimating the age of the insect by its relative development will give an approximate number of days since death.

Other biological evidence, such as the presence or absence of certain insects in the soil under the body, can give clues as to how long the body has lain on the ground. Even the growth of tree roots that have pierced a body has been used to measure how long a body has been buried.

Autopsy

Autopsies are conducted if circumstances indicate criminal death or there is suspicion of it. In the mortuary, the pathologist examines any wounds, bruises, and broken bones to discover how and with what they were inflicted and whether they were the cause of death. As well as establishing the cause of death, the pathologist also collects trace evidence from the body, such as clothes, fragments of metal from a broken blade, foreign hairs, or fragments of someone else's skin from beneath the victim's nails. The external examination of wounds, stabs, and cuts is often extremely important in establishing the sequence of events and in many cases is more important than the internal examination. The body is photographed and sketched, and the size and position of the wounds are described. Routine samples of tissues and bodily fluids are also taken.

During the autopsy the pathologist looks for signs of poisoning or drug overdose. Samples of the blood, urine, and organs are retained for analyses by a toxicologist. Analysis is then carried out to identify the substance responsible. The liver is the most common organ saved for analysis, as it concentrates many drugs, making them identifiable when blood and urine concentrations have declined.

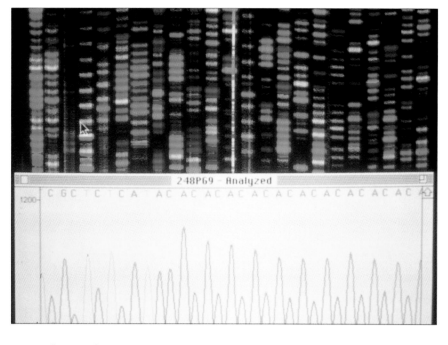

248P69 - Analyzed

C GC T C A AC AC AC AC AC AC AC AC AC AC A

DNA fingerprints are printed here on photographic film (background). The fingerprints are analyzed by computers (foreground).

Sexual assault

The examination of victims of sexual offenses is one of the most difficult tasks for forensic scientists. About two-thirds of examinations are for rape investigations, and the rest involve murder or other violent crimes. Police surgeons, clinical forensic physicians, or gynecologists deal with sexual offenses. The rape victim is asked to stand on paper while undressing so that any trace evidence that may fall off is caught and analyzed, along with the clothing. The victim must then undergo a full physical examination. The body surface is inspected for bruises, abrasions, and signs of a struggle. If bite marks are discovered, a forensic orthodontist will check them, and swabs are taken to try to obtain the attacker's saliva. The pubic hair is combed to find foreign hairs, and vaginal and anal swabs are taken to collect semen for DNA profiling. Since the victim of the sexual assault may find this physical examination as invasive as the attack, officers carrying out these tasks must do so with great sensitivity, and psychological counseling is commonly provided to victims.

PSYCHOLOGICAL PROFILING

Psychological profiling is the examination of all aspects of the crime, often with the help of a forensic psychologist, in order to build up a picture of the sort of person who committed the offense. This picture can be remarkably complete, including the suspect's likely age, sex, occupation, disorders, upbringing, marital status, education, hobbies, probable type of home, and even a suspect's physical appearance. Psychological profiling is used mostly by behavioral scientists and the police to narrow down an investigation to suspects who possess certain behavioral and personality features that are revealed by the way a crime was committed. The primary goal is to aid police in cutting down their suspect list. Robert K. Ressler and colleges of the FBI first developed psychological profiling by interviewing convicted killers. They listed their individual characteristics, the type of victim, the nature of the attack, and their behavior before, during, and after the crime. In doing this study Ressler began to build up a series of descriptions, or profiles, of typical violent criminals. Profiling itself, however, does not identify a specific suspect; profilers simply sketch the general character of the perpetrator.

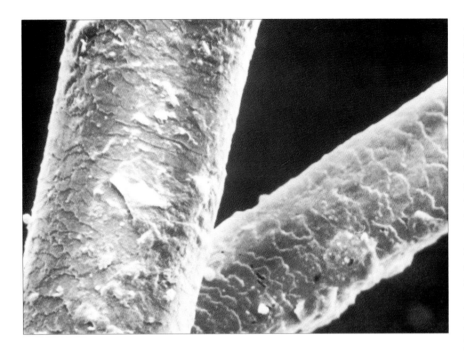

Electron micrograph of human hair, showing the overlapping plates of keratin that make up its outer covering. Forensic scientists have assembled collections of human and other animal hairs, as well as natural and synthetic fibers, to aid identification.

Serology

Serology is the investigation of whole blood and blood serum. It is an invaluable tool in the identification of suspects and is also useful in identification of charred human remains. Semen, saliva, and sweat are also examined using serological methods.

Blood typing is commonly used to show that bloodstains on weapons or clothing could have come from a suspect or victim. Some people's blood type can be identified from their sweat and saliva. Although blood typing is extremely useful, it is not specific to individuals, and many people will have the same blood type. Identification using DNA is much more exact. In recent times, DNA profiling has largely overtaken blood typing, as it can almost irrefutably identify a single individual, with the chance of a mistake much less than one in a million.

WHODUNIT

The four blood groups: A, B, AB, and O (see BLOOD) are familiar to most people. However, there are a variety of other ways of categorizing blood; most are based on the presence of different types of protein. One particular protein was found to be present in the blood of some people but not others. The presence of the protein, or lack of it, is referred to as the Rh (for rhesus) factor because it was first discovered in the blood of a rhesus monkey. If blood contains this protein, it is Rh positive (Rh+), if it does not, it is Rh negative (Rh–).

Serologists use at least ten typing systems to analyze blood, so, when given two blood samples, the serologist can calculate the level of probability that the two samples came from the same person.

For instance in the average mixed Caucasian population, the ABO system occurs in the following percentages: 39.2 percent have A blood; 12.7 percent have B; 43.5 percent have O; and 4.5 percent have AB blood.

Blood also contains other substances that help identify it. Two of these are phophoglucomutase (PGM) and haptoglobin (Hp). These two proteins occur in differing numbers of people. If two samples are found to be AB, PGM2, and Hp1, the probability that they are from the same person is 1 in 3,000—1 person in 3,000 will have blood of this composition. However, if the two samples are O, PGM1, and Hp 2-1, then the probability that they are from the same person is 1 in 8. Either finding could make it far more likely that a suspected person committed the crime.

Analysis of DNA

DNA is found in all body cells that contain a nucleus; it occurs in chromosomes, the cells' genetic material. Any hairs, skin cells, blood, or semen left at the scene of the crime can be used to establish a DNA profile of the offender. DNA profiling determines the sequence of nucleotides (the building blocks of DNA) in part of a DNA strand. Scientists analyze a small number of sequences of DNA that are known to vary a great deal among individuals. These sequences are thought to be specific to the individual. Analysis of DNA is therefore a powerful tool to forensic investigators.

DNA profiling does not, however, give a whole individual genome. This task would be too time consuming, since there are millions of nucleotides in human DNA.

The fact that only a small part of the DNA is used has caused controversy over the reliability of DNA profiles; as a result a number of state courts reject DNA evidence on the grounds that it may not be unique. However, the chances of an innocent person having the same DNA profile as the true criminal is many millions to one. In recent years many falsely convicted prisoners have been released on the strength of DNA analyses.

A DNA profile is obtained by using RFLP (restriction fragment length polymorphism). Cell nuclei are isolated from the sample. DNA is extracted and cut into fragments by biological catalysts called restriction enzymes. The fragments are separated using electricity (electrophoresis) and radioactively tagged. Radioactive markers allow the DNA profile to be visualized onto photographic film. DNA profiles from crime-scene evidence can now be compared with DNA profiles from the suspect. A more recent variation to this method is VNTR (variable number tandem repeats), which relies on the fact that DNA has a large number of repeating sequences of A-T and C-G pairs (see DNA).

There are, however, problems with DNA profiling. Firstly, it can take weeks before the results are available. Second, only very small quantities of DNA are usually available, although a remarkable laboratory technique called PCR (polymerase chain reaction) can reproduce a million or more copies of a single short length of DNA. However, as this method multiplies only a single DNA fragment, the profile is less reliable. A further problem is that forensic DNA samples are often collected as dead cells, and genetic material may degrade after cell death. Quick discovery and analysis of the evidence is therefore the top priority.

T. JACKSON

See also: BLOOD; DNA; FIBERS; LIVER AND GALLBLADDER; MEDICINE, HISTORY OF.

Further reading:

Evans, C. 1998. *The Casebook of Forensic Detection: How Science Solved 100 of the World's Most Baffling Crimes.* New York: Wiley & Sons.

FOREST BIRDS

All the world's great tracts of forest, from the cold northern taiga to the steamy jungles of Southeast Asia and the Amazon, accommodate varied bird communities. Some species inhabit the dense forest interior, exploiting every niche from the forest floor to the canopy; others live at the woodland's edge, feeding in open country and returning to roost. Some species live in very specific forest habitats, perhaps feeding on a single species or group of plants found only in certain areas. Most birds are active during the day, although some venture out at night.

The relationship between these birds and the forests they inhabit is a reciprocal one. For just as the birds themselves are well adapted to their habitat, the forest depends on these winged occupants for its renewal. Forest birds play an important role as agents of seed dispersal, and many forest plants surround their seeds with succulent flesh to attract fruit-eating birds such as toucans and hornbills. Many forest flowers rely on birds such as hummingbirds and lorikeets for pollination (see POLLINATION).

Forests provide resident birds with all their needs: food, shelter, and nest sites. However, many of these birds are at great risk as humans destroy the forests. Unlike bird species that travel vast distances to breed or hunt, many forest birds fly only short distances. In contrast to temperate forest species, relatively few subtropical and tropical species migrate.

Adaptations for survival

Forest-dwelling birds have a number of adaptations to aid survival. For example, many have short, stubby wings, which give them greater maneuverability in flight among the trees but which are then less suitable for long-distance migration. In addition, many are well equipped for climbing or running. One arrangement, providing a better grip for clambering among the branches, is zygodactyly: the two outer toes point backward and the two inner ones point forward. Zygodactyly is seen in woodpeckers, parrots, and cuckoos. Many such birds also have strong, curved claws and bills to improve grasp.

Woodpeckers (family Picidae) use their strong bills to bore into bark in search of insects. They also drum their beaks against trees as a territorial signal.

CORE FACTS

- Forest birds have many adaptations to their habitat, such as short stubby wings for flying among the trees, grasping feet with strong curved claws for clambering up branches, and color camouflage.
- Some forest birds build their nests high up in the trees, while others build theirs on the forest floor.
- Forest birds communicate mainly by calling, rather than through sight.
- There are many species of forest birds found throughout the world, in coniferous forests, temperate forests, and tropical rain forests.

Ground-dwelling species, such as the cassowaries of Australia and New Guinea, have long, strong legs for running and feet with long, sharp claws, which they use to scratch the ground for food. Most ground-dwelling birds are omnivorous.

Many forest birds are camouflaged from predators by their color. High-level residents, such as parrots and trogons that occupy the tropical rainforest canopy, are colored green, although some are gaudy blues and reds. Species living lower down in the trees, such as goatsuckers and nighthawks (known as nightjars in the Old World) are mottled shades of brown and gray and thus almost impossible to detect against a tree trunk or branch. Similarly, many ground-dwelling birds are speckled in shades of gray and brown to blend in with the foliage and dappled light of the forest floor.

Nesting in the forest

Many forest birds build their nests high in the trees. Few predators can reach or find the well-concealed nest. The young of most birds nesting up in the trees

---

CONNECTIONS

● The varied species of birds that inhabit woodland and forest display a huge range of **ADAPTATION** to their environment.

● Many forest birds have elaborate **COURTSHIP** displays.

*The ovenbird (*Seiurus aurocapillus*) nests on the ground or in the branches of trees where it is better protected from predators. The nest looks like a dutch oven, hence the bird's name.*

NIGHT BIRDS OF THE FOREST

Some species of forest birds are nocturnal, moving about and feeding at night and resting during the day. Other species are crepuscular: they are active at twilight and again toward dawn but are rarely to be found on the move in broad daylight. Most of these birds are specialized to prey on creatures such as insects and small rodents that are out and about only at night. All night birds, except for the short-sighted New Zealand kiwi, have excellent vision to help them find their way in the dark. Most also seem to have very good hearing.

The nocturnal species have several other things in common. In particular, they are all masters of concealment while resting during the day. Most nest in holes or burrows or in dense foliage, where they are usually safe from detection by predators. Also, they tend to be the same color as their background, making them even harder to see. Another shared characteristic is the response to threat: if an intruder comes on the scene, a nocturnal bird keeps very still.

The best-known and most abundant of night birds are the owls. There are 130 or so species of owls distributed widely throughout the world, and they make up over half of all bird species that are active at night. Whereas many owls also hunt by day, nightjars and nighthawks are almost always dusk or dawn birds. The nightjar family falls into two groups. One of these, the nighthawks, is present only in the New World. Birds in this group have rictal bristles, rather like cats' whiskers. North American nightjars, including the whippoorwill, poorwill, and chuckwill's widow, have names that echo the sounds they make, as they flit tirelessly through the trees on a hot summer's night. One of these, the poorwill, has the habit—extraordinary for a bird—of hibernating during winter, or at least during cold periods in the winter, remaining inactive until the spring.

Across the Pacific, relatives of the nightjar are the frogmouths of Southeast Asia and Australia. They, too, have good camouflage and soft plumage, but their large, flat bills are triangular and hooked. They swoop on insects from their perches instead of taking them on the wing. The squat little owlet frogmouths of Australia have mixed hunting techniques, taking prey either on the ground or in flight.

are described as being nidicolous (nest inhabiting) or altricial. They hatch at an early stage of development and are often blind, naked, and helpless. They are totally dependent on the parents for food.

Species such as nighthawks and game birds, such as grouse and pheasants, build their nests on the ground, where the risk of predation is higher. In contrast to the eggs of tree-nesting birds, the eggs of ground-nesting birds are often speckled or mottled in shades of browns and creams for camouflage. Their young, already well developed by the time they hatch, are known as nidifugous (nest fleeing) or precocial. Their eyes are open, and they have a covering of warm down feathers that double as camouflage. These chicks leave the nest within a few days or even within moments of the last one hatching and can run around and feed themselves without needing their parents.

Keeping in touch

Maintaining contact can be difficult in dense vegetation, and clear calls that carry a considerable distance are an essential means of communication. The different layers of the forest have different acoustical properties, and birds use the calls that carry best in the layers where they live. Ground dwellers have loud calls, while many species living in the middle and lower layers of the forest use simple, repetitive songs. In the canopy, the calls change to higher frequencies as the forest becomes more open and sound travels better. The canopy-dwelling hornbills of the Old World tropics have hollow, helmetlike casques on top of their large bills, which help to amplify their calls.

Other forest dwellers have alternative means of communication. Most pigeons and doves, for instance, have soft, quiet calls, but when disturbed, they take to the wing with a loud, flapping flight that warns other birds of danger. As well as making their loud calls, woodpeckers also drum their bills against tree trunks to proclaim territory.

Coniferous forests

The taiga (northernmost part of the coniferous forest) extends across northern Europe, Asia, and North America. There are few tree species, but many glacier-hewn lakes, slow-flowing rivers, and swamps. The forest is immensely cold and covered with snow from November through March.

Thrushes, crows, jays, and woodpeckers also thrive in the taiga. They, along with small mammals, attract predators such as northern goshawks (*Accipter gentilis*) and golden eagles (*Aquila crisaetus*). Here, too, as in other coniferous forests, are the 50 or so species of birds, including crossbills, nutcrackers, and pine grosbeaks, that have become specialized to feed on the seeds of larch, spruce, and pine. Common birds at ground level in the taiga include blue, ruffed, and spruce grouse, gray jays, and varied thrushes living on pine needles, catkins, buds, and berries.

In summer, great flocks of birds, including the tits and bramblings of Europe and Asia and the warblers and some chickadees of North American, migrate to the northern forest to nest and rear their young.

These seasonal visitors, drawn in part by the summer invasion of insects feeding on the conifers, are themselves preyed upon by the local carnivores.

Temperate forests

South of the taiga, the climate becomes gentler, and the deciduous or mixed forests of the temperate zones are more densely populated with birds than the cold forests to the north. Here there is bird noise all around: snatches of songbird repertoire, alarm calls, the drumming of a woodpecker's bill against a tree, the clatter of wings as a pigeon flies up when it is disturbed. Yet, in summer, with the trees in leaf, the birds are very hard to see.

In the fall, acorns are plentiful. These are a favorite food of plump forest birds such as jays (family Corvidae), wood pigeons (*Columba palumba*), and Eurasian nutcrackers (*Nucifraga caryocatactes*). Except for the pigeons, these birds all store acorns for winter. Some smaller, insect-eating birds, such as tits and tree creepers, remain in the forest all year round, surviving the winter by foraging around for insect eggs and pupae and seeds, in the case of tits. Other insect eaters, including warblers, migrate south in the winter in search of more plentiful food.

Tropical rain forests

There are more birds in the tropical rain forests than any other habitat in the world. From the dense understory to the high canopy, this is a lush environment, teeming with wildlife. Compared with birds elsewhere, rain forest birds have a huge variety of plants and animals on which to feed.

Central and South America

The region with the greatest number of birds is the neotropical region (Central and South America and the islands of the Caribbean), which contains the largest area of continuous rain forest in the world. Roughly half of all bird species either breed in this region or visit when winter falls over the Northern Hemisphere. Many of the birds found here, including macaws, motmots, toucans, tanagers, hummingbirds, and parrots, are among the most colorful anywhere in the world. There are 37 species of toucans. Gregarious, noisy canopy dwellers usually found moving around in small flocks, toucans are quite large, usually 13 to 26 inches (33 to 66 cm) from bill to tail. They are distinguished by their huge technicolor bills, which they use to pluck fruit.

One of the most peculiar birds in the Amazon basin is the hoatzin (*Opisthocomus hoazin*). It nests near water, and its chick is ideally adapted for life among the branches. The hoatzin chick is naked on hatching but is quite capable of looking after itself. Leaving its nest within a few days of hatching, it climbs around in the branches with the help of two large claws on the "elbow" of each wing. If danger approaches, the chick drops into the water below and then swims to the nearest branch before clambering back to the vicinity of its nest. By the time the chick fledges, it has lost its claws and can no longer swim.

In broad terms, rain forest dwellers tend to be specialized to their own particular level. In the Central American rain forest, for example, tinamous and curassows live on the forest floor, flower-piercers and hummingbirds live in the understory, and woodpeckers, trogons, jacamars, and puffbirds live higher up. In the canopy are toucans and parrots. High above the trees, wheeling and darting in endless pursuit of insects, are those acrobatic fliers, the swifts.

The colorful trogons are common in the forests of Central and South America, Africa, and Asia. They are quite large for arboreal (tree-living) birds, measuring 9 to 15 inches (23 to 38 cm) in length. Trogons are usually seen alone or in pairs or, rarely, in small family groups. The most spectacular trogon is the quetzal (*Pharomachrus mocino*), which has a metallic green back, a bright red underside, and long tail plumes, in the case of the male. The quetzal ranges from southern Mexico to western Panama.

Africa

In contrast to rain forests of the neotropical region, African rain forests have far fewer species, and the

*The keel-billed toucan (*Ramphastos sulfuratus*) lives in the rain forests of Central and South America. Its brightly colored bill is curved to pluck fruit from the trees.*

PARROTS AND PARAKEETS

Parrots are the best known of all tropical birds. There are more than 300 species, ranging from the large blue-and-gold macaw of the Central and South American rain forests to the nectar-sipping lories of the Pacific islands. Parrots are ideally adapted for life in the trees. Many are shades of green to camouflage them amid the leafy forest canopy in which they live. However, some species, in particular the macaws, are brilliantly colored. Parrots have a very characteristic strong bill, used for a range of tasks from preening to crushing hard seeds and nuts. The bill also serves as a grappling hook when climbing among the branches. Parrots' feet are unusual in that they are zygodactylous (the two outer toes face backward), which, in addition to giving them a very strong grasp, also enables the feet to be used like hands, to manipulate objects.

Parrots are brilliant mimics. The gray parrot of Africa (*Psittacus erithacus*, shown below) imitates the calls of other birds in the wild. Parrots in captivity will mimic household noises and human speech. This trait has made them popular pets, which, along with habitat loss, is threatening their survival. Many species are endangered, while the paradise parrot (*Psephotus pulcherrimus*) of Australia may now be extinct: the last sighting of a paradise parrot was in 1927.

Like all forest birds, parrots also depend for their survival on the future of the forests. As humans cut down and remove the rain forest for lumber and for farmland, they destroy the birds' habitats and put them in danger of extinction.

AT RISK

number of individuals tend to be rather low. Here the great majority of birds are small insect eaters such as the flycatchers, bulbuls, and babblers. A phenomenon of the tropical forest is the presence of mixed-species flocks made up of dozens of such little birds, which move through the trees hunting their own particular food. The groups disturb the vegetation, flushing out insects.

Overhead in the canopy, larger birds such as hornbills, turacos, and parrots fly from branch to branch in search of fruit. There is also a small group of large birds, such as the Congo peacock (*Afropavo congensis*), that, having largely abandoned flight, moves around the forest floor.

Asia

Trees of the Southeast Asian rain forests are taller than related species in Africa and the New World, with the emergents (the tallest trees of the forest, reaching above the canopy) often soaring to a height of more than 225 feet (70 m). Birds of the emergent zone include swifts, eagles that prey on lizards, bats, and rodents, and aggressive little birds of prey called falconets that, although hardly bigger than sparrows, look like falcons and prey on large insects and small birds. The largest birds of the Asian rain forest canopy are the hornbills, which feed on fruit and insects and nest in cavities in the trees.

Australia and New Zealand

Australia and New Zealand have two distinct types of forest—temperate and tropical—each supporting a unique selection of plant and animal life. The temperate forests of New Zealand, with only two native species of land mammals (both bats), are unusual in that their principal herbivores are birds: three species of flightless kiwis and the kakapo (*Strigops habroptilus*), a ground parrot.

Many other birds are unique to the region, including the birds of paradise and bowerbirds of tropical New Guinea, famous for their exotic plumage, showy courtship displays, and building of bowers, which some decorate with objects of a particular color. No less elegant are the lyrebirds of the temperate forests of eastern Australia. Like the parrots that abound in both temperate and tropical forests of Australia, lyrebirds are also very accomplished mimics (see COMMUNICATION).

K. McCALLUM

See also: BIRDS; BIRDS OF PREY; COMMUNICATION; POLLINATION; TAIGA BIOMES; TEMPERATE FOREST BIOMES; TROPICAL RAIN FOREST BIOMES.

Further reading:

Burton, R. 2001. *The World of the Hummingbird*. Toronto: Firefly Books.
Eastman, J., and A. Hansen. 1998. *Birds of Forest, Yard, and Thicket*. Mechanicsburg, Pa.: Stackpole Books.
Jordan, R., and J. Pattison. 1999. *African Parrots*. Surrey, BC: Hancock House Publishing Limited.

FOSSEY, DIAN

An unconventional U.S. zoologist, Dian Fossey (1932–1985) devoted her life to studying and protecting African mountain gorillas. Apart from making important observations on the social structure of gorilla society, she raised awareness of the dangers faced by gorillas, which are now protected by governments and international organizations.

Early life

Dian Fossey was born in Fairfax, California, in 1932. Her parents were divorced when she was six because of her father's heavy drinking. Kitty, her mother, remarried a year later. Her stepfather, Richard Price, was a strict disciplinarian who insisted that Fossey eat all her meals in the kitchen with the housekeeper until she was 10 years old. One of the few people to show her any affection was her Uncle Albert. Perhaps because she was a lonely child, Fossey developed a lifelong affection for animals.

In 1950 she enrolled as a preveterinary medical student at the University of California in Davis. However, she found studying science a struggle, and when she failed her second year after getting low grades in chemistry and physics, she transferred to San Jose State College to study occupational therapy, a course that would allow her to work with damaged children. She graduated in 1954.

Fossey worked in several hospitals before becoming director of occupational therapy at the Kosair Children's Hospital in Louisville, Kentucky. She had a natural affinity with emotionally and physically disabled children, describing them as "like wild animals penned up with no hope of escape." Although she loved her work, Fossey dreamed of traveling to Africa and seeing wild animals. She was inspired by the writings of George Schaller, who had spent a year studying the behavior of mountain gorillas in Zaire. However, such a trip would cost thousands of dollars. Her attempts to persuade her parents to back a bank loan for the trip proved unsuccessful, but she remained undaunted. She took out a mortgage

against her next three years' earnings and on September 26, 1963, set off for Africa.

Meeting Louis Leakey

Fossey wanted to achieve two things while in Africa: to see mountain gorillas and to meet Louis Leakey, the famous paleoanthropologist. After a safari trip she set off for Olduvai Gorge, Leakey's field site. On the morning of her arrival, Leakey had just uncovered part of a fossil giraffe. As he was showing Fossey the specimen, she slipped, fell into the excavation, sprained her ankle, and vomited over the fossil. It was hardly an auspicious meeting, but in the course of conversation, Leakey and Fossey discovered a common interest in gorillas. Leakey thought gorillas might provide insights into human evolution, his field of interest.

Two weeks later, battling with asthma and a still-painful ankle, Fossey struggled up the 10,000 feet Virunga volcanoes in Zaire and had her first sighting of the elusive animals that were to dominate the rest of her life—mountain gorillas.

Fossey returned to the United States and did not see Louis Leakey again until 1966, when he came to Louisville to give a lecture. He was also looking for someone willing to take on a long-term study of mountain gorillas, similar to that being carried out in Gombe, Tanzania, by Jane Goodall on chimpanzees. Fossey's enthusiasm and determination more than made up for her lack of suitable qualifications, more so because Leakey considered qualified scientists overtrained and also believed that women had a greater aptitude for this sort of work than men.

After many years of work, gorillas allowed Dian Fossey to join in their groups.

CONNECTIONS

● The paleoanthropologist Louis Leakey promoted the study of **BEHAVIOR** in **PRIMATES**, hoping to supplement his research into **HUMAN EVOLUTION**. The success of Jane Goodall's chimpanzee study in Gombe was an important factor leading to Fossey's long-term investigation of mountain gorilla behavior.

CORE FACTS

- Fossey's work on gorilla behavior changed the popular view of gorillas as savage beasts, showing them instead to be peaceful animals (unless provoked) living in family groups.
- The high public profile of the mountain gorilla is due mainly to Fossey, who promoted the gentle nature of the gorilla and at the same time warned of the danger of their extinction.
- Fossey's direct approach to handling poaching, which included shooting cattle that wandered into Virunga National Park, made her unpopular with local people and probably led to her murder.

Dian Fossey with her team in Rwanda.

In 1970 Fossey left Karisoke to complete her PhD at Cambridge University, England. She regarded a PhD as a necessary evil; formal qualifications were essential to receive funding, and a doctorate would allow her to take on graduate students to help with research.

Back to the Virungas

Fossey returned to Africa in December 1966, much against the wishes of her parents. After visiting Jane Goodall in Gombe, to learn about her methods of study, and seeing Leakey, who by this time had returned to Nairobi, she drove to her field site with wildlife photographer Alan Root, who helped to set up camp. He departed two days later, leaving Fossey with two African employees with whom she could not communicate, as she could not speak their language

At first she found camp life difficult; the climate was cold and wet, and the thin mountain air made breathing difficult. It was a lonely existence, but Fossey soon became engrossed in her work. She kept a detailed diary of her experiences with the gorillas and managed to win their confidence by imitating the right sounds and postures. After six months she got within 30 feet (9m) of the apes, possibly because they had been habituated by Schaller two years earlier.

Civil war in Zaire forced Fossey to flee her camp in July 1967. However, she was undeterred and within weeks returned to the Rwandan side of the Virunga volcanoes and set up another camp. The gorillas here were more wary, and it took much longer to be accepted by them.

Karisoke Research Center

Fossey spent most of the last 18 years of her life at her new camp, which later became an international center for gorilla research. She led an increasingly isolated existence as her attachment to the gorillas grew. Her approach to studying animal behavior was based on empathy and affection rather than dispassionate academic observation. She named all the gorillas, her favorite being a young male called Digit that would come and play with her. The group to which Digit belonged was dominated by a silverback, which Fossey called Uncle Bert, after her own uncle. A visiting National Geographic photographer, Bob Campbell, filmed Fossey with her gorillas. The pictures caused a sensation—for the first time they showed friendly physical contact between an ape and a human.

The war on poachers

Throughout her stay in Virunga National Park, Fossey became increasingly aware of the problem of poaching. Gorillas were caught for meat or to obtain their heads and hands to sell as trophies. Poachers also killed mother gorillas as well as other protective members of the family group in their quest to get babies to supply to zoos. Sometimes wire snares and traps set for smaller prey would injure gorillas, and they would die from wound infections. Fossey realized that if poaching continued on this scale, the mountain gorilla would soon be extinct.

On New Year's Day 1978, one of Fossey's students found the body of Digit. His head and hands had been hacked off. He had been killed defending his family. Uncle Bert was killed six months later. Fossey had a mercurial temper at the best of times, and she now resorted to drastic measures to drive away the poachers. She told the local Tutsi herders she was a sorceress and burned the houses of those she thought were responsible for poaching. She shot their cattle if they strayed into the Virunga National Park and armed her students with guns, a policy she called "active conservation." She also began an international campaign to stop poaching by setting up the Digit Fund to publicize the plight of the gorillas and finance gorilla patrols in the park.

In 1981 Fossey returned to the United States and became an associate professor at Cornell University, Ithaca, New York. The move gave her a chance to escape the rising tension at Karisoke and write a book about the gorillas, called *Gorillas in the Mist* (1983). The book, which recounted observations of her field research, was an immediate success and was later made into a film (1988). Fossey returned to Rwanda in 1983, but her enemies had not forgotten her. She was found murdered in her cabin on December 27, 1985. Her head had been split open by a blow from a machete. She was buried at Karisoke alongside Digit. Apart from her name, her headstone simply reads "No one loved gorillas more." Her murderer was never found.

B. MORGAN/K. DENNIS-BRYAN

See also: CONSERVATION; SOCIAL ORGANIZATION.

Further reading

Fossey, D. 1983. *Gorillas in the Mist*. New York: Mariner Books.
Schaller, G. B., and T. L. Matthews. 1998. *Light Shining Through the Mist: Dian Fossey*. Washington, D.C.: National Geographic Society.
Weber, B., and A. Vedder. *In the Kingdom of Gorillas. The Quest to Save Rwanda's Mountain Gorillas*. London: Aurum Press, 2002.

FOSSILS

Fossils are the preserved remains of prehistoric organisms or traces of their activity

Fossils are the preserved remains of prehistoric organisms or evidence of their existence. The earliest fossils are of organisms that lived hundreds of millions of years ago—a time so ancient that scientists refer to it as "deep time." Finding and studying fossils is a fascinating biological treasure hunt that allows people to piece together the long history of life on Earth. The word *fossil* actually means "that which is dug up," although this meaning is now limited to describe only the unearthed remains or indications of past life on Earth. Paleontology is the use of fossils to study this ancient life and its evolution through time.

Two types of fossils

Fossils can be divided into two types: body fossils and trace fossils. Body fossils are the actual bodily remains of an organism or an imprint or cast of those remains. Trace fossils are just that: traces such as burrows, trails, footprints, or coprolites (fossil dung) that give an indication of the activities and behavior of the animal that left them.

Most fossils are dug up or found on dry land, although that land may once have been part of an ancient sea, and the fossil organism probably lived in or near that sea. Marine fossils are more abundant than terrestrial ones, as many are invertebrates, which have a longer evolutionary history and are more numerous than vertebrates. Fossils are usually found embedded in sedimentary rock, where ancient layers of sand, mud, or other sediments have built up and become compressed over time to form the rock. Most sedimentary rocks are laid down in water. Cuttings, quarries, cliffs, caves, and exposed sedimentary seashores are good places to hunt for fossils.

How fossils form

Not all organisms become fossils after they die. Most just rot away and disappear. Soft body parts are either quickly eaten by predators or decay through bacterial action and are nearly always lost to the fossilization process. In addition, the organism may be crushed or torn apart so that it ends up in separate pieces. What makes a fossil different is what happens to an organism both immediately after it dies and during the prolonged period when it undergoes the process known as fossilization. In fossilization the organism's relatively fragile organic structure is commonly replaced with a harder and more durable one.

Because fossilization requires particular conditions, there are many gaps in the fossil record. The process starts with burial: for example, an organism dies and sinks to the bottom of the sea, river, or lake. It then becomes covered with sand or mud, which shuts off the supply of oxygen. Since oxygen is needed for the normal process of decomposition, the buried organism is removed from the cycle of decay and thus has a better-than-average chance of being preserved.

These fossils in amber clearly show completely preserved plant remains.

The organism's hard materials, such as shells, bones, teeth, and wood, provided they are buried quickly, are those that are most likely to become fossils. They gradually become covered by sediments, which protects them from further decay and disintegration.

Most fossils are found in what was once ocean. As ocean sediments pile up, water is expelled, and the particles tend to pull together and stick to one another (a process known as coherence). In this way, shale, limestone, or sandstone rocks, made up from the prevailing sediments, form around the developing fossil. Harder rocks, such as limestone, tend to preserve the full three-dimensional structure; in softer materials,

CORE FACTS

- Fossils are any evidence of ancient life that is preserved in rocks.
- There are two types of fossils: body fossils, which represent physical remains of organisms, and trace fossils, which include trails, footprints, and burrows.
- Fossilization commonly involves a dead organism's organic structure being replaced by much harder material, such as calcite, iron sulphide, or quartz.
- A fossil's age can often be calculated by radioactive dating.
- Fossil fuels (coal, gas, and petroleum) are the fossilized remains of plants that lived up to 340 million years ago.

CONNECTIONS

- Fossilization provides much of the evidence for the study of the **EVOLUTION** of life on Earth.

- Information on the **EXTINCTION** of animals and plants can be gained from the study of fossils.

- Studying fossils has also given humans a better understanding of **HUMAN EVOLUTION**.

THE PILTDOWN MAN AND THE MISSING LINKS

The evolution of the modern human being from apelike ancestors is one of paleontology's greatest puzzles. The fossil record is incomplete, and the "missing links" have long been sought. In 1912 the fossilized remains of a skull, half human and half ape, was discovered in Britain and unveiled to an astonished public. Discovered by an English lawyer, Charles Dawson, the skull was the fulfilment of a 50-year-old prophecy from Charles Darwin's theory of natural selection and provided the ideal missing link between humans and apes. The skull combined the high brow of an intelligent hominid with a jawbone resembling that of an ape. Crude flint tools and bones of long-extinct animals were found with the skull in a Sussex gravel pit and seemed to show that the skull's owner had lived long before the time of Neandertals. Since skeletal remains of Neandertals were already well known, this half human, half ape was greeted with much enthusiasm.

In 1953, however, the skull was denounced as a forgery. It was found to be simply the amalgamation of a recent human skull and the jawbone of a modern orang-utan. The so-called Piltdown Man had fooled scientists for more than 40 years.

such as shale, specimens become flattened.

Once final burial has taken place, the slow and gradual process of fossilization can begin. The physical and chemical processes (called diagenesis) that actually preserve the remains occur. The skeleton of a vertebrate such as an ichthyosaur (an aquatic reptile), for example, will eventually become a mineralized replica: a fossil made of stone. Natural bones are a mixture of protein fibers (collagen) and mineralized binding substance (hydroxyapatite). During the fossilization process, the protein part gradually disappears and is replaced by minerals such as calcite, iron sulphide, or quartz. This process is known as molecular substitution.

Petrifaction

Another rarer mechanism of preservation is petrifaction. In this process, the original fossil is replaced molecule by molecule to produce a perfect replica. In Yellowstone National Park, the silicified tree trunks from a sequence of 30 forests, one growing on top of the other, still exist, following the destruction of the woodland by volcanic eruptions 50 million years ago. The petrified forests of Arizona provide another example of trees buried and infiltrated with minerals.

Animals can also be petrified. The muscles of a 350 million year-old shark have been preserved in this way. Soft body parts are rarely preserved in the fossil record. The famous Burgess Shale bed in British Columbia, however, has provided many specimens of trilobites and other arthropods complete with limbs, antennae, and gut contents. As yet no conclusive explanation has been given for this remarkable preservation, termed a conservation *lagerstatten* (German for fossil bonanza).

Complete preservation

Under very rare conditions, the whole organism is preserved, with hair, skin, and internal organs still intact and recognizable. Such complete preservation occurs under glacial conditions, in which the body is quickly frozen and covered with ice, and thus, microbial activity is minimized. Woolly mammoths and rhinos have been found in Siberia and Alaska. Their stomachs still contained undigested grasses and their flesh, after 45,000 years, was found to be still edible. Frozen human remains have also been discovered. In 1991, for example, scientists discovered the remains of a 5,000-year-old man in an Austrian glacier.

Some organisms, particularly insects, are fossilized as complete specimens in amber. Amber is the yellow fossilized resin from coniferous trees. The insects preserved in the sticky resin appear very lifelike, as they were unaware of the danger of the resin when they became stuck and covered in it. In one case, a spider with silken threads emerging from its spinnerets was forever immobilized and preserved in a bead of amber.

Peat bogs also hold many clues to the past, and many long-dead and fossilized human specimens have been dug from their midst. One of the most famous was the Tollund man found in 1950 in a Danish peat bog. After 2,000 years, many features are still visible

Petrifaction of this log has resulted in the replacement of the original fossil with quartz.

in minute detail, from the leather hat on his head to the hairs and pores on his face. As peat bogs are very acidic, bacteria cannot survive, the result being little or no putrefaction (rotting), and thus, organisms become fossils.

Natural petroleum seeping to the surface and forming asphalt pools, such as the 25,000 year-old La Brea Tar Pits in Los Angeles, California, led to a sticky end for many ancient animals. Whole food chains, from the original herbivore victim, to the carnivore that thought it had found easy game, and the scavenger trying to finish the remains, are preserved in some of these pools. Finally, in extremely hot and dry areas, mummification or rapid dehydration of a body may occur, yet another route to a body's preservation. Specimens of a giant sloth preserved in this way have been found in New Mexico.

Plant fossils

Many plants are fossilized. Coal, for example, is made up of remains of ancient plants such as giant club mosses and horsetails. However, compression for as much as 345 million years has blurred their structure, and thus, it is indecipherable for detailed study. Plants that are preserved on fine clay or silt as impressions or outlines can more easily be studied and often yield impressive detail, such as the structure of the leaves. Some fine specimens of Eocene plants have been found in the clay pits at Puryear, Tennessee.

In other cases, plant material may be subject to carbonization. This process occurs when plants are deposited in low oxygen conditions, as found in swamps or still water. The soft parts of the plant decay through water and chemical action, leaving the more stable carbon elements to settle as sediment, which forms black shale, a mudstone with high concentrations of organic matter.

Plant pollen is very distinctive and can be studied under high-power electron microscopes. Fossil pollen can provide information about ancient plant communities and climatic change.

Trace fossils

Trace fossils are formed when an overlying layer of sediment fills the tracks made by an animal to give a positive impression. They include the various tracks made on the ocean floor by ancient invertebrates such as worms, starfish, snails, and trilobites, as well as the larger land tracks of dinosaurs and human ancestors. Permanent burrows, the homes of animals such as burrowing worms, bivalves, and sea urchins can also be preserved. Such tracks and trails provide accurate information about the motion, stride, normal pace, and even lifestyle and habits of the animal that made them. Fossil footprints and coprolites, for example, are often the only record of some prehistoric animals, such as the late Triassic reptiles that were the ancestors of dinosaurs.

How fossils are dated

Fossils are themselves part of the geological dating process, since each stratum or rock layer contains fossils of organisms that inhabited that layer. In undisturbed

*Pictured is a body fossil of the leaves of the fern **Mariopteris nervosa**.*

THE RISE AND FALL OF TRILOBITES

Trilobites (the name means three lobed) were early arthropods. Trilobites are some of the best-known and most extensively collected fossils. They were the dominant and most advanced marine life-forms in the lower Paleozoic era, some 550 million years ago, and represented the first massive radiation of the arthropods. They evolved rapidly, producing thousands of different species and spreading extensively, and their remains are found on every continent.

The extensive remains left behind by these animals have provided a wealth of knowledge on their structure and lifestyles. Their bodies were segmented, except in the regions of the head and tail, and some species could curl up into a protective ball much as modern pill bugs do. Most were small, measuring less than 4 inches (10 cm), although a few were much larger and reached lengths of up to 28 inches (70 cm). In many species, the eyes were well developed and, where preserved, represent one of the first recorded examples of a vision system in the animal kingdom.

Trilobites existed in a wide range of habitats; most were filter-feeding scavengers living on the ocean bottom in shallow waters. Others were free swimmers and hunters that lived in deeper waters. Trilobite life history was similar to that of many modern-day arthropod species. Periods of growth were followed by the molting of their outer covering (carapace) when a new segment grew. It is the carapace rather than the whole organism that is found most commonly in a fossilized form.

Trilobites prospered throughout the Ordovician period (500 million to 425 million years ago) but gradually decreased in diversity through the Silurian and Devonian periods (425 million to 405 million years ago and 405 million to 345 million years ago, respectively). By the Carboniferous period (345 million to 280 million years ago), only one relatively unspecialized family remained, and at the end of the Permian period, 230 million years ago, this family, too, became extinct.

rock, the lowest layer will contain the oldest fossils, but movements of Earth's crust (to form mountain ranges, for example) heave up the lower beds and expose fossils long buried. Finding similar fossils thousands of miles apart in rocks belonging to different continents has also allowed geologists to correlate and date the age of the rocks relative to one another. As some fossils give such a good indication of the age of the surrounding rock, they are often used in the detection of oil and petroleum deposits.

The age of a fossil is usually obtained through radioactive dating. The dating is based on the fact that a known proportion of atmospheric carbon is radioactive, occurring as a radioactive isotope (carbon 14 as opposed to the nonradioactive and more common carbon 12). Plants, when alive, absorb carbon dioxide for photosynthesis and pass the fixed carbon along the food chain to various animal species. When they die, organisms absorb no new material. These radioactive isotopes decay (break down) to form more stable elements according to a known timetable. A fossilized bone can be dated by the amount of carbon 14 remaining compared with the relative amounts of carbon 14 available at the time of its formation. However, this technique becomes less accurate if specimens are older than 40,000 years, because carbon 14 decays relatively quickly, having a half-life of only about 5,730 years. The amount of carbon 14 remaining in older fossils is often too small to quantify. Other elements, such as rubidium, can be used as alternatives. Rubidium may be found in suitable quantities in rock close to the fossil-bearing rock layers rather than in the fossil itself and can be measured. Often several different dating methods are used for greater accuracy.

Why scientists study fossils

Fossils provide much interesting information on Earth's past, both in terms of the creatures that lived here and the changes in climate and environment. Britain, for example, was once much warmer than it now is. In the River Thames fossils of hippopotamuses haved been discovered that are dated before the final glaciation. These animals are limited now to the warmer regions of Africa.

Most of what scientists know about the evolution of organisms has been learned from the fossil record. The fossil evidence is also supported by information from fields as diverse as embryology, molecular genetics, and comparative anatomy, providing a mass of indisputable information on the evolutionary links between organisms on Earth.

The oldest identifiable fossils are those of bacteria. These date from about 3.5 billion years ago and represent the earliest life-forms on Earth. Bacteria are single-celled prokaryotes (cells without an enclosed nucleus). The oldest eukaryotic fossils (animals, plants, and fungi with an enclosed nucleus) are of unicellular organisms and date from about 1.5 billion years ago. Such remains give us insight into early life on Earth. The fossil record has provided many examples of evolutionary change within a single lineage

LUCY

The question of what came first in humans, two-legged gait (bipedalism) or the larger brain, was the cause of much heated debate at the beginning of the 20th century. The discovery of Piltdown man had apparently solved this problem at least for 40 years, but the debate was reopened when the find was discovered to be a hoax. The discovery of a fossil skeleton, nicknamed Lucy, by the U.S. paleontologist Donald Johanson in 1974, in the Afar region of northeastern Ethiopia finally provided the answer. Her skeleton was a rare find, being almost complete, and gave exciting information on human evolution.

Lucy belonged to one of the *Australopithecus* species of apes, *Australopithecus afarensis*, the most primitive of the Australopithicine species, which existed three to four million years ago. Lucy's skeleton was that of a female individual about 4 feet in height, and since her wisdom teeth had erupted, she was believed to be about 20 years of age. Her teeth were midway between those of modern humans and chimps, with canine teeth of medium length. Her skull capacity was smaller than modern humans, but the most exciting feature of her skeleton was the fact that the pelvic, leg, and foot bones proved that Lucy and her contemporaries were already bipedal. The archeologist Mary Leakey provided further evidence when, in 1976, she found footprints of three bipedal individuals at Laetoli in Tanzania dating from around the same time as Lucy. Bipedalism is now accepted as one of the earliest features in the evolution of human beings, preceding the formation of a larger brain.

DISCOVERERS

(the line of descent from a common ancestor), a change known as phyletic change, and fulfills the expectations of Charles Darwin's theory of natural selection. The fossil history of the horse, for example, clearly shows the gradual reduction in toes and the modifications of the leg bones and teeth that have led, after 60 million years, to the modern horse.

J. STIRLING

See also: LIVING FOSSILS; OCEAN HABITATS.

Further reading:

Fortey, R. 1999. *Life: A Natural History of the First Four Billion Years of Life on Earth*. Vancouver: Vintage Books. Palmer, D., et al. 1999. *Encyclopedia of Dinosaurs and Prehistoric Creatures*. New York: Simon & Schuster.

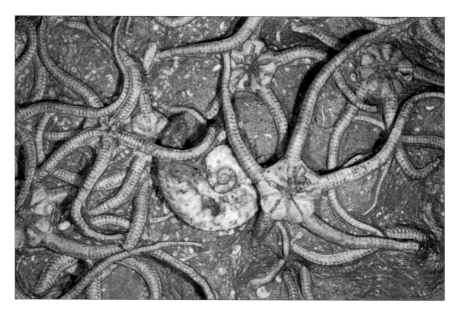

These are body fossils of the eophiuoid Palaeocoma egertoni *and an ammonite (at the center).*

FRANKLIN, ROSALIND

Rosalind Franklin provided images of DNA that helped to confirm its double helical structure

A brilliant scientist who died young, Rosalind Elsie Franklin (1920–1958) was first an industrial chemist working on coal and then a molecular biologist who worked on viruses (particularly the tobacco mosaic virus). She contributed to the discovery of the double helical structure of DNA. Franklin died in 1958, four years before British biophysicist Francis Crick (b. 1916), U.S. geneticist James Watson (b. 1928), and British biophysicist Maurice Wilkins (b. 1916) were awarded the Nobel Prize for physiology or medicine.

Early life
Rosalind Franklin was born in London on July 25, 1920, the second of five children. She was educated at St Paul's Girls School, London, where her keen intelligence and dedicated nature were recognized and encouraged early on. However, her decision at the age of 15 to become a scientist was not wholly welcomed by her father because the family had no previous connection with science. Initially he refused to pay her college fees but eventually gave in when his wife voiced her support and an aunt offered to provide the money. In 1938 Franklin passed the entrance exam and went to Newnham College, Cambridge, one of the few U.K. women's colleges at the time, where she studied physical chemistry. She graduated in 1941 but was disappointed not to get a first-class degree. Franklin attributed this to having worked herself into a state of exhaustion before the final examinations. She was, however, awarded a graduate fellowship to investigate gas-phase chromatography under noted chemist Ronald Norrish (1897–1978), but she left after a year.

Physical chemistry research
In 1942 Franklin was appointed assistant research officer at the British Coal Utilization Research Association. While working there, Franklin established a reputation for painstaking and solid work. She applied her expertise in physical chemistry to the structure of coal and charcoal, gathering data for her thesis, which was entitled *The Physical Chemistry of Solid Colloids with Special Relation to Coal and Related*

Rosalind Franklin achieved a great deal as a scientist in her short and difficult career. It is tempting to wonder how much more she would have achieved had she lived longer.

Materials. She obtained her PhD from Cambridge in 1945. By the age of 26, she had published five papers and interested other scientists in the field of high-strength carbon fibers. Between 1947 and 1950 Franklin worked in Paris at the Laboratoire Central des Services Chimiques de l'Etat. As a *chercheur* (researcher), Franklin developed her skill in X-ray diffraction techniques by working on problems of carbon structure, especially graphitization of carbon at high temperatures. It was her skill with X-ray crystallography that led to her research work on the structure of DNA (deoxyribonucleic acid).

The switch to biochemistry
While working on coal, Franklin had been introduced to a scientist named John Randall, whose biophysics laboratory was involved with investigating the structure of DNA. Franklin had recognized the growing importance of studying biological molecules, and so when she was awarded a research fellowship in 1951, she joined Randall's Medical Research Council Biophysics Research Unit at King's College London. British biophysicist Maurice

CORE FACTS
- Franklin's achievements were made at a time when there were few women scientists, and as a result she often felt isolated in her work.
- While working on coal, Frankin helped launch the field of high-strength carbon fibers.
- The X-ray diffraction techniques used in mapping the structure of DNA were markedly improved by Franklin.
- Franklin's research on viruses was instrumental in founding the field of structural virology.

CONNECTIONS

● Franklin's contribution to the discovery of the structure of **DNA** was once often overlooked, credit going only to the Nobel Prize winners **CRICK**, Watson, and Wilkins.

● Franklin used **X RAYS** to obtain diffraction images of DNA and also worked on **VIRUSES**, including the tobacco mosaic virus.

Wilkins, who later shared the 1962 Nobel Prize with Crick and Watson, was already working there.

Maurice Hugh Fredrick Wilkins was born on December 15, 1916 at Pongaroa in New Zealand. When he was six, he was brought to England by his parents, educated in Birmingham, and went on to study physics at St John's College, Cambridge, graduating in 1938. His first position was as research assistant to John Randall at Birmingham University working on the luminescence of solids. After gaining his PhD in 1940, Wilkins applied his knowledge to the World War II effort and was involved in projects such as improving cathode-ray radar screens. The technology he developed is still in use. He then worked on uranium isotopes, after which he spent a short time in California as part of the Manhattan Project, a U.S. initiative concerning nuclear physics that resulted in the dropping of atomic bombs on Japan. Wilkins returned to Britain in 1945 when the war ended. He again started to work with John Randall, this time at the University of St Andrews, Scotland, where he was employed as a lecturer in physics. Like Franklin, he too gradually became interested in biophysics, using methodologies from previously unrelated disciplines. Wilkins wanted to use his knowledge in a positive way after his wartime experiences. So when Randall's biophysics group moved to King's College London in 1946, Wilkins went too.

By the time Franklin arrived at the laboratory, Wilkins had already obtained diffraction pictures of DNA taken by Raymond Gosling, a graduate student assigned to work under Rosalind. Wilkins was also aware that sharper images could be obtained under higher humidity. Although Franklin was uniquely suited to the difficult task of setting up X-ray fraction equipment and applying it to the complex DNA molecule, she found herself in an environment that was hostile to female scientists and eventually came into conflict with Wilkins. Much has been written about their somewhat testy relationship. It seems that the problem may have started because Wilkins was under the impression he was getting an assistant, while Franklin thought she was taking over the X-ray diffrection work on DNA. Despite this situation, she and Gosling conducted a systematic study into the effects of humidity on X-ray imaging, and Franklin succeeded in collecting clear X-ray diffraction images of DNA molecules, despite the difficulties of the material. She also analyzed them in detail, establishing that DNA existed in two forms, A and B, in dynamic equilibrium. This finding was consistent with the helical structure proposed in 1950 by Wilkins. However, Franklin was never entirely convinced that DNA had a helical structure and sought further experimental evidence to resolve the matter. In the meantime, Wilkins showed her work (initially without her knowledge) to Watson and Crick, who then published their now famous paper on the structure of DNA in the magazine *Nature* (April 25, 1953).

Franklin received little credit for her work on DNA at first, even though she supplied Watson and Crick with vital data and images and pointed out various errors in their first unpublished model of the DNA molecule. She supported having phosphates on the outside of the helix, as well as discovering that DNA has A and B forms. Franklin and Gosling's paper on DNA, which was in draft form in March 1953, was finally published in *Nature* on July 25, 1953.

Too short a life

Because of the difficulties she experienced at King's College, Franklin decided to look for another position. In 1953 she transferred to Birkbeck College, London, to work in the crystallography laboratory of Professor J. Bernal. She was supported by grants from both the British Agricultural Research Council and the U.S. Department of Health. She continued to publish papers from her earlier work on coal but also completed writing up her research on DNA and started to study the structure of the tobacco mosaic virus (TMV) and other viruses. She and her team established among other things that TMV particles were hollow, not solid, as was previously thought. Between 1953 and 1958, Franklin produced 17 papers on this subject, even though she had been diagnosed with ovarian cancer, very possibly caused by the effects of X rays. In 1956 Franklin had the first of three operations. She continued working for another two years, becoming interested in the polio virus, but died at the age of 37 on April 16, 1958. Wilkins survives and remains an outspoken campaigner against nuclear warfare.

L. VENOLIA / K. DENNIS-BRYAN

See also: ANALYTICAL TECHNIQUES; BIOLOGY, HISTORY AND PHILOSOPHY OF.

Further reading

Maddox, B. 2002. *Rosalind Franklin and the Discovery of the Double Helix Structure of DNA*. London: HarperCollins.
Senker, C. 2002. *Rosalind Franklin*. *Scientists Who Made History*. Austin: Raintree / Steck Vaughn.

X-RAY DIFFRACTION

X-ray diffraction was the technique used by Franklin to obtain high-quality images of the DNA molecule (B form). For a molecule to be "seen," the distance between its constituent atoms must be at least half the wavelength of the light being used to view it. Normal light has too great a wavelength (hence, molecules are invisible), and so X rays, which also have a reasonable degree of spatial coherence, are used. The DNA is prepared in a crystalline form to give it a repetitive structure, each unit being identical to the next. When the X-ray beam hits the crystal, the electrons surrounding each atom of the molecule bend the X rays into a characteristic pattern called the X-ray diffraction pattern (see ANALYTICAL TECHNIQUES). The image obtained is usually a series of discrete spots arranged in circles around the beam. The position and brightness of the spots provide information about the crystal. Franklin's pictures were produced in the early 1950s, when X-ray diffraction was still in its infancy. However, the quality of her work was such that Watson knew immediately when he saw the X rays that they confirmed the double helical structure of DNA that he and Crick had been working on. It is possible that this X-ray technique caused Franklin's early death.

FROGS AND TOADS

Frogs and toads are tailless amphibians in the order Anura

Early zoologists sowed the seeds of endless confusion when they chose to distinguish between one slimy little creature that jumps and another dry, warty one that walks by calling the first a frog and the second a toad. At the time, only one type of each of these creatures was known: the common frog of Europe (later to be known as *Rana temporaria*) and the common toad of Europe (*Bufo bufo*).

Investigation has revealed, however, that there is no real scientific difference between frogs and toads, and some families contain both. Members of the largest frog family, Ranidae (containing more than 700 species) are still often called true frogs, while the family Bufonidae (more than 330 species) contains what are sometimes known as the true toads. For the most part, however, scientists simply use the term *frog* for all such creatures, whether slimy or dry, smooth, or warty.

CORE FACTS

- Frogs and toads are tailless amphibians in the order Anura. Modern frogs first appeared on Earth at least 150 million years ago.
- Although frogs tend to have moist, smooth skin and toads are dry, there is no scientific difference between them.
- Frogs and toads are found in most regions of the world.
- Most frogs and toads breed in water. In both, the larval stage is a gill-breathing tadpole.

Frogs and toads belong to the order Anura—amphibians without a tail. There are more than 3,800 species, ranging in size from the tiny *Psyllophryne didactyla* of Brazil, whose body is less than ⅖ inch (1 cm) long, to the goliath frog (*Conraua goliath*) of West Africa, which may grow to over 12 inches (30 cm). One of the largest frogs in North America is the bullfrog (*Rana catesbeiana*), which can grow to 6 inches (15 cm) in length. The leopard frog (*Rana pipiens*) is familiar from dissections in biology classes.

Most frogs and toads lay their eggs in water. The larval stage is the aquatic, gill-breathing tadpole, which metamorphoses (changes) into the adult.

Body shape

Frogs and toads are easily recognizable, with their short, fat bodies, flat heads, large mouths, and well-defined limbs. Their shape depends largely on lifestyle and habitat. Most move by leaping, and so the back legs are usually much larger and stronger than the front legs. Frogs can easily leap distances up to ten times their body length and sometimes up to 40 times. Some species (mainly toads) rarely jump; they move by walking and so have smaller back legs. Tree frogs are smaller than most terrestrial frogs and have sticky disks on their fingertips so they can cling to branches and leaves. The skin of the belly can also press tightly against a surface. Aquatic frogs are streamlined for swimming and have long back legs and large webbed feet.

A Malayan horned toad (Megophrys nasuta). Horned toads are specialized for burrowing, using the sharp ridges on their heads to dig.

CONNECTIONS

- Frogs and toads produce poisons from special glands in their **SKIN** to deter **PREDATORS**, an effective form of **DEFENSE**.

- In the late 1940s and 1950s, scientists used the clawed frog (*Xenopus laevis*) to study the complete development from the embryonic stage to **METAMORPHOSIS.** This work formed the basis for studies into the development of other **AMPHIBIANS.**

A poison-dart frog (Dendrobates pumilio) from Costa Rica. The bright colors warn predators that the frog is poisonous.

Distribution

Frogs are found in most regions of the world except very cold, dry habitats and some inaccessible oceanic islands. Many species live in swamps and marshes or alongside rivers, streams, and lakes. In wetlands they forage around the water's edge, ready to jump in to escape predators. Only one species, the crab-eating frog (*Rana cancr ivora*) of Asia, lives in salt water. Tropical forests also support many species: some live in the trees, others on the forest floor. Several species of frogs spend their entire lives underground in burrows or chambers.

Avoiding predators

Frogs rely mainly on camouflage to escape detection from a range of predators, which may include mammals, birds, snakes, and even other frogs. Most frogs are shades of brown or green, patterned to blend in with their surroundings. Species that live among leaves or reeds are often bright green. They include many species of tree frogs, several of which resemble lichen and are perfectly camouflaged when resting

on lichen-covered tree trunks. Frogs living on the forest floor amid leaf litter are often shades of brown to match the dead leaves.

Many cryptically colored frogs have a gaudy patch of skin on their flanks and thighs. These brightly colored or patterned patches, known as flash markings, are concealed when the frog is at rest, only becoming exposed when it straightens its legs to leap away. *Agalychnis calcarifer*, a tree frog of Central and South America, has a green body when resting, but when it moves, orange and black stripes on its flanks and thighs are exposed. It could be that these markings exist to confuse predators: when the frog leaps, the predator's eye is surprised by them, but when the frog lands, they disappear.

Other species, however, are brightly colored, and their dramatic livery is believed to warn predators that they are poisonous or foul tasting. This situation is most evident in the case of poison-dart frogs (see box left), which are usually colored in brilliant shades of red, yellow, and orange and strikingly patterned. These frogs are diurnal (active during the day). Their toxicity and warning coloration protect them so effectively that there is no need for them to hide by day as many other species must do.

The defensive armory of frogs and toads includes poison glands in the skin that secrete toxic or bad-tasting substances to deter attackers. The biochemical composition of the toxins, their strength, and the position of the issuing glands vary between species. Many secrete alkaloids, known as batrachotoxins, which can be lethal in high doses.

Senses

Frogs have well-developed vision and hearing. They have large eyes with pupils that close down to a small slit on exposure to bright light in order to protect

DEADLY WEAPONS

All frogs produce noxious or toxic substances. The most deadly toxins are those of the so-called poison-dart frogs of Central and South America (genera *Dendrobates* and *Phyllobates*). These frogs are named for the Amazon Indians' use of the poison on their blow darts. As well as a very strong alkaloid called batrachotoxin, they produce a lethal mixture containing several other alkaloid toxins (see ALKALOIDS). One of the deadliest species, only described by scientists in 1978, is the brilliant orange or yellow *Phyllobates terribilis* of western Colombia. Its skin contains substances 20 times more toxic than those produced by any other poison dart frog. A single frog of this species may yield 1,900 micrograms (µg) of a poison, less than 200 µg of which can kill an adult human.

the sensitive cells of the retina. The slit may be vertical or, less often, horizontal. Most frogs possess a third eyelid, properly called the nictitating membrane, to protect the eye from dust.

The ears, located just behind the eyes, are detectable by the circular disk of the tympanum, the eardrum. Frogs are capable of vocalization (unlike other amphibians) and produce a great variety of croaks, trills, clicks, and whistles, unique to each species, to define their territories and attract mates. Most of these sounds are made when the frog exhales a large volume of air. The air vibrates the vocal cords in the larynx. As the frog calls, it inflates one or more vocal sacs (chambers that open off the mouth), and doing so modulates the sound.

Adaptations for survival

In addition to keen senses, frogs have a number of physiological adaptations to aid their survival. Besides breathing through their lungs, they also breathe through their skin—cutaneous respiration. Thus, they can absorb oxygen from water or air through their skin. The skin must be kept moist for this process to occur, so many frogs have a slimy coating. Frogs living in dry places cannot breathe through their skin and rely instead on their enlarged lungs.

Most frogs do not drink but absorb moisture through their skin, either from the water or from moist soil. The most important means of maintaining water balance is by regulating the amount of water absorbed against the amount excreted. Aquatic frogs must limit the amount of water retained in their body and therefore, they excrete urine containing waste products, mainly in the form of ammonia, diluted by large amounts of water.

Terrestrial species must limit the amount of water excreted. They get rid of their waste products as urea, which is less toxic than ammonia and can be held in the body and excreted less frequently in a small amount of water. Terrestrial frogs can store large quantities of water (up to 20 to 30 percent of their body mass) in their bladder. Thus, they can forage farther from water.

Temperature regulation

Like reptiles, amphibians are cold-blooded (see COLD-BLOODED ANIMALS). They cannot control their body temperature internally (as birds and mammals can) but must rely on external sources for warmth. However, because of the risk of drying out, most frogs cannot bask in the Sun, as reptiles can. Frogs function best at temperatures between 68° and 86 °F (20° and 30 °C). They have a critical minimum temperature (usually around 37 °F, or 3 °C) below which they cannot move at all and a critical maximum temperature (around 104 °F, or 40 °C) above which they die from heat exhaustion. Frogs from temperate regions often hibernate underground to avoid cold winter weather. Similarly, in hot regions frogs are active during the cooler parts of the year but estivate (lie dormant) underground in summer to avoid the heat (see HIBERNATION).

THE LIFE OF TADPOLES

Frogs have an aquatic, free-swimming larval stage called a tadpole. Unlike adult frogs, tadpoles have a tail and no limbs, and they breathe through gills (see GILLS AND SPIRACLES). Their shape and size vary with their habitat. Tadpoles that live in calm, quiet waters such as ponds tend to have round, plump bodies; those that live in the faster-moving waters of rivers and streams have slender, streamlined bodies. The mouth of tadpoles that live in fast-moving waters is often modified into suckerlike disks, which enables them to cling onto rocks or vegetation. Some species also have an adhesive disk on the abdomen.

Most tadpoles are herbivorous, feeding largely on algae and bacteria. They have rows of horny rasping teeth arranged around a small mouth, which they use to scrape algae and bacteria growing on leaves or rocks. They also feed on fragments of soft or decaying plants. Some tadpoles feed by taking in gulps of water and filtering out suspended particles. Because plant material takes longer to digest than animal material, tadpoles have a very long gut, which, coiled in a spiral inside the abdomen, is often visible through the body wall. Some species are predatory, feeding on small aquatic arthropods and even tadpoles of their own or other species. Some feed on the eggs of other frogs.

In some species, the tadpoles are supplied with enough yolk so that they do not need to feed. After hatching, the tadpole continues to develop, drawing on its yolk reserves until it metamorphoses into a frog.

Some species of frogs have no tadpole stage; the larvae develop within the egg, emerging as tiny frogs, a phenomenon known as direct development.
In the Surinam toad (*Pipa pipa*), the young frogs emerge from eggs carried in depressions on their mother's back. In a few species fertilization is internal: the developing embryos are kept inside the female, who gives birth to live young.

A CLOSER LOOK

Feeding

All adult frogs are carnivorous, opportunistic feeders who swallow their food whole. The size of their (mostly live) prey depends on the size of their mouth. To help swallow large prey, the frog retracts one or both of its eyeballs into its skull. The eyeballs are pressed down into the flexible roof of the mouth, and this maneuver helps to force the prey down the frog's throat. The eyeballs rest in a tough casing to protect them while the frog is swallowing.

Some frogs are active hunters. Others, relying on their camouflage, lie in wait to catch their prey. Most have a sticky tongue, attached at the front of the mouth, which is flicked out to catch prey. Some species catch prey by lunging and grabbing it in their mouth. Most feed on invertebrates, such as beetles, slugs, snails, and worms, although larger species also eat small vertebrates, including rodents, fish, young birds, snakes, and even other frogs. A few species eat some plant material as well.

Reproduction and development

Unlike the eggs of reptiles and birds, amphibian eggs are not enclosed in a shell. The eggs dry out, and the embryos die if they are not kept moist. Thus, like other amphibians, frogs return to water to breed. Many breed in streams and rivers, while others breed in small temporary pools. Tree frogs breed in the water that collects between the bases of leaves, or in holes high up in trees.

During the breeding season, adults migrate to their breeding sites. Males produce species-specific mating calls to attract a mate. In most frogs, fertilization is external. Once a male has attracted a female, he sits on her back to fertilize her eggs as she releases them. Because of the difficulty of clinging onto the back of a slippery female, breeding males of most species develop structures known as nuptial pads: areas of rough skin on the outer edge of the thumbs. In the tailed frog (*Ascaphus truei*), however, fertilization is internal: the male transfers the sperm directly into the female's body.

The eggs are covered in layers of a jelly, secreted by the female. This jelly protects the eggs from harmful microorganisms and from abrasive damage caused by water movement. In some species, including the large *Bufo* toads, the jelly also contains noxious substances to deter predators such as fish.

Not all frogs lay their eggs in water. Many tree frogs attach their eggs to leaves or twigs overhanging streams. When the tadpoles hatch, they drop into the water below. Other species lay their eggs near water, and when they hatch, the tadpoles wriggle toward the water. Poison-dart frogs lay their eggs on land and guard them until they hatch. The tadpoles then wriggle onto the parent's back to be carried to water to continue their development.

Inside the egg, the embryo grows and hatches out as a tadpole. The tadpole eventually metamorphoses into an adult frog. In most species, metamorphosis occurs within two to three months. However, frogs whose tadpoles live in temporary pools of water have

to develop quickly before the pool dries up. Tadpoles of the spadefoot toads (*Scaphiopus* spp.) of North America, for example, metamorphose a couple of weeks after hatching. In contrast, tadpoles of the American bullfrog (*Rana catesbeiana*) can take up to three years to develop.

K. MCCALLUM

Some frogs carry their eggs until they are ready to hatch. The male European midwife toad (Alytes obstetricians) carries the eggs for about a month before releasing them into a pool when they are ready to hatch.

See also: ALKALOIDS; CAECILIANS; COLD-BLOODED ANIMALS; GILLS AND SPIRACLES; HIBERNATION; SALAMANDERS AND NEWTS; VERTEBRATES.

Further reading:

Beebee, T. 2000. *Frogs and Toads*. London: Whittet Books Ltd.
Hofrichter, R., ed. 2000. *Amphibians: The World of Frogs, Toads, Salamanders, and Newts*. Toronto: Firefly Books.

COMING ONTO LAND

In vertebrates, the transition from an aquatic to a terrestrial lifestyle began during the middle to late Devonian period (405 to 345 million years ago), when a fish ancestor gave rise to the first tetrapods (vertebrates with four limbs). Scientists believe the first tetrapod evolved from a group of fish known as lobe-fins in shallow, freshwater lakes. The earliest known tetrapod, *Ichthyostega*, was about 3 feet (1 m) long with a fish-shaped body and head, a finned tail, and four stout limbs, enabling it to move on land, perhaps feeding on the shores of shallow pools.

By the end of the Devonian period (345 million years ago), *Ichthyostega*, the first known amphibian, and its relatives had died out. However, by then the tetrapod lineage had given rise to two viable branches: one the ancestor of modern amphibians, the other the line from which reptiles evolved. Most scientists agree that all present-day amphibians (salamanders, newts, and caecilians, as well as frogs and toads) arose from a common ancestor.

The earliest known frog is *Triadobatrachus*, from early Triassic fossils (about 230 to 220 million years ago). It is placed in its own order, Proanura, which means "before frogs." There is a gap of 50 to 60 million years in the fossil record before any other frogs show up. The next species to appear, from about 150 million years ago onward, are similar to modern frogs and are grouped in the same order (Anura).

EVOLUTION

FRUITS AND FRUIT PLANTS

A fruit is the mature form of the fertilized ovary of a plant

Fruit-bearing plants have been an important source of food for people throughout human history. In the hunter-gatherer phase of human development, people knew which fruits were edible and which were harmful and passed on this information from one generation to the next. When humans began to lead more settled existences—domesticating animals and growing crops—they cultivated fruiting plants. Deliberate selection for larger and higher quality fruits over thousands of years has resulted in the familiar fruits of modern day.

What exactly are fruits? In terms of the way that people eat fruits and vegetables, fruits are seen as a dessert food, and vegetables are seen as savory food. However, botanists have a different definition. Botanists define a fruit as the part of a flowering plant that contains the seeds. Thus, such familiar "vegetables" as tomatoes (*Lycopersicon esculentum*), green beans (*Phaseolus vulgaris*), and peas (*Pisum sativum*) are fruits. Tomatoes and string beans are eaten as whole fruits; in contrast, people discard the pods of peas and eat the seeds. Nuts, such as the hazelnut (*Corylus* spp.), acorn (*Quercus* spp.), and coconut (*Cocos nucifera*), as well as berries, such as the blueberry (*Vaccinium* spp.), are all botanically fruits.

Fruits and reproduction

Flowers are the reproductive organs of flowering plants (see FLOWERS AND FLOWER STRUCTURE). The male parts of the plant are the anthers and the filaments, which together form the stamens, and they produce pollen grains, which contain the male reproductive cells. The female parts of the plant are the stigma, style, and ovary, which together form the pistil. The ovary contains the ovules, which contain the female reproductive cells.

The purpose of the fruit is to surround and protect the seeds and often to aid in dispersal as well. The variation in shape, type, and size of fruit is important for the seed's protection and dispersal.

The crab apple, of the rose family (Rosaceae), is a typical temperate fruit-bearing plant.

For example, the fruit of the familiar dandelion (*Taraxacum* spp.) bears a silky-hair "parachute" called the pappus, which is adapted to aid dispersal with the passing wind; the fruits of maple trees (*Acer* spp.) bear winglike blade and can spiral in the wind before reaching the ground several hundred feet from their source.

Fleshy fruits that ripen and fall from the mother plant may decay on the ground. The seeds, containing the next generation as an embryo, germinate and a new plant grows. Many fleshy fruits, particularly berries, are eaten by birds and animals. The seeds that are spat out or pass through the animals' digestive system allow the plant to grow in a new location, where the new and the parent plants are not competing for space, light, water, and nutrients.

Nuts and other dry fruits may be carried off in the fall by squirrels (*Sciurus* spp.), chipmunks (*Tamias* spp.), or other animals and buried as a food store. If they are not eaten during the winter, new plants germinate in the spring. Fruits with burs, such as the familiar cocklebur (*Xanthium strumarium*), can cling to an animal's fur and be carried for miles. The cocklebur is actually enclosed in a woody shell called the involucre, with barbed hooks extending like tiny Velcro fasteners waiting for a passing animal to carry the bur's seed to a new location.

Fertilization

Before most plants can develop fruit and seeds, fertilization must first occur (see FERTILIZATION). When the ovule has been fertilized by a pollen grain, the flower undergoes a change. Usually, the anthers and stigma wither, and the petals fall off. The ovary enlarges and becomes the fruit, and the fertilized ovules become the seeds.

CORE FACTS

- A fruit is the mature form of a plant's fertilized ovary, which contains the seeds for future generations.
- Many foods commonly thought of as vegetables are in fact fruits.
- Fruits are divided into simple fruits (developed from a single ovary) and compound fruits (developed from several ovaries).
- Selection and cultivation of plants bearing larger and higher-quality fruits over thousands of years have resulted in the familiar fruits now available.
- The rose family (Rosaceae) is probably one of the most important groups of fruit-bearing plants and includes apples, pears, and strawberries.

CONNECTIONS

- Seeds are the products of fertilized ovules (see **SEEDS AND SEED DISPERSAL**).

- Modern fruit cultivation is becoming increasingly dependent upon the use of **FERTILIZERS** and **PESTICIDES** to achieve maximum yields.

- The changing face of **AGRICULTURE** in the United States has involved a greater use of **GENETIC ENGINEERING** in the production of fruit crops with larger yields, better flavors, and a more attractive appearance.

The pineapple is a common multiple compound fruit.

pericarp is dry when ripe, like the pod of a bean, or fleshy like that of a tomato. When a simple fruit ripens, its pericarp will either open to shed the seeds or remain closed. A fruit with a pericarp that opens is said to be dehiscent. Such fruits as peas and beans are dehiscent. Fruits with a closed pericarp, such as many nuts and grains, are called indehiscent.

Fleshy simple fruits can be classified as berries, drupes, or pomes. Berries are defined by scientists as having a completely fleshy pericarp. For example, the pericarp of the grape ripens into a fleshy, edible pulp. (It should be remembered that the botanist's definition of a berry is not the same as the one in common usage. To the botanist, oranges, tomatoes, watermelons [*Citrullus lanatus*], bananas, and green peppers [*Capsicum annuum*] are berries.) Berries with a leathery pericarp, such as watermelons, are called pepos. Oranges and other citrus fruits have a leather-like rind and are called hesperidiums.

Drupes have a hard, woody endocarp (pit or stone) surrounding the seed. Surrounding the pit is the soft, fleshy (usually edible) mesocarp. The exterior layer (exocarp) of drupes is usually a soft, thin skin. Familiar drupes are olives (*Olea europaea*), peaches (*Prunus persica*), plums (*P. domestica*), and cherries (*P. avium* and *P. cerasus*). Pomes are simple fleshy fruits, such as apples (*Malus* spp.) or pears (*Pyrus* spp.), whse often inedible core is the true fruit, which has a semihard pericarp surrounded by a fleshy but firm and greatly swollen receptacle (the surface at the tip of the flower stalk that bears the various flower parts).

In addition to the fleshy simple fruits, there are also dry simple fruits. These include such grains as corn (*Zea mays*), rice (*Oryza sativa*), and wheat (*Triticum* spp.), and pods of beans and peas, as well as milkweed. Many nuts, including acorns and hazelnuts, are also classified as dry simple fruits with a single, usually edible, seed and a hard pericarp or shell. Some nuts, such as the almond (*Prunus dulcis*), are actually the hard endocarp and seed of a drupe, while pecans (*Carya illinoinensis*), walnuts (*Juglans* spp.), and chestnuts (*Castanea* spp.) are seeds, the usually leathery pericarp having been removed. The hard shell of a coconut is the endocarp stripped of its thick, fibrous layer (coir), which is the mesocarp.

Compound fruits are the product of two or more ovaries in one or more flowers. There are two types of compound fruits: aggregate and multiple. A single gathering of ripened ovaries produced by one flower is called an aggregate. Common aggregate compound fruits are strawberries (*Fragaria ananassa*) and raspberries (*Rubus idaeus*).

Multiple compound fruits are the result of many individual flowers that join to form a single fleshy mass as it matures. The pineapple (*Ananas comosus*) is a multiple compound fruit. It consists of several hundred individual flowers that fuse together during the maturation process, forming a single edible fruit. Other multiple fruits are figs (*Ficus carica*), mulberries (*Morus* spp.), and breadfruits (*Artocarpus altilis*).

Most plants must undergo the normal fertilization process, but in certain cultivated plants, such as seedless grapefruits (*Citrus paradisi*), oranges (*C. sinensis*), grapes (*Vitis vinifera*), and bananas (*Musa* spp.), fruit is produced without fertilization by a process known as parthenocarpy from the Greek words *parthenos*, which means "virgin" and *carpos*, "fruit." Most commercial perennial fruit crops (having a life cycle lasting more than two years) are propagated asexually by grafting (see page 794).

Simple and compound fruits

Botanists classify a fruit by its structure: simple or compound. A simple fruit is the product of a single ovary. A compound fruit, as the name suggests, is composed of two or more ovaries.

In a mature fruit, in which the seed is fully developed, the ovary wall is composed of three layers: the outside layer, known as the exocarp; the middle layer, the mesocarp; and the interior layer, the endocarp. The three layers together form the pericarp.

Most fruits are composed of a single ripened ovary and are thus simple. Simple fruits are further divided into fleshy or dry, depending on whether the fruit's

Types of fruit plants

With the exception of olives, fruit plants generally require a considerable amount of moisture. Depending on the climatic conditions necessary for growth, fruits can be classified into three basic types:

• **Temperate fruits** are found in the geographic regions between the hot tropics and the frigid polar zones. These wide regions include most of the world's populated areas, covering much of Europe and North America, as well as large areas of Asia, parts of South America, South Africa, Australia, and New Zealand. Familiar temperate fruits are apples, pears, peaches, cherries, grapes, apricots (*Prunus armeniaca*), and plums. Bush-grown berries, such as the blueberry, cranberry (*Vaccinium oxycoccos*), and raspberry, are other temperate fruits. Nuts are also temperate fruits, and include acorns and hazelnuts.

• **Subtropical fruits** are grown in regions that remain mild to warm throughout the year. Some fruits grown in these regions can survive a mild frost, but most cannot. The most common type of subtropical fruits are the various citrus fruits, including oranges, grapefruits, lemons (*Citrus limon*), and limes (*C. aurantiifolia*). Other familiar subtropical fruits include figs, dates (*Phoenix dactylifera*), olives, and avocados (*Persea americana*).

• **Tropical fruits**, as the name implies, are grown strictly in tropical regions and are unable to survive even a light frost. The most common of these fruits are bananas and pineapples. Others include mangoes (*Mangifera indica*), papayas (*Carica papaya*), acerolas (*Malpighia glabra*), and, in tropical Asian zones, the litchi (*Litchi chinensis*).

Fruits and humankind

Ever since the earliest human began gathering food, it is clear that fruits have been an essential part of human lives. Anthropologists have uncovered evidence that many modern-day fruits date back to prehistoric times. They include the most important food crops: wheat, corn, and rice (see GRAINS). Although there is considerable controversy over the origins of wheat, it is known that it was grown in China as early as 2700 BCE and by even earlier lake dwellers in Switzerland. Wheat was also grown around 2300 BCE along the banks of the Indus River in northwestern India and along fertile riverbanks in early Mesopotamia (in present-day Iraq; see AGRICULTURE). Corn, also called maize, is the New World's major contribution to the development of fruits of this sort. Grains of corn have been found in Inca tombs.

A comparatively new fruit to become widespread in the human diet is the tomato. Native to the mountainous regions of Peru, Ecuador, and Bolivia, the tomato was carried by migrating people into Central America and Mexico about 2,000 years ago. The Spaniards carried it back to Europe, where for centuries it was regarded solely as an ornamental plant.

From Europe the tomato came to the United States. Few accepted the fruit, thinking that, like its close relative the deadly nightshade (*Atropa belladonna*), it was poisonous. Around the time of the U.S. Civil War (1861–1865), the popularity of the tomato began to grow, and it is now one of the most popular cultivated plants, with more than 200 known varieties.

Science and fruits

The process of selective breeding of fruits has been known for centuries. By constantly selecting the most desirable plant and using it for breeding the next generation, the fruit strain can be altered to meet the needs of the grower or market. Individual plants are selected for their color, taste, texture, ability to withstand undesirable weather conditions, and high

The reproductive organs and fruit structure of a simple fleshy fruit.

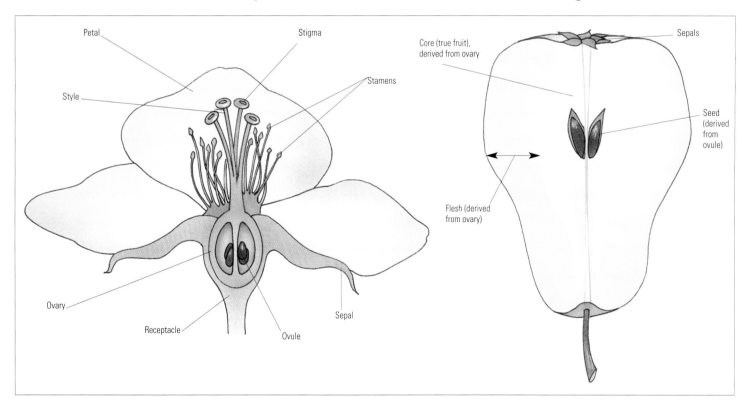

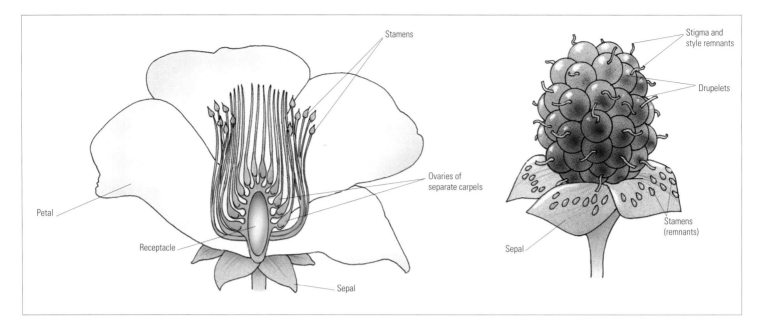

Stamens

Ovaries of
separate carpels

Petal

Receptacle

Sepal

Stigma and
style remnants

Drupelets

Stamens
(remnants)

Sepal

**The flower and fruit
structure of an aggregate
compound fruit.**

productivity. Once a plant with the desired characteristics has been produced, it is propagated vegetatively by selecting and growing parts of the plant, such as the stem, roots, or buds, to develop new tissues identical to the parent fruit plant. Most fruits are propagated vegetatively by grafting. A bud or section of a stem from one plant (the scion) is joined to a root or the root plus the stem of another plant (the stock).

In the United States, grape growers have used the selective breeding process to generate major new strains of fruit. The fox grape (*Vitis labrusca*) of New England, for example, has led to the creation of such new cultivars as the Concord, Catawba, Delaware, and Niagara. Apples such as the Winesap, Macintosh, and Greenings are all recent cultivars grown to meet the taste of the marketplace.

When an individual fruit plant develops a random genetic change, it is known as a mutation. Horticulturists often use mutant strains, called sports, to improve the breed. The original Delicious apple, for example, was pale red and striped. One grower noticed that several branches on one of his trees bore apples of a solid red color. He grafted these apple-bearing branches onto the rootstocks of another tree and developed the deep red variety known as a Red Delicious apple.

PHYLLOXERA

Certain species of grapes are native to New England. A century after vineyards had been established in the colonies, by the grafting of European varieties onto local stocks, France imported large numbers of American vines in the mid-19th century. These vines were infected with an aphidlike insect, phylloxera, which lived by sucking the sap from the roots. Although the American vines were largely resistant to its attack, European vines were not, and within 20 years most of the French vineyards had been destroyed. The only solution was to replant with phylloxera-resistant rootstocks from the United States, and by 1890 nearly 6 million acres (2.4 million ha) of French vineyards were flourishing once more. In the 1990s, phylloxera made a limited reappearance in southern France, but the use of modern pesticides kept it under control.

Growers also cross the pollen of one plant with a desirable trait into the flower of a plant with another desirable trait. The resulting plant is a hybrid of the two chosen plants. Hybridization has led to the development of plants by genetic engineering, in which the genes from one plant are merged with the genes of another to create a new variety.

The growing science of genetic engineering has had a major impact on the development of new and improved fruit. Although the technique remains controversial, it is allowing horticulturists to develop, with a great deal of precision, fruit with specific characteristics. A major development occurred in 1994, when the Flavr Savr tomato was introduced. For years, tomatoes were picked green before being sent to the market, and their taste and texture were far inferior to a vine-ripened tomato. Each tomato has about 100,000 genes: by discovering which genes control the ripening process and altering them to allow the fruit to remain fresh longer, scientists developed a new strain of fruit.

Modern versus ancient fruits
In general, familiar modern cultivated fruits tend to be larger and sweeter than any wild ancestor. For example, wild pears and apples are small, hard, and rather bitter. On the island of Socotra, south of the Arabian peninsula, grows a wild species of pomegranate (*Punica protopunica*), the fruits of which are miniature versions of the better-known fruit (*P. granatum*). On the Mediterranean island of Crete and in western Turkey grows a wild species of date palm (*Phoenix theophrasti*), the fruits of which are much smaller than familiar dates, with thin, sweet flesh around the seed.

ECONOMICALLY IMPORTANT FRUITS
The rose family
In terms of the popular definition of a fruit, probably the most important group of fruit-bearing plants is the rose family (Rosaceae), which contains most of the fruit trees commonly grown in temperate climates. Fruit types include pomes, such as apples and pears,

which are formed from the fleshy but firm swollen receptacle surrounding the semihard, seed-bearing ovary. Apples have been cultivated since primitive times. Soon after Europeans settled in the United States, apples were successfully introduced. In 1997 the United States produced more than 9.8 billion pounds (4.5 billion kg) of apples at a value of about $1 billion; Washington, New York, Michigan, and California are the major apple-producing states.

Drupes in the family Rosaceae, such as plums, cherries, peaches, nectarines, and apricots, all have a fleshy outer zone (called the mesocarp) surrounding the stone, a single seed enclosed in a hard, woody case (called the endocarp). Some members of the Rosaceae are shrubs or climbers. Examples include blackberries and raspberrries (*Rubus* spp.), the fruits of which are aggregate compound fruits with clusters of drupelets (miniature drupes).

One member of the Rosaceae family that has no woody growth is the strawberry. Instead it is low growing, with tufts of leaves and long wiry trailing runners, which root and produce new plants at points along their length. Another aggregate compound fruit, the strawberry is a swollen, fleshy receptacle with numerous ovaries embedded in it near the surface.

Citrus fruits

Another important family of fruit-bearing trees is the Rutaceae, which includes all the citrus fruits (oranges, lemons, limes, and grapefruit). The genus *Citrus* originated in eastern Asia but was introduced long ago to southwestern Asia and the Mediterranean region. With the cold (but not frosty) wet winters and hot dry summers, citrus trees thrive in a Mediterranean climate, although they need irrigation during the dry season. Oranges, the most popular citrus fruit, are grown in the warmer Mediterranean regions, such as Israel, Greece, southern Spain, and Morocco, as well as in the southern United States, South Africa, China, and southern Japan. The southern portion of the United States (Florida in particular) is the world's largest producer of oranges.

The other major citrus fruits, lemons and limes, are believed to have originated in the warm, subtropical regions east of the Himalayas and northern Myanmar (Burma). The grapefruit, on the other hand, is thought to have originated in Malaysia as a mutation of the pomelo (*Citrus maxima*), a similar looking fruit. Grapefruit entered the New World via Jamaica during the 17th century.

Vines

The vine family (Vitaceae) is of great economic and cultural importance in certain parts of the world because it includes the grapevine, *Vitis vinifera*.

Grapes are one of the oldest domesticated fruits. Scientists know that their cultivation goes back at least 6,000 years—they are pictured in Egyptian tombs. Their cultivation spread successfully along the Mediterranean coasts and now includes many other parts of the world.

When the European grape was first introduced into the Americas during colonial days, strains of plant diseases unique to the region prevented the development of agricultural grape production. Fortunately, local species of grapes existed that were immune to these diseases, and the colonists learned to graft onto them and establish local vineyards. Grapes, for both wine and dessert use (as well as for raisin production), are third only to apples and oranges as the leading cash fruit crop in the United States. In 1997 more than 13.7 billion pounds (6.2 billion kg) of grapes were produced at a value exceeding $3.1 billion.

Olives

The olive family includes the olive tree, which is native to and cultivated extensively in the Mediterranean basin. In fact, olives are the main crop in countries, such as Greece, where the mountainous, hilly, and dry terrain is perfectly suited to this type of agriculture.

Olives will grow up to altitudes of about 2,500 feet (760 m). The fruits are pressed to extract the valuable olive oil. Some fruit is pickled for eating in salads and for use in cooking.

The apple is an example of a simple fruit. It has the second highest volume of production in the United States after the orange, and has been grown and cultivated since early times.

Oranges are an extremely valuable cash crop. Citrus fruits, such as oranges, grow best in a Mediterranean climate.

Tropical fruits

The tropics are especially rich in fruit-bearing plants, such as bananas, mangoes, and avocados. Many of these are now widely cultivated on a commercial scale, not only in the tropics and subtropics but also in temperate parts of the world. This important trade in exotic fruits has developed during the 20th century as a result of improved cultivation techniques and more efficient distribution.

The wild ancestors of these tropical fruits are restricted to regions: for example, bananas, mangoes, litchis, rambutans (*Nephelium lappaceum*), mangosteens (*Garcinia mangostana*), and durians (*Durio zibethinus*) come from Southeast Asia; figs, dates, and pomegranates from western Asia; pineapples from South America; and avocados from Central America.

Bananas are interesting plants in that they do not produce seeds within their fruits. The wild ancestors and their relatives have small, barely edible fruits that split open to reveal large, rock-hard seeds, whereas cultivated bananas and similar plantains have become sterile during their process of domestication. They are propagated vegetatively (asexually) by detaching suckers (underground sideshoots) from the base of the plant. The banana plant, although resembling a palm tree, is a giant herb whose stems (actually a pseudostem formed from overlapping leaf sheaths) die down after flowering and fruiting and are continually replaced by suckers.

Modern fruit cultivation

Modern cultivation of fruiting plants and trees concentrates on achieving the maximum yield of fruit in the space available. For example, apples may be grown as cordons (trees trained to grow along a support),
whereby the apple variety is grafted (vegetative propagation carried out by attaching a bud or shoot of one plant onto the stems and roots of another) onto a dwarfing (less vigorous) rootstock. Growth is restricted to a single stem, which is trained diagonally up a wire. Grafting is useful for achieving optimal conditions: the waist-high apple trees are crowded together in long rows, with enough space between for mechanical harvesters to operate.

In warmer, drier countries, salad crops such as tomatoes, peppers, and cucumbers (*Cucumis sativus*) are grown intensively in greenhouses with controlled irrigation. The shelter provided by the glass or plastic helps to maintain high temperatures for the ripening of the fruits, retains humidity in what would otherwise be too dry an environment, and protects the growing plants from wind damage. A tomato plant grown under optimal conditions in such a greenhouse can develop a stem up to 33 feet (10 m) long, with clusters of fruit at intervals of approximately 10 inches (25 cm) that are harvested as they mature.

B. LEERBURGER / N. TURLAND

See also: FERTILIZATION; FLOWERS AND FLOWER STRUCTURE; GRAINS; HORMONES; SELECTIVE BREEDING.

Further reading:

Bond, R., ed. 1985. *All about Citrus and Subtropical Fruits.* Des Moines, Iowa: Meredith Corporation/Ortho Books.
Ferguson, B., ed. 1987. *All about Growing Fruits, Berries, and Nuts.* Des Moines, Iowa: Meredith Corporation/Ortho Books.
Tate, D. 1999. *Tropical Fruit.* Singapore: Archipelago Press, an imprint of Editions Didier Millet.

FUNGI KINGDOM

Fungi, multicellular, eukaryotic organisms that lack chlorophyll, make up one of the five kingdoms

Fungi, including these toadstools, lack chlorophyll, the green pigment needed for photosynthesis.

Molds and mildews, rusts and smuts, mushrooms and toadstools are all fungi. There are around 77,000 named species in the Fungi kingdom, and probably many more exist. Although they may look like plants, fungi are unlike plants in many important ways. Fungi have filamentous bodies and cell walls made of chitin. Plants are made of box-shaped cells and have cell walls made of cellulose. One of the most striking differences between fungi and plants is their color. Plants are green because they contain chlorophyll; fungi do not contain this pigment (although some are green). Consequently, fungi are unable to carry out photosynthesis to produce their own food. Instead, like animals, fungi are heterotrophs: organisms that get their nutritional substances by digesting other organisms, living or dead. Fungi secrete digestive enzymes into their surroundings and absorb nutrients from the organisms to which they are attached.

Fungi can be beneficial or detrimental to other organisms. In the soil, fungi are often beneficial and act as decomposers, breaking down organic matter such as dead leaves, wood, and rotting carcasses to recycle nutrients through the ecosystem: when they feed, they recycle elements such as carbon, nitrogen, and hydrogen into a form that can be used by other organisms.

Above ground, people put fungi to good use. For example, yeasts are used to make bread, beer, and wine. They cause changes in the carbohydrates of fruit and grains through fermentation (see FERMENTATION), producing ethanol and carbon dioxide. Drugs derived from fungi include penicillins, an important class of antibiotics (see the box on page 799), and cyclosporin, the first immunosuppressive agent used to prevent the rejection of transplanted organs. Some edible species, such as the "supermarket mushroom," *Agaricus brunnescens*, are grown commercially.

However, fungi can also destroy crops by attacking roots, shoots, foliage, and fruits and causing plant diseases, such as leaf spots, blights, and brown areas on fruits. Trees also fall victim to fungal attack. In recent decades, the worst fungal outbreak was Dutch elm disease, caused by the fungus *Ceratocystis ulmi*, which swept North America and Europe in the mid-1900s, devastating well-established elm trees. In the home, molds cause foods to spoil, and mildews ruin clothes and furnishings.

All fungi, except single-celled yeasts, consist of fine, tubelike filaments called hyphae. Hyphae are

CORE FACTS

- There are around 77,000 known species of fungi. They include molds, mildews, mushrooms, and toadstools.
- All fungi are made up of fine tubes, called hyphae, that form a meshlike body, the mycelium.
- All fungi gain energy from other organisms and are either saprophytic, parasitic, or symbiotic.
- Although some fungi cause disease in plants and animals, others have a beneficial effect as recyclers of organic material.

CONNECTIONS

● Certain fungal spores, usually those that are dispersed in the air by the wind, may contribute to the onset of an **ALLERGY**. Common allergies include **ASTHMA** and hayfever.

● Fungi that break down plant and animal debris, releasing the organic nutrients into the **ATMOSPHERE**, contribute to the **CARBON CYCLE** and **NITROGEN CYCLE**.

THE EVOLUTION OF FUNGI

The origin of fungi is obscure, and the fossil record is very poor. However, fungi probably did not appear until the beginning of the Paleozoic era, some 570 million years ago. All fungi are eukaryotic (each cell contains a nucleus). They consist of hyphae (fine branching tubes) and are heterotrophic (cannot synthesize their own food). Some fungi are terrestrial but are thought to have evolved from aquatic forms because the more primitive eukaryotic fungi (protoctistan) have motile stages (in which they swim in water) and are primarily aquatic. However, fungi living in aquatic habitats do not have a motile stage, a fact that suggests they originally derived from terrestrial forms. Many mycologists now believe that most fungi evolved from ancestral flagellates (algal or protozoan organisms bearing flagella, or whiplike swimming organs).

All fungi, as is the case for all cells, have a prokaryotic ancestor (that is, an organism whose cells do not have a nucleus). Scientists generally believe that a primitive eukaryotic cell evolved through endosymbiosis (living within another organism for mutual benefit). That is, cell organelles of eukaryotic cells were at one time free-living prokaryotes. From this primitive eukaryotic cell, four separate lines of evolution occurred: the fungi, protist, plant, and animal kingdoms.

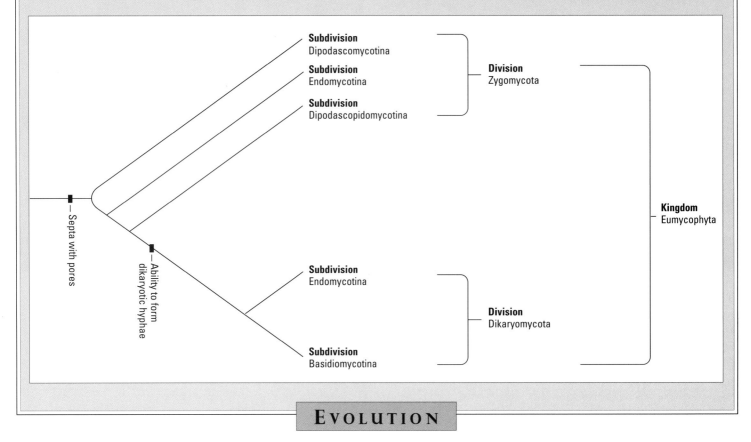

EVOLUTION

made up of a tough carbohydrate called chitin (also present in the hard exoskeleton of insects, arachnids, and crustaceans). Chitin strengthens the hyphae, which grow to form a loose meshwork called a mycelium. This mycelium, not the spongy and sometimes colorful fruiting body (seen above ground as a mushroom), is the true body of the fungus.

Fungi have a vegetative phase (in which hyphae develop), and a reproductive phase (in which spores are produced). The appearance of the hyphae is used to identify the genus and species of fungus, although the fruiting body, which is above ground, is easier to observe. Hyphae may be a white fuzz or they may grow into a three-dimensional network that is large enough to hold in a human hand.

Propagation and dispersal

Spores are the most common propagative unit of fungi and may be produced asexually or sexually. The characteristics of spores, such as color and mode of production, can also be used to identify individ-ual fungal species. In addition, the complex walls of the spores, with up to three distinct layers, can be stained and identified.

Fungi are able to take advantage of different environmental conditions and produce a large number of spores very quickly. Desiccation (drying out) or air movement around the fruiting bodies causes the spores to be released. If the spores settle on organic matter and the environmental conditions are favorable, they germinate, producing new hyphae.

Asexual reproduction can be very efficient, and it can occur at any time of the year for some fungi. Sexual reproduction requires specific conditions for the nuclei of the gametes (reproductive cells) to come together and fuse into a zygote. Combining different genetic material ensures that the population is varied and can adapt to changing conditions.

Survival strategy

Most fungal spores are dispersed in the air. This method is effective for survival, since thousands of spores may be distributed over a wide area, perhaps over thousands of miles, and thus, they have a better chance of germinating. Some spores are discharged with force: for example, those of the puff mushrooms are sent out in a visible cloud.

A type of fungus called cap mushrooms release their spores in a circular pattern. If the spores germinate in a uniform environment, such as a lawn, they produce a mycelium meshwork. The mushrooms grow near the outer perimeter of the circle, where nutrients are more abundant, and form a "fairy ring." Each year the circumference of the ring expands and may reach 98 feet (30 m) or more in diameter.

Some fungi are parasitic, and some are even predatory. When dispersed spores of these fungi land on a suitable host, they grow on the host's outer surface and produce germ tubes, which invade the host, either by penetrating the outer layer or by entering through pores in the surface of the host (the stomata).

Survey of the fungi kingdom

Scientists estimate that only about 30 percent of fungi have been identified worldwide, although some 70,000 known species have been studied. Scientists have devised a number of different ways of classifying fungi. One commonly used system groups fungi into the kingdom Eumycophyta, which has two divisions: Zygomycota and Dikaryomycota. Zygomycota is a group of terrestrial fungi, which reproduce sexually by conjugation (union) of the gametangia (gamete-producing structures). This division represents less than 1 percent of fungi species but includes common fungi that colonize sugary or starchy foods in a warm, moist environment. The black bread mold, *Rhizopus stolonifer*, is a household example.

Sexual reproduction produces a thick-walled spore called a zygosporangium, which undergoes meiosis (cell division in which the chromosome number is halved; see CELL BIOLOGY) to produce spores that germinate into new hyphae. The more common asexual spores are black and can be found on bread and peaches or horse and bat dung.

The remaining 99 percent of known fungi, belonging to the division Dikaryomycota, have a greater ecological range than the zygomycotan fungi and are often found in drier conditions. The hyphae of dikaryomycotan fungi are narrow and have cross walls (called septa), which strengthen them and prevent them from collapsing. These fungi grow on a variety of foods, such as cellulose, lignin produced by plants, and keratin (a component of animal skin, horn, and hair; see HAIR; HORN; SKIN).

Within the Dikaryomycota are two groups: basidiomycetes (club fungi), and ascomycetes (sac fungi). Basidiomycetes are larger fungi and include toadstools, puffballs, stinkhorns, rusts, and smuts, which are a problem to farmers and market gardeners, and the fungus *Serpula lacrimans*, which is the source of dry rot in building timbers. Basidiomycetes reproduce using spores.

The largest (in terms of species numbers) and most varied class of fungi consists of ascomycetes (molds, yeasts, truffles, and morels) that reproduce both sexually and asexually. This class includes: powdery mildews, which often affect rose bushes; some edible mushrooms, such as the morel or the highly prized

Fungi will live anywhere they can find nourishment, and most will grow on plant cellulose or on the keratin in animal skin, horn, and hair. Shown above is a bird's-nest fungus (Cyathus striatus).

THE WONDER DRUG

The British microbiologist Alexander Fleming (1881–1955) is credited with the accidental discovery, in 1928, of penicillin, the first antibiotic. It was not until 1941 that a partially purified form of penicillin (derived from *Penicillium notatum*, an ascomycete) came into medical use through the work of Howard Florey (1898–1968) and Ernst Chain (1906–1979). It revolutionized medical practice, by preventing countless deaths from serious infection. Development of a fermentation technique in the United States during World War II (1939–1945) enabled large quantities of the antibiotic to be produced. Its availability to wounded soldiers toward the end of the war greatly reduced mortality among casualties.

Penicillin prevents the formation of the bacterial cell wall. Many natural forms of penicillin have been identified, and penicillin G remains the antibiotic of choice against a number of life-threatening

infections, as well as the sexually transmitted diseases gonorrhea and syphilis. As with other antibiotics, the overuse of penicillin has resulted in resistant strains of bacteria, which produce an enzyme, penicillinase, which destroys the drug.

Penicillin G, a natural product of fermentation, is injected into the bloodstream. It cannot be taken orally because it is destroyed by the acidity of the stomach. By adding phenoxyacetic acid to the fermentation medium, a new form, penicillin V, was produced, which is acid stable and can be taken orally. By adding side chains chemically to the penicillin produced by the fungus *P. notatum,* a range of semisynthetic penicillins has been produced that are resistant to penicillinase. Penicillin and other antibiotics are ineffective against viral infections, which include the common cold, influenza, and HIV.

A CLOSER LOOK

The fruiting body of a **Morchella** *fungus, which is an ascomycete. Ascomycetes reproduce both sexually and asexually.*

lifestyles, becoming saprophytic (living on dead and decaying organic matter), parasitic (living on other living organisms), or symbiotic (living with another organism for mutual benefit).

Saprophytic fungi, having almost exclusive access to large quantities of dead plant and animal material, are nature's most abundant terrestrial recyclers. They produce toxic metabolites, called mycotoxins, which can be poisonous or carcinogenic (cancer causing).

Parasitic fungi, which cause a majority of the plant diseases, are detrimental to agriculture, food processing, horticulture, and the timber trade. Millions of dollars are spent each year to prevent severe fungal attacks. Parasitic fungi also cause disease in humans and animals. Those that infect humans mostly colonize the exterior of the body (the skin, nails, and hair), although fungal infection can also make its way inside the body, causing serious illness.

The most common mutualistic fungi (living in symbiosis with other organisms) are mycorrhizae and lichens. Mycorrhizae have a special relationship with the roots of many plants. Woodland mushrooms, for example, find nourishment from tree roots and, in return, provide extra minerals for the tree. Some moorland plants, like heather (which lacks root hairs), depend on a mycorrhizal arrangement for their survival in poor soils.

A lichen is the result of a close association between an alga and a fungus (see LICHENS). Lichens are unique, since they take on a form and function unlike that of either partner. They colonize bare ground and rocks, and are found in almost every habitat on Earth, especially harsh environments such as the hot, dry deserts in the southwestern United States and the cold, dry deserts of Antarctica. Lichens have been used by scientists as ecological indicators because they are very sensitive to air pollution, especially sulfur dioxide.

truffle; yeasts; and the ergot fungus, *Claviceps purpurea*, which, infecting rye, caused widespread outbreaks of the disease called ergotism in medieval Europe in those who had eaten contaminated rye. Ergotism produces hallucinations and convulsions, and may have been the basis for the 1692 Salem witch crisis.

Choice of lifestyles

For fungi to secrete enzymes that break down complex organic matter into simple molecules absorbable by the fungi's hyphae, they must adopt one of three

Dangerous pastime

Many mushrooms are safe to eat. However, gathering mushrooms can be a dangerous occupation because it is often difficult to tell edible mushrooms apart from poisonous species. It is not simply a question of mushrooms being safe and toadstools being poisonous. Mushroom experts, called mycologists, use the word *mushroom* to describe any of the larger basidiomycetes; they hardly ever use the word *toadstool*. To be safe in all cases, it takes an expert to know the good fungi from the bad.

E. SHUBERT

See also: CELL BIOLOGY; FERMENTATION; FLEMING, ALEXANDER; HAIR; HORNS; LICHENS; MOLDS AND MILDEWS; MUSHROOMS AND TOADSTOOLS; SAPROPHYTES; SKIN.

Further reading:
Jennings, D. H. 1999. *Fungal Biology: Understanding the Fungal Lifestyle.* New York: Springer Verlag.
Larone, D. H. 2002. *Medically Important Fungi: A Guide to Identification.* Washington, D.C.: American Society for Microbiology.

WHOLESALE DESTRUCTION

Many fungi have caused widespread destruction to plant communities, horticultural enterprises, and agricultural crops. The chestnut blight, caused by an ascomycete, killed almost all mature chestnut trees in North America. Wheat rust caused epidemics in the United States during the 1930s, destroying wheat crops and creating financial ruin for many prairie farmers. Southern corn blight caused an epidemic in 1970, destroying most of the crop in several states. Dutch elm disease has destroyed the beautiful shade tree, the American elm, in cities across the United States. There are innumerable fungi that cause plant diseases, affecting wheat, barley, rye, corn, lettuce, tomato, fruits, and trees. Gaining a better knowledge of the basic biology of fungi will enable scientists to exploit their beneficial uses more fully while keeping their destructive potential at bay.

A CLOSER LOOK

GAIA HYPOTHESIS

The Gaia hypothesis suggests that the Earth is a living organism able to regulate its own environment

Gaia (pronounced *guy-uh*) is the name of the Greek goddess of Earth. It is also the name of an important hypothesis that may explain the persistence of life on Earth for almost four billion years. The Gaia hypothesis was first suggested in the 1970s by the British scientist James Lovelock (b. 1919). In the 1960s he was working with the U.S. space program to determine if there was life on Mars. During this time, he realized that a planet's atmosphere could provide clues about the presence of life, because organisms use the atmosphere to transfer raw materials and waste products.

Lovelock also noted a similarity between the atmospheres of Mars and Venus, Earth's lifeless neighbors. The atmosphere on Mars is about 95 percent carbon dioxide and 3 percent nitrogen, with only tiny amounts of water and oxygen. Although Venus has a much denser atmosphere, the proportion of gases in it are about the same as that on Mars. According to the laws of chemistry and physics, Mars, Venus, and Earth should have atmospheres similar to each other. However, Earth's atmosphere is about 79 percent nitrogen, 21 percent oxygen, and 0.03 percent carbon dioxide. Earth's atmosphere is different to that on Mars or Venus because life has changed it.

In the beginning

When life began, Earth's atmosphere was probably mostly carbon dioxide, with some water vapor and nitrogen (gases produced naturally by volcanoes). Any oxygen would have reacted with other elements to form compounds, so there would have been little of the free oxygen that exists now.

Lightning causes nitrogen (N_2) to react with water (H_2O) to give nitric acid (HNO_3) and ammonia (NH_3). Both compounds dissolve in water and are removed from the atmosphere by rain. When rain strikes the ground, nitric acid and ammonia react with substances in rocks to form nitrates (No_3), which are then washed into the oceans. So in a world without life, most of the nitrogen should be in the ocean, not the atmosphere. Again, Earth's

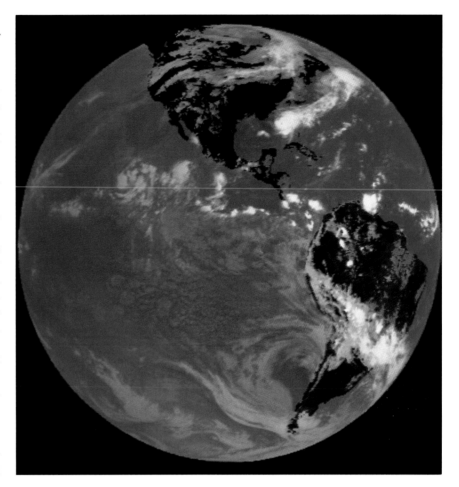

present atmosphere is different. Scientists think that the first forms of life were probably anaerobic bacteria (those that cannot live in the presence of oxygen). Living in the ocean, these bacteria converted dissolved nitrates to nitrogen gas, which began to accumulate in the atmosphere. This process also released oxygen, but this oxygen reacted with other compounds and still did not accumulate significantly in Earth's atmosphere.

Oxygen did not persist in the atmosphere until organisms capable of photosynthesis developed. They used energy from the Sun to convert carbon dioxide and water to sugars and oxygen (see PHOTOSYNTHESIS). The first such organisms were blue-green algae (cyanobacteria). As these organisms became more plentiful, they removed more carbon dioxide from the atmosphere and produced more oxygen. Eventually, the cyanobacteria produced so much oxygen that the original anaerobic bacteria, being intolerant of oxygen, could not survive everywhere. These organisms now exist only in places where there is no oxygen, such as on the deep-sea floor, in waterlogged soils, and in the intestines of animals.

So Earth's atmosphere is different from its neighboring planets, because some bacteria released nitrogen, while others absorbed carbon dioxide and released oxygen. These processes are ongoing.

Satellite pictures from space have allowed humans to see Earth as a whole—a living system with many complex, interconnecting parts.

CONNECTIONS

● The Gaia hypothesis states that Earth is a living organism with its own mechanisms of **HOMEOSTASIS**.

● Humans have been putting increasing amounts of **CARBON DIOXIDE** into the **ATMOSPHERE**. The result may be **GLOBAL WARMING**, which would disrupt living systems on Earth.

CORE FACTS

■ The Gaia hypothesis was proposed by the British scientist James Lovelock in the 1970s.

■ The hypothesis states that Earth is a self-regulating living organism able to maintain conditions favorable for life to survive.

■ Evidence for the Gaia hypothesis includes the fact that Earth's atmosphere, unlike those of its closest planetary neighbors, Mars and Venus, contains nitrogen and oxygen. In addition, living organisms interact with the nonliving part of Earth to keep the temperature stable, even as the Sun becomes hotter.

JAMES LOVELOCK

James Lovelock (right, in 1987) is a rarity—an independent scientist. While most scientists work for research establishments or universities, Lovelock's laboratory is in a cabin in Cornwall, England. Being independent allows him to study whatever interests him. His studies have taken him into the fields of chemistry, medicine, cybernetics, and marine biology. Not having a regular salary, Lovelock has relied on his many inventions and books to support his family and his research.

Born in England in 1919, James Lovelock holds a PhD in medicine from the University of London and has taught at Yale, the Baylor University College of Medicine, and Harvard. His first book proposed the Gaia hypothesis and was simply titled Gaia. It was published in 1979.

Please Shut the Gate

Coombe Mill Experimental Station

DISCOVERERS

Life regulates the environment

The idea that life changes the environment is not new, but Lovelock took the idea a step further. In 1972 he proposed the controversial Gaia hypothesis, which states that life regulates the environment to keep conditions favorable for life to survive. Since then, Lovelock has gone on to propose that Earth itself can be viewed as being alive. He calls this living Earth Gaia. Gaia is composed of all the living things on the planet, as well as the rocks, the oceans, and the air, and a complex interaction exists between the living and the nonliving.

For life to regulate the environment, there must be a feedback mechanism should the changes it causes become too extreme. Thus, conditions are kept within the narrow limits needed to ensure the survival of life. In organisms, the term that describes the maintenance of constant conditions in the body is *homeostasis* (see HOMEOSTASIS). According to the Gaia hypothesis, life keeps Earth in homeostasis.

There are several phenomena that may support the Gaia hypothesis. One is that life on Earth has survived several collisions with huge meteorites. Such collisions would have been more devastating than any nuclear weapon and would have hurled enough dust into the atmosphere to block out life-giving light from the Sun. The last such collision is proposed to have happened 65 million years ago, when about 70 percent of species on Earth were wiped out, including the dinosaurs. However, life persisted and thrived, as new organisms, including mammals, developed. Despite the catastrophe, the environment recovered, and organisms were once

again able to thrive, probably helped by the homeostatic effects of life itself.

Another phenomenon that supports the Gaia hypothesis is that the temperature of the Earth has stayed relatively constant since life began around four billion years ago. This fact is more remarkable than it seems, because the Sun is much hotter now than it was when life first appeared on Earth. Life may regulate climate in two ways: clouds reflect the Sun's heat, and carbon dioxide absorbs the Sun's heat; both involve living organisms that interact with the nonliving environment.

• Cloud reflection: Clouds are formed by water droplets. The water droplets form when water vapor condenses around a microscopic particle called a cloud condensing nucleus (CCN). If there are few CCNs, clouds form with fewer, but larger water droplets. If there are many CCNs, clouds form with more, smaller droplets. Small droplets form whiter clouds that reflect more of the Sun's light and exert a cooling effect on Earth.

In the ocean, microscopic algae produce a gas called dimethyl sulfide (DMS), a source of CCNs. The warmer the climate, the more algae grow and the more DMS they produce. The more DMS they produce, the more white clouds are formed, thus more light is reflected from the Sun, and Earth becomes cooler. A cooler Earth then reduces the amount of algae and DMS and white clouds, thus exerting a warming effect on Earth, and so on (see the diagram opposite).

• Carbon dioxide: Carbon dioxide is a powerful greenhouse gas, trapping heat from the Sun (see GLOBAL WARMING). The more carbon dioxide present in the atmosphere, the more of the Sun's heat is trapped and the warmer Earth becomes. The less carbon dioxide present in the atmosphere, the less heat is trapped and the cooler Earth becomes.

There are many ways in which living things are involved in the removal of carbon dioxide from the environment (see CARBON CYCLE). Like cyanobacteria, plants take up carbon dioxide in the process of photosynthesis. When they die, many plants (and the carbon in their tissues) are eventually buried and compressed deep underground. Fossil fuels, such as coal and oil, are formed in this way.

Water from rain reacts with carbon dioxide in the air and the soil to form carbonic acid (H_2CO_3), which in turn reacts with the rocks to release calcium and bicarbonate (HCO_3^-). Both the carbonic acid and the bicarbonate are then washed into the oceans, where minute organisms convert them into calcium carbonate ($CaCO_3$) to make their shells. When these organisms die, their shells sink slowly to the ocean bottom and form sediments, locking up the carbon they contain in the process.

The uptake of carbon dioxide depends on the temperature. As Earth warms, the tropical areas expand, increasing the amount of plant and bacterial life and the extraction of carbon dioxide from the atmosphere. As Earth cools, the tropical areas recede, and the organisms extract less carbon

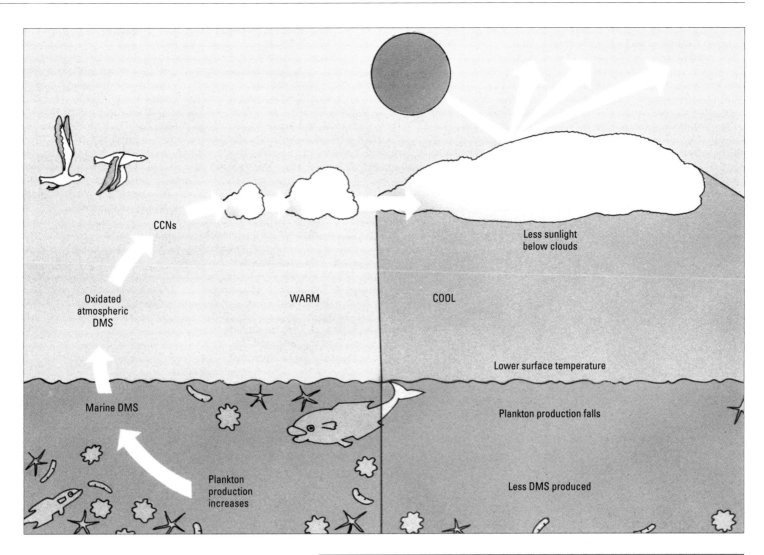

The cloud–algae theory suggests that algae regulate Earth's temperature through their effect on clouds.

dioxide. This feedback mechanism is consistent with the Gaia hypothesis.

Criticisms

Many scientists reject the Gaia hypothesis. They argue that for life to regulate the environment to keep conditions favorable for life's survival, Earth must have both intelligence and a purpose. Lovelock answers such criticisms with the Daisyworld model (see right). However, whether the Gaia hypothesis is right or wrong may be less important than what it has done. It has generated new lines of scientific inquiry and provided a model for analyzing and predicting environmental change, and it has given a view of Earth as a resilient and vibrant fusion of the living and nonliving.

M. ALLEN

See also: CARBON CYCLE; DESERTIFICATION; EVOLUTION; PHOTOSYNTHESIS.

Further reading:

Kump, L. R., et al. 1999. *The Earth System*. Upper Saddle River, N.J.: Prentice Hall.
Lovelock, J. 2000. *Gaia: A New Look at Life on Earth*. New York: Oxford University Press.

THE DAISYWORLD MODEL

James Lovelock's fictional Daisyworld is a planet on which the only organisms are two species of daisies; one is black, the other white. Neither species of daisy will grow if the planet is too hot or too cold. Daisyworld's Sun is like that of Earth: it becomes hotter as it gets older.

At first the planet is cool, and there are an equal number of black and white daisies. However, the black daisies grow better because they absorb more of the Sun's energy than the white daisies, which reflect the light. Over time, many white daisies die. The larger proportion of black daisies makes the planet hotter, because they cover so much of its surface and absorb so much energy. Eventually, the black daisies absorb so much energy from the Sun they begin to get too hot and die. The white daisies begin to thrive, however, because they can keep cooler by reflecting the Sun's energy. Soon they cover the planet and reflect so much energy that the planet cools.

After billions of years, the Sun becomes so hot that even the white daisies die, but for all those years, the daisies regulated the climate, and both species survived longer than they would have if either had been the only color present. Many scientists believe that Earth will ultimately suffer a similar fate. In a few billion years, the Sun will become so warm that life will no longer be able to control the temperature of Earth's environment.

Daisyworld is a computer model of a simple planet. It shows how life can regulate climate without having a purpose or intelligence. More complex models with more organisms and more colors of daisies have shown that life can regulate climate more effectively. It also shows how organisms that can regulate the environment cooperatively are more likely to survive.

A CLOSER LOOK

GENE THERAPY

Gene therapy normally refers to the introduction of a corrective gene into a person's cells to treat genetic disease

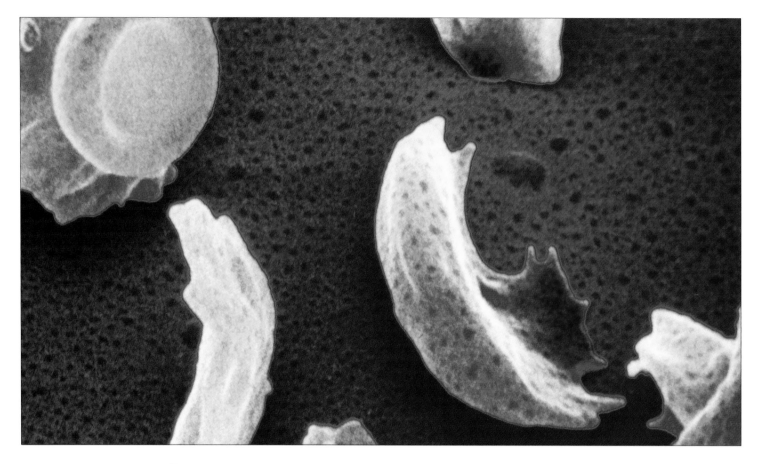

Sickle cells seen with a normal red blood cell. Sickle-cell anemia is one of the condition that responds to gene therapy.

CONNECTIONS

● Gene therapy employs **GENETIC ENGINEERING** techniques, including the use of **VIRUSES** to insert corrective genes into a patient's malfunctioning cells.

● Gene therapy offers the potential for treating a wide range of **GENETIC DISEASES**, from **DEGENERATIVE BRAIN DISEASE**, such as **ALZHEIMER'S DISEASE**, to certain forms of **CANCER**.

In 1999, two boys with severe combined immuno-deficiency disease (SCID) were successfully treated with a corrective gene for their condition. Children with SCID are unable to fight most forms of infection. Their body's immune system lacks white blood cells (T- and B-lymphocytes) and consequently the antibodies necessary to combat infection (see IMMUNE SYSTEMS). The boys inherited a form of SCID caused by a defective gene that encodes for a surface receptor on lymphocytes that allows them to respond to growth factors. Without the receptor the immune system cells do not develop properly.

The treatment involved removing blood cells (precursor cells) from the boys and introducing a virus that contained the functional gene for the receptor into the isolated stem cells (see STEM CELLS). Once placed back into the the patients' body, these cells restored the complete immune system as though the disease had never existed. Without this treatment, children with this form of SCID could survive only in the sterile environment of a plastic bubble, which protected them from contact with disease-causing agents.

Gene therapy trials on SCID patients were performed as early as 1990, but in every case before 1999, patients were also given simultaneous drug treatments. It was never clear whether the drug therapy or the gene therapy caused the improvement of the condition. For the boys treated in 1999 and in subsequent trials, no additional supportive drug treatments were given.

Only after these trials were performed was it clear that gene therapy could be performed safely to produce an apparent cure for disease. Despite this remarkable success, the early promise of gene therapy has yet to be fulfilled because of technical difficulties. Even in the successful SCID case, doctors do not know whether the immune system will function for a normal lifespan. Nevertheless, gene therapy holds great promise.

Human genes

A gene is a unit of inheritance. It is also a specific sequence of DNA (deoxyribonucleic acid; see DNA) in a human cell. Genes are carried on chromosomes,

CORE FACTS

■ Gene therapy works by replacing or supplementing genes or by correcting a faulty gene's function to produce a cure for an inherited or acquired disease.

■ Gene therapy has not yet fulfilled all its early promise because of the many technical problems involved.

■ Corrective genes can be delivered to target cells in various ways, ranging from viral vectors to microinjection, but all methods have their drawbacks.

■ A common problem in gene therapy is failure of the corrective gene to be properly expressed in target cells.

■ Gene therapy offers the long-term potential for treating hundreds of genetic diseases.

which are packaged within the nucleus of cells. Put simply, a gene affects a particular feature or trait, such as eye color, hair color, or ear shape. Barring spontaneous alterations in human genes (mutations), all human characteristics are produced by the genes a person inherits from his or her parents. However, the expression of genes is sensitive to environmental conditions. For example, poor diet may cause individuals not to reach their genetically determined full height.

The expression of human genes is usually much more complex than this simple picture suggests, however. Most human traits are determined by more than one gene, and even a single human gene is often not one discrete sequence of DNA. Commonly human genes comprise several lengths of DNA (called exons) interspersed with other lengths of DNA (called introns). Proper expression of the gene requires the splicing together of exons and removal of the intron units. This rearrangement takes place after the DNA is transcribed into a messenger RNA. To complicate the process further, the expression of most genes is regulated in each cell by protein factors that are themselves the products of other genes. Thus, in order to understand the nature of genetic disease in humans, it is necessary to understand a complete network of related genes and the regulation of their products. These daunting complexities must be overcome for gene therapy to succeed.

Human genetic diseases

One way or another, the genes people inherit probably influence their susceptibility to almost every disease they encounter. However, there are some genetic defects that specifically cause disease. These inherited (genetic) diseases number at least 4,000. They include conditions such as hemophilia (a condition in which the blood does not clot properly), Huntington's disease (a degenerative brain condition), and cystic fibrosis (where the mucus of the lungs and digestive system is unusually sticky). In each case, these disorders are the result of a mutation in a single human gene. Other conditions, such as increased susceptibility to certain types of cancer, are influenced by several different genes. In genetic diseases, an abnormal gene usually exerts its effect by producing a nonfunctioning or poorly functioning protein or enzyme. This deficiency causes the signs and symptoms of the disease.

Somatic and germ-line gene therapy

Gene therapy works on the principle of replacing, supplementing, or correcting a faulty gene to produce a cure for an inherited or a genetically influenced disease. At its simplest, there are two forms of gene therapy: somatic and germ line. Somatic gene therapy, currently the focus of trials on both humans and other animals, involves using corrective procedures on the faulty genes of somatic (body) cells. These are nonreproductive. Alterations to such cells are not inherited by the offspring of treated patients.

Germ-line gene therapy, on the other hand, involves corrective genetic procedures that are inherited by a patient's offspring. These gene-therapy procedures act on the germ line (sperm or egg cells) or the reproductive cells that give rise to them. Currently, research on germ-line intervention is strictly limited to nonhuman animals, because of the technical and ethical challenges it poses.

The source of corrective genes

Before gene therapy can be considered, researchers must isolate the faulty protein or enzyme that is the cause of the disease. The correct sequence of the fully functional protein must also be known so that the gene can be manufactured using genetic engineering techniques. Once this goal is achieved, the fundamental challenge for gene therapists is to insert the corrective gene in the patient's targeted cells and get the gene to operate correctly.

Delivery systems

Fundamental to most types of gene therapy is finding a means to deliver the corrective gene into the nucleus of targeted cells. For the purpose of correcting faulty gene function, the therapeutic gene must lie within the nucleus of the cell for it to be expressed (for the protein product of the gene to be manufactured in appropriate quantities). Delivering the corrective gene into the target nucleus is in itself a major technical challenge. There are two broad approaches. The ex vivo (outside the body) approach involves removing targeted cells from the patient and then genetically modifying the cells in the laboratory. The cells are then returned to the patient. This approach was used in the successful human gene-therapy experiments described above.

In the laboratory, corrective genes can be introduced into cells using electrical currents that open up channels in the cell membrane (electroporation) or by direct microinjection of DNA into the cell's nucleus. These methods are not very efficient, however, and although the corrective gene may end up

Corrective genes are added to compensate for a defective gene. Corrective genes integrated into a chromosome will be passed on to daughter cells when the cell replicates.

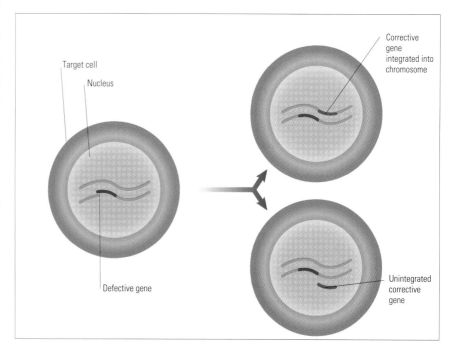

Target cell

Nucleus

Corrective gene integrated into chromosome

Defective gene

Unintegrated corrective gene

REPAIRING GENES

Most gene-therapy approaches involve adding a corrective gene, but there are potential alternatives. One involves repairing a defective gene, rather than replacing or supplementing its function. Some of the mutations that cause an inherited disease condition affect only a very small part of a gene, involving one or a few nucleotides in a human gene that is perhaps 1,000 to 2,000 nucleotides long. For example, sickle-cell anemia is caused by a mutation that affects a single nucleotide in the gene that codes for part of the hemoglobin molecule (the pigment molecule in red blood cells that carries oxygen). This single minor change causes red blood cells to distort, so reducing their capacity to carry oxygen to body tissues. Patient's symptoms include fatigue, headaches, and shortness of breath. Taking another example, more than 70 percent of cases of cystic fibrosis are attributable to the deletion of three nucleotides from a single gene.

Since 1993 researchers in Philadelphia have been experimenting with mobilizing the target cell's own DNA repair mechanism to correct damaged genes. Human DNA is double stranded, with the sequence of nucleotides on one strand being complementary to those on the other so that the two strands fit together. Researchers can manufacture a complementary strand of DNA for the correct version of a gene. Potentially, when this strand pairs with a DNA strand from the malfunctioning gene, the two fit together, except at the place where the strands mismatch; there a bulge forms between the two strands. Natural DNA repair mechanisms scan for such bulges and attempt to repair them. If the corrective DNA can be suitably engineered, it could encourage DNA repair mechanisms to repair the faulty DNA strand. Initial experiments in vitro (in laboratory glassware), with the right mixture of chemicals, have shown that the sickle-cell mutation can be corrected in this fashion, but this success is still a long way from showing that the mechanism is viable for use in vivo (in living organisms).

A CLOSER LOOK

in the cell's nucleus, it rarely becomes incorporated into the cell's chromosomes. This inserted gene is less stable than the other genes in the nucleus, and the new gene is not copied when the cell divides. So the effect of the therapeutic gene is short-lived.

A better approach is to use natural biological agents that are supremely adapted to inserting genes into chromosomes. These agents include viruses. Viruses are themselves disease-causing agents, and to be used for gene therapy, they are normally weakened or inactivated first to remove or minimize their potentially harmful effects. Some of the virus's genetic material, DNA or RNA (ribonucleic acid), is removed, and the therapeutic gene inserted. The modified virus cannot multiply in the patient, but its therapeutic genetic payload can be inserted in the chromosomes of the host cell. When the host cells divide, the therapeutic gene is duplicated, too, and passed on to the next generation of cells, thus providing long-term corrective action to the patient.

The ex vivo approach works well for use with dispersed tissues, such as bone marrow. For discrete organs, the in vivo (in living organisms) approach is commonly used. Modified viruses are used as a vector to deliver the genetic payload to target cells within the body. The means of delivery varies depending on the nature of the virus, the disease being treated, and the target organ. For example, the first in vivo human gene-therapy trials involved cystic fibrosis patients. They contain an attenuated (weakened) adenovirus containing the therapeutic gene.

Adenoviruses naturally seek out the lungs and can be used as live vaccines against respiratory infections without serious side effects. Unfortunately the use of adenovirus vectors in treating cystic fibrosis was not very successful in part because of the immunological response the virus produces in patients.

Viral vectors

Choosing a suitable viral vector to deliver a genetic payload involves considering several factors. First, the virus must be specific for the target body cells and be capable of efficiently infecting those cells. Second, the virus must be capable of being attenuated so that it is not directly harmful. Third, it must be able to be cultured and manipulated safely in the laboratory and grown in high concentrations (high titer). Fourth, the virus must be capable of carrying and inserting the therapeutic gene. Fifth, the virus should be able to evade the patient's immune system. If it does not do so, then cells "infected" with the therapeutic gene will be targeted for attack by the patient's immune system. The very cells that could treat the patient's disease will be recognized as foreign and knocked out by the immune system.

Retroviruses are RNA viruses (they contain a core of RNA rather than DNA). They also contain the enzyme reverse transcriptase. This enzyme catalyzes the conversion of RNA into DNA, which is inserted into the DNA of host cells that are actively dividing. Retroviral vectors are popular for ex vivo delivery to cultured cells, where cells such as blood cells can be readily removed and replaced. However, more recent research has enabled retroviral vectors to be used in vivo. Although retroviruses are versatile as therapeutic-gene vectors, they also have a number of disadvantages. Researchers have little or no control over where precisely a retrovirus inserts a therapeutic gene into a human chromosome or how many copies of the gene it inserts. The genetic payload could be inserted within another human gene, thus altering or disrupting its expression. Perhaps worse, it could disrupt a regulatory gene that controls the cell cycle and cell division. The cell would die or perhaps be transformed into a cancer cell. Although such harmful occurrences have a low probability, such possibilities must be weighed in the balance. Finally, human genes tend to be large, and retroviruses can accommodate only small human genes or downsized versions of larger genes. Usually, regulatory regions that are necessary for the gene to function well are omitted, and so the efficiency of gene expression is markedly lowered.

Adenoviruses are another group of viruses in popular use in gene therapy. Adenoviruses contain double-stranded DNA linked with protein. Although they, unlike retroviruses, insert their genetic payload into the nucleus, it is not integrated into the host cell's chromosomes. On the plus side, the problem of chromosomal disruption is avoided, but on the minus side, the therapeutic gene is not copied when the cell divides, so treatment may require repeated administration of the viral vector. Also, adenoviruses are more likely than retroviruses to be recognized by the immune system, so triggering an inflammatory response. When adenoviral treatment is repeated, immune attack against infected cells is hastened. To minimize such problems, some researchers have been developing stealth adenoviral vectors that do not contain any of the original viral genes. Such "gutted" viruses are being developed for injection into muscles to treat muscular dystrophy.

A third major group of viruses is being utilized in gene therapy studies, the parvoviruses (viruses containing double-stranded DNA with sealed ends). The adeno-associated virus (AAV) looks to be among the most promising for gene therapy. Like the retroviruses, AAV can insert its genetic payload into human chromosomes and does not seem to trigger immune responses. Also, it can infect non-dividing as well as dividing cells. On the minus side, the virus is difficult and expensive to grow in large quantities, and it is poorly taken up by target cells. As is clear, none of the current viral vectors are ideal. Researchers are presently exploring the use of other viral vectors, including Herpes simplex, the virus associated with cold sores and genital herpes.

Nonviral vectors

Several nonviral approaches to therapeutic gene delivery are available. Gene uptake by cells is low using these approaches, but they offer the potential for introducing therapeutic genes along with their regulatory components. In ex vivo methods, a high voltage can be applied to a mixture of target cells and DNA in suspension. In this process, called electroporation, DNA is taken up through pores in the cell membrane, but relatively little enters the nucleus.

Some researchers use manufactured liposomes as delivery vehicles. The liposomes are microscopic vesicles (sacs) created from lipids that resemble those found in the target cell's membranes. Researchers insert corrective DNA into the liposomes, which fuse with the cell membrane and empty their contents into the cell. Some of the delivered DNA finds its way into the nucleus although the process is inefficient. A variation on this theme is the construction of DNA-molecular conjugates. Gene-containing DNA samples are mixed with amino acids or proteins with a natural affinity for cell surfaces. Some of these proteins bind specifically to the cell-surface receptors. The DNA-molecular conjugates are taken up by the cells via endocytosis (engulfing), and some DNA may end up inside the cell.

Gene expression

Inserting a corrective gene into a target nucleus is only part of the gene-therapy challenge. Once there, the gene has to be expressed. In a normally functioning cell, various factors cause a gene to be switched on and off to suit the cell's metabolism. These factors require DNA binding sites near the genes they regulate to either enhance or repress the transcription of the gene. These regulatory sites are called promoters, and gene promoters carry bind-

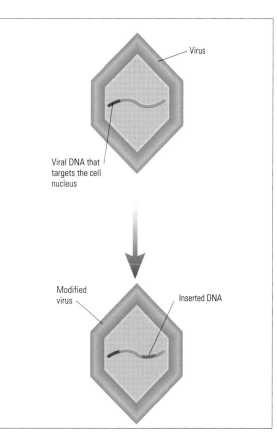

Labels: Virus; Viral DNA that targets the cell nucleus; Modified virus; Inserted DNA

Viruses are modified for gene therapy by retaining the genes that target a cell's nucleus, deleting the harmful genes, and replacing them with corrective genes.

ing sites for regulatory factors as well as RNA polymerase, the enzyme that manufactures mRNA from DNA. Typically, the promoter is located at the front of the gene it regulates. Unfortunately, promoters for human genes are often large, owing to the number of factors that work together to fine-tune gene regulation. Researchers find difficulty packaging large promoters within viruses. Often, researchers resort to other strategies, such as using promoters that are native to the virus or manufacturing artificial promoters. Some workers have developed promoters that are switched on by the antibiotic tetracycline. The promoters can be activated according to the level of tetracycline administered to the patient. None of these solutions is ideal, and the best results

THE JESSE GELSINGER CASE

Until September 1999, no one had died as a result of gene therapy. In that month, 18-year-old Jesse Gelsinger attended the University of Pennsylvania's Institute for Human Gene Therapy to take part in a clinical study for ornithine transcarbamylase (OTC) deficiency. In OTC the liver cannot break down ammonia (a harmful waste product) in the normal way, blood concentrations of ammonia can rise to harmful levels. The condition can be controlled by conventional treatments. In Jesse's case, clinical researchers were testing gene therapy using an adenovirus with a corrective gene. Jesse inhaled the modified virus, but within four days he died from a massive inflammatory response in his lungs. The other patients in the trial appeared unharmed. A thorough investigation revealed an unexpected failure in Jesse's immune response to check rising inflammation. However, several thousand people have taken part in gene-therapy trials, and this is the only recorded treatment-related death.

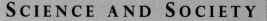

SCIENCE AND SOCIETY

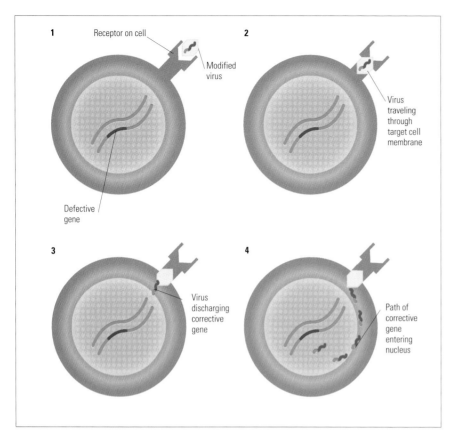

1

Receptor on cell

Modified virus

Defective gene

2

Virus traveling through target cell membrane

3

Virus discharging corrective gene

4

Path of corrective gene entering nucleus

Gene therapy uses the fact that viruses attach to receptors on a cell membrane. Once attached, they discharge their contents into the cells, which in turn work their way into the nucleus.

the corrective gene, levels of gene expression are rarely high enough. The natural expression of genes is regulated in a complex manner, and researchers are still in the process of unravelling this complexity.

Third, inserting a corrective gene may have an unintended deleterious effect somewhere else in the human genome. Some recent research with viral vectors to treat AIDS has shown that HIV infection itself can influence the way that corrective genes are integrated into chromosomes.

There are strong arguments in favor of gene-therapy research continuing. Even the trials so far have added years of healthy life to many patients. Traditional approaches to treating debilitating genetic diseases often involve drug treatment to provide something with a similar effect to the missing enzyme or other protein the defective gene cannot provide. Even if such treatment is available, and often it is not, the treatment may be prohibitively expensive, and it must be taken continuously throughout the person's life. Gene therapy offers the potential to treat the condition at its source. At its best, a single gene therapy could provide a permanent cure for the patient and potentially at much smaller cost than other forms of treatment or healthcare.

tend to come when the viral vector carries the corrective gene's promoter together with the gene. Then the corrective gene is expressed as naturally as possible. Low levels of gene expression continue to hamper gene-therapy advances. Improving levels of gene expression remains a key focus for research.

Taking stock

In the 1980s trials on animals suggested that gene therapy, by inserting corrective genes into targeted animal cells, might correct certain genetic diseases. The results of the trials were very mixed, but some of the most successful led to the first partially successful human trials in 1990. Since then, animal and human trials have continued to produce very mixed results. Arguably, the most successful results are with human patients suffering from severe combined immunodeficiency disease (SCID), as already described. The ex vivo approach using retroviruses has yielded high levels of corrective gene expression among patients over several years. Young people who previously had to live in isolation bubbles can now live more-or-less normal lives. With so much time and expense involved and with such mixed results following apparent early successes, it was not surprising that federal agencies, health specialists, and the public began to question the value of gene-therapy research. In 1996 the U.S. National Institutes of Health (NIH) tightened the requirements for approving gene-therapy trials. Those trials that are now approved should have a greater likelihood of yielding beneficial results.

What are the major hurdles that remain? First, the gene delivery vehicles that introduce DNA into target cells are inefficient. Second, following delivery of

Future prospects

After years of effort, the complete assembly of the entire human genome sequence was published simultaneously by the privately funded Celera Corporation and a publicly funded consortium of laboratories called the Human Genome Project. The compilation of the complete human genome sequence is a dazzling accomplishment and a critical milestone for the successful treatment of human disease. Remarkably, these publications show that humans have far fewer genes than previously believed, somewhere between 30,000 and 50,000. The findings are spurring on the discovery of previously unknown genes for genetic diseases and increasing understanding of regulatory mechanisms for those genes that are known. They are shedding light on how immune reactions might be suppressed or circumvented so that engineered viruses can safely deliver their therapeutic payload to cells. Greater knowledge of the human genome and its gene products will accelerate advances in all stages of gene therapy. Unless there are major setbacks, by the second half of the 21st century, gene therapy will have come of age. By then, perhaps hundreds of genetic diseases will be treatable if not curable.

T. DAY

See also: BLOOD; DNA; GENETICS; HUMAN GENOME PROJECT; IMMUNE SYSTEMS; STEM CELLS.

Further reading:

Kresina, T. F., ed. 2001. *An Introduction to Molecular Medicine and Gene Therapy.* New York: Wiley-Liss. Peltonen, L., and V. A. McKusick. 2001. Dissecting human disease in the posteconomic era. *Science* 291: 1224–1229.

GENETICALLY MODIFIED FOODS

Genetically modified foods have properties specifically altered by genetic engineering

The term *genetically modified foods* (GM foods or GMFs) commonly refers to food products derived from crop plants that are created using sophisticated genetic engineering techniques.

Using the tools of molecular biology, plant geneticists can transfer simple genetic traits to crop plants from wild relatives, distantly related plants, or even nonplant organisms, such as animals and bacteria. Traditionally, selective breeding of crops for desired traits (such as disease resistance or high crop yield) was a gradual process of selecting individuals with the desired traits and crossing them generation after generation to produce strains with required characteristics. Genetic engineering methods involving recombinant DNA technology shortcut this process. Genetic modification in this manner offers a high-precision tool for creating new strains with beneficial characteristics, including strains that would never normally occur in nature (see SELECTIVE BREEDING).

The first GM food product to be licensed for U.S. consumption was a tomato strain called Flavr Savr. The producers used genetic engineering to introduce a specific inhibitor of the tomato skin enzyme polygalacturonase. This enzyme causes ripe tomatoes to soften. By inhibiting the enzyme, vine-ripened tomatoes stayed fresh for a longer time. This property is particularly useful for tomatoes that are shipped great distances. However, the Flavr Savr was withdrawn from the market for commercial reasons.

The technology

GM food technology depends on the production of transgenic plants (plants that contain genes that have been manufactured and inserted by genetic engineering methods). The genes are stably incorporated into the plant cell's genome. The genome refers to the entire assemblage of chromosomes in a plant cell's nucleus, the genes that are located on these chromosomes, and the sequences of DNA (deoxyribonucleic acid) that make up the genes. To produce transgenic plants, researchers target those plant cells that are capable of growing to produce an entire new plant (so-called totipotent cells; see STEM CELLS). There are

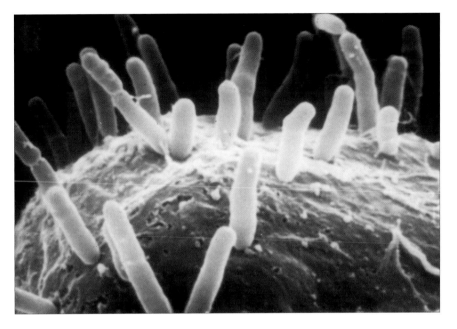

Agrobacterium tumefaciens, *the bacterium used extensively to genetically modify foods*.

several ways of inserting genes, but two methods are most popular: microprojectile bombardment and using a bacterium. With the microprojectile bombardment approach, a particle gun is used to propel tungsten or gold beads coated with genetic material through the cell wall, across membranes, and into the cell. Most cells die from the damage inflicted, but in a few cases the genetic material enters the nucleus and transforms the cell. The novel genetic material DNA is incorporated into the genome, and the new gene's characteristics are expressed.

The most common method of gene insertion uses the bacterium *Agrobacterium tumefaciens*. This organism causes crown gall disease in some plant species. It does so by inserting a plasmid (a ring of DNA separate from the bacterium's main chromosome) into the plant cells it infects. The plasmid carries genes that cause uncontrolled cell division, the result being a tumor in the host plant. Plant geneticists can engineer the bacterium so that it no longer inserts tumor-causing genes but instead introduces a novel gene selected to confer chosen properties.

Whichever method of gene insertion is used, researchers must be able to identify rapidly which plant cells have been transformed correctly. To this end, they insert other genes as genetic markers that are inserted alongside the novel genes. For example, genes that confer antibiotic resistance or herbicide resistance can be inserted. The treated plant cells are then grown in a medium containing the appropriate antibiotic or herbicide, and only those plant cells that have been correctly transformed will be able to survive and grow.

Potential benefits of GM crops

The global human population has risen above 6 billion, and is likely to double by 2050. Many plant

CORE FACTS

- ▦ Genetic modification involves introducing novel genes into food plants using genetic engineering methods involving recombinant DNA technology.
- ▦ The potential benefits of GM foods include lowering production costs, raising crop yield, and reducing impact on the environment through less use of chemical pesticides and herbicides.
- ▦ The major concerns about GM foods center on unintended effects on the environment and human health and issues of economic inequality and control.

CONNECTIONS

- ● The production of genetically modified foods employs **GENETIC ENGINEERING** techniques, including the use of **BACTERIA** to insert novel genes into targeted plant cells.

- ● Genetic modification potentially offers much greater speed and precision than traditional **SELECTIVE BREEDING** of plants.

- ● GM crop plants are produced commercially that are resistant to specific **PLANT DISEASES** and **PESTICIDES**.

A gun fires microscopic beads into a plant cell to allow foreign DNA to travel into the cell's nucleus, where the foreign DNA can become part of the cell's genome. Some cells do not survive this treatment, but those that do acquire new characteristics.

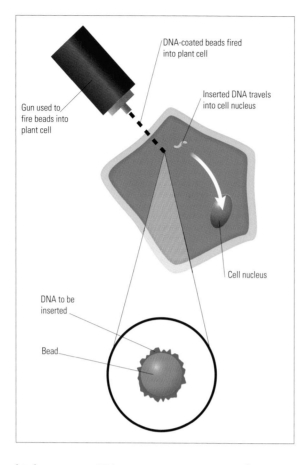

DNA-coated beads fired into plant cell

Gun used to fire beads into plant cell

Inserted DNA travels into cell nucleus

Cell nucleus

DNA to be inserted

Bead

biologists see GM crops as a major contributor to meeting the world population's growing demand for food. Crop plants that are genetically resistant to herbicides top the list of commercial GM forms.

Applying chemical herbicides to kill weeds, without harming the crop, is costly. It usually requires repeated applications, and thus, high levels of herbicide enter the environment. The agricultural and biotechnological (agri-biotech) company Monsanto has created a strain of GM soybeans that are resistant to Roundup, a potent herbicide. A single application of Roundup kills weeds but leaves the crop

PREVALENCE OF GM CROPS AND FOOD PRODUCTS

According to figures published in January 2002, 5.5 million farmers worldwide grew GM crops. In total, the crops covered more than 120 million acres (50 million hectares), about twice the size of the state of Oregon. The main GM crop producers are Argentina, Canada, China, and the United States, with U.S. farmers producing more than half.

Soybeans and corn are the two most widely grown commercial GM crops, followed by cotton, rapeseed (canola), and potatoes. In 2000 about three-quarters of GM crops were modified for tolerance against herbicides (weed killers), and about 20 percent for resistance to insect pests.

By 2000 the U.S. Food and Drug Administration (FDA) and the U.S. Department of Agriculture (USDA) had passed 40 types of GM plants for commercial harvesting. In the United States, GM soybean and corn derivatives are widely used as food additives. They are incorporated into hundreds of foods, including breakfast cereals, cooking oils, and candies. It is likely that almost all people in the United States have eaten GM products at one time or another.

A CLOSER LOOK

plant unharmed, thus lowering costs and potentially reducing environmental impact.

The use of chemical insecticides to kill crop pests is very costly and pollutes the environment. Consumers are also rightly suspicious of consuming pesticide-treated foods. While some consumers and farmers favor organic farming methods, researchers have engineered a corn plant that contains genes from the bacterium *Bacillus thuringiensis* (Bt). Bt produces a natural insecticide that protects it from being eaten by mosquito larvae. This insecticide also kills an important insect pest, the corn borer. Introducing Bt genes into corn plants avoids having to treat the crop with chemical pesticides and potentially reduces farming costs. Similarly, many plant biologists are working to create GM plants that are resistant to diseases caused by viruses, bacteria, and fungi.

Many GM crops are targeted at profitable Western markets, for example, fruits, and vegetables that have enhanced appearance and longer shelf life, although the latter may reduce nutritional values. Other novel developments include GM potato plants that contain an antifreeze gene taken from polar fish. The gene gives plant seedlings tolerance against cold temperatures so that seedlings can be planted early with less concern about frost damage. However, some GM plants are also targeted at markets in developing countries with the aim of alleviating problems in less wealthy communities. For example, some researchers have a long-term aim to develop GM tomatoes and potatoes that manufacture vaccines that would offer the eater protection against conditions such as bacterial dysentery and measles.

In developing countries, some communities are malnourished because local people depend largely on a staple food, such as polished rice, that does not provide a well-balanced range of vitamins and minerals. For such reasons, visual impairment due to vitamin A deficiency is common in some communities. Researchers in Switzerland have developed a GM strain of rice, golden rice, which is rich in vitamin A, and could be grown by communities to help alleviate this dietary deficiency.

As world population increases, land previously unsuitable for plant cultivation may well be pressed into use. Researchers around the world are currently seeking to develop GM plants that will grow in inhospitable places, such as drought-ridden regions and places where the soil has a high salt content.

Potential risks of GM crops and foods

Many sectors of the community, from environmental activists and religious organizations to scientists and government officials, have raised concerns about GM foods. Their concerns fall largely into three categories: environmental impacts, human health risks, and economic questions.

In 1999 an article published in the scientific journal *Nature* showed high mortality rates among monarch butterfly caterpillars fed the pollen from Bt corn genetically-engineered to produce natural insecticide. The study was prompted by concern that pollen from Bt corn could blow onto milkweed plants growing alongside fields. Monarch caterpillars eat milkweed leaves, not corn, but they might inadvertently eat the insecticide-laced pollen. Scientists argue over the accuracy and validity of this study, but it does highlight a general concern, that GM crops may be having unintended effects on other organisms.

Another worry is that engineered genes could be transferred from crop plants to weeds, and thus produce superweeds that have the protective properties of the crop plants. In this way, weeds could become resistant to herbicides and insect pests and could then spread almost uncontrolled. Possible solutions to this problem involve more genetic engineering. The most likely cause of gene transfer from plant to plant is via pollen, which contains the male gamete. GM plants could be created that are male sterile and so would not produce pollen. However, in this case, the crop would need to be planted with fresh GM seed each year. Many farmers in developing countries rely on harvesting their own seed for next year's crop and could not afford to buy new GM seeds each year. An alternative approach is to genetically engineer the plant so that its pollen does not contain the natural insecticide, even if other parts of the plant do. A less technical approach to the problem would be to create buffer zones of non-GM crops around each field of GM crops beyond which the pollen of the GM crop would not blow. The non-GM crops would not be harvested. Scientists argue about how wide the buffer zone would need to be, but at 20 to 100 feet (6 to 30 m) across, it would probably not be economically viable, even if it could be enforced.

A third environmental concern is that insect pests will rapidly become resistant to the natural insecticides produced by GM crops. A fourth worry is that the antibiotic-resistance genes used as genetic markers in some GM crops could lead to the creation of superbacteria that are multiply resistant to antibiotics, thus posing a major public health threat. Potential risks to human health are largely unknown, and introducing novel genes into an existing plant could create new chemicals to which some people might be allergic. The plant's altered biochemistry might produce unforeseen effects, such as higher levels of potentially toxic substances or markedly altered the nutritional value. Thorough testing of GM foods and proper labeling of GM products has been called for. In the early 2000s, a panel set up by the Royal Society in Britain reported that many international regulators said that GM crops should be "substantially equivalent" to non-GM breeds, but they had not agreed precisely what the phrase means. The panel recommended that agreement be reached before commercial GM food production starts in the United Kingdom.

As for economic concerns, agri-biotech companies obviously invest large amounts of money in bringing their GM products to market and expect to make a return on their investment. Some consumer advocates are concerned that agribusinesses have too great a control on the crop market because of the patents they are taking out on genetically engineered strains, a situation that could force seed prices up. One effect could be to widen the gap of opportunity between prosperous and poor countries.

The future

GM foods offer enormous potential, but there are still unresolved concerns. GM crops are flourishing in some parts of the world but have yet to be grown commercially in Britain and several other European countries. In these countries, agencies that regulate food and agriculture will not allow commercial GM crop production until the results of ongoing environmental and health trials are evaluated.

T. DAY

See also: AGRICULTURE; BIOTECHNOLOGY; DNA; STEM CELLS.

Further reading:

Altieri, M. A. 2001. *Genetic Engineering in Agriculture.* Oakland, Calif.: Food First/ Institute for Food and Development Policy.
Lambrecht, B. 2001. *Dinner at the New Gene Café.* New York: St. Martin's Press.
Marshall, E. L. 1999. *High-Tech Harvest: A Look at Genetically Engineered Foods.* London: Franklin Watt.

Bacterial plasmids are used as the carriers of new DNA to infect a plant cell and thus enable it to have new characteristics.

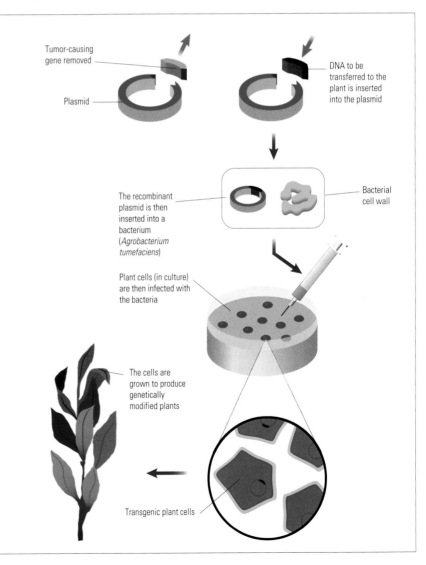

Tumor-causing gene removed

DNA to be transferred to the plant is inserted into the plasmid

Plasmid

The recombinant plasmid is then inserted into a bacterium (*Agrobacterium tumefaciens*)

Bacterial cell wall

Plant cells (in culture) are then infected with the bacteria

The cells are grown to produce genetically modified plants

Transgenic plant cells

GENETIC DISEASES

A child undergoing treatment for cystic fibrosis, an autosomal recessive hereditary disease.

CONNECTIONS

● The introduction of a corrective gene into someone's cells to treat genetic disease is called **GENE THERAPY**.

● Genetic diseases are determined by information held on the **CHROMOSOMES**.

Genes provide instructions to cells to make proteins that the body requires to grow and function. A defective gene may have mild, moderate, or fatal consequences, depending on the role of the protein for which the gene codes. Genetic diseases occur when there is a mutation in a single gene or a set of genes (see MUTATION). A mutation is a change in the DNA sequence of a gene (see DNA). Sometimes whole chromosomes (see CHROMOSOMES), the long strands of DNA and protein that carry genes, may be abnormal and thus may lead to disease. Thanks to new medical advances, once-fatal genetic diseases can now often be managed, with a better quality of life.

How heredity works

In each organism, every cell contains an identical copy of its complete genetic information (its genome), which is divided into units called chromosomes. Humans are diploid organisms (having paired chromosomes), and each body cell contains 23 pairs

Genetic diseases are determined by an individual's genetic makeup

of chromosomes, including a pair of sex chromosomes. Women have two full-length sex chromosomes, called X chromosomes, while men have one large (X) and one small (Y) chromosome. The number of genes found on each chromosome varies with the size of the given chromosome.

One chromosome of each pair is inherited from the mother and the other is inherited from the father. Genes exist in varieties called alleles. If a child inherits the same alleles from both parents, the child is said to be homozygous for that allele. If the child inherits two different alleles for one allele, it is said to be heterozygous for that particular characteristic (see GENETICS).

When an individual is heterozygous for any one gene, one of the alleles may dominate the other. Sometimes this situation occurs because a product made by the dominant allele masks the product of the other, recessive, allele. Often it occurs because the recessive gene does not make any product, and the dominant gene wins out by default. For some pairs of genes, neither will be dominant, and both characteristics will be expressed at the same time, the result being codominance. Other times the combination of one dominant and one recessive copy produces an intermediate trait. This combination is called incomplete dominance. An example of incomplete dominance is the pink flower produced by the progeny of a white and a red snapdragon.

GENETIC DISEASES

Genetic diseases may be categorized as chromosome abnormalities, single-gene disorders, multifactorial disorders, and mitochondrial disorders.

Chromosomal abnormality

Chromosomal abnormality occurs when chromosomes, or large segments of them, are duplicated, missing, or altered in some way. A deviation from the normal number of 46 chromosomes (aneuploidy) is by far the most common form of genetic defect in humans. Aneuploidy occurs when meiosis, the process of cell division to produce a sperm or egg, is faulty (see CELL BIOLOGY).

One well-known aneuploid condition, Down syndrome, affects about 1 in every 700 children born in

---

CORE FACTS

■ Genetic diseases range from simple color blindness to fatal diseases.

■ It is possible to screen pregnant women for a number of genetic diseases.

■ Genetic diseases can be grouped into chromosomal abnormalities, single-gene disorders, multifactorial disorders, and mitochondrial disorders.

the United States. People with Down syndrome have additional copies of one or part of a chromosome, producing a genetic and consequentially a biochemical imbalance during development. Down syndrome includes characteristic facial features, short stature, heart defects, mental retardation, and susceptibility to infection. The most common form of Down syndrome is also called trisomy 21 because people with it have three copies of chromosome 21.

Other forms of aneuploidy may involve duplication, deletion, or translocation (movement) of parts of chromosomes so that the chromosome content is changed, even if the chromosome number is not. Translocation occurs when a section of a chromosome is moved. Translocation occurs in a form of Down syndrome, where a section of chromosome 21 is moved to the tip of another chromosome.

Single-gene disorders

Occasionally, a mutation causes the product of a single gene to be missing or altered. About 1 in 100 babies is born with a disorder that is caused by a single faulty gene. Inheritance caused by genes on the 22 pairs of chromosomes other than the sex chromosomes is autosomal. Autosomal traits are equally common in both sexes.

Autosomal recessive traits

Thousands of genetic diseases are known to be inherited as recessive alleles. When the alleles are recessive, their effects are seen only in the homozygous state, in other words, if both parents contribute the recessive allele to their baby. The frequency of the recessive gene in the population will determine how often two of these genes come together. In many cases, they are passed down by individuals who are heterozygous and have no knowledge that they carry the recessive allele. Thus, two unsuspecting carriers may produce a child with the disorder seemingly "out of the blue." Marriages between closely related couples, or those breeding strictly within a given population increases the chance of these disorders occurring. For example, Tay-Sachs disease, a metabolic disorder, is extremely rare in almost all populations but has a higher frequency (about 1 in 4,000 births) in Ashkenazi Jews.

PRENATAL SCREENING AND GENETIC COUNSELING

Once a woman becomes pregnant, there are various tests that can detect disorders in the fetus. The cost of screening is high, and the type of screening carried out is determined by the population. In Sardinia, for example, thalassemia, an inherited disorder of hemoglobin synthesis, is screened for in the general population.

Amniocentesis and chorionic villus sampling can be used to screen for cystic fibrosis, diabetes, hemophilia, Huntington's disease, sickle-cell anemia, and many other gene defects. DNA probes can be used for detecting defective genes in fetuses, newborns, and adult carriers, such as those for sickle-cell anemia and Huntington's disease.

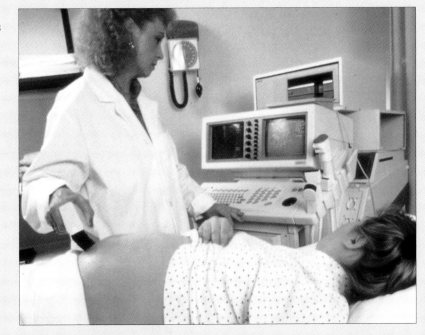

Ultrasound scanning provides a valuable diagnostic aid in determining the condition and growth of unborn children.

wall into the uterus. Amniotic fluid surrounding the fetus is then withdrawn, and the cells studied for chromosomal abnormalities. Amniocentesis is usually done between weeks 14 and 18 of pregnancy. The procedure is associated with a very low risk of miscarriage.

Chorionic villus sampling (CVS) allows cells from the fetal chorionic membranes, part of the fetal portion of the placenta, to be sampled. This test is usually carried out between weeks 8 and 11 of pregnancy. The risk of spontaneous miscarriage is highest in the early weeks of pregnancy and is increased slightly by the CVS test.

Ultrasound scanning is used to check that the fetus is developing correctly. High-frequency sound waves are passed through the mother's abdomen and converted into visual signals on a screen.

Fetoscopy involves the insertion of a fine optic telescope through the mother's abdominal wall. The fetus can be closely observed, and it also possible to take samples of its skin or blood. Amniocentesis requires a fine needle to be inserted through the mother's abdominal

Genetic counseling provides people with information about genetic disorders from experienced counselors. Topics include the likelihood of two people having an afflicted child, the psychological effects such a child might have on other family members, and the financial cost of the disorder in terms of treatment and any necessary life changes, as well as information on relevant options, including prenatal diagnosis and abortion. Genetic counseling thus gives people information to make an informed and independent choice.

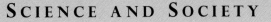

SCIENCE AND SOCIETY

When two people both carrying a gene for a particular recessive abnormality in the heterozygous state have children, a quarter of the children are likely to have the abnormality, and three-quarters will be normal. However, two-thirds of the unaffected children will be carriers of the recessive allele and therefore carriers of the disease. If only one parent is heterozygous, all the children will appear normal, but half will be carriers.

Sickle-cell anemia

Sickle-cell anemia is caused by a mutation in the gene for hemoglobin, which carries oxygen in the blood (see ANEMIA). The abnormal hemoglobin causes the red blood cells to become sickle shaped instead of doughnut shaped. The misshapen blood cells clog blood vessels and thus restrict blood supply to the tissues. Circulatory problems may lead to brain damage and even paralysis. Most sufferers die in their teens and twenties. However, sickle-cell anemia is one of several recessive genetic disorders that confers an advantage in heterozygous carriers in some environments by providing resistance to certain forms of malaria.

Cystic fibrosis

Cystic fibrosis is the most common serious genetic disorder among Caucasians. The cystic fibrosis gene causes a failure in the proper functioning of glands that produce mucus. As a result, the glands produce mucus that is abnormally thick and sticky, and it clogs up body passageways, such as those in the intestines and respiratory system. Malnutrition often occurs, because digestion is impaired, and recurring lung infections lead to chronic heart disease. Life expectancy for those with cystic fibrosis has improved with new drugs and heart and lung transplants.

Tay-Sachs disease

In this disease, one of the enzymes that catalyze the breakdown of a fat molecule called N-acylsphingosine, is faulty. As a result, a product in the breakdown pathway of fat accumulates in the brain cells of the child. The child appears to develop normally for the first five months of life. By eight months, the child has lost alertness; blindness, deafness, the onset of seizures, and progressive loss of muscular control follow.

Autosomal dominant traits

If a parent has an autosomal chromosome carrying a gene causing a dominant abnormality, his or her chances of having an affected child are one in two. Unlike cases of recessive inheritance, these conditions run in families. Two examples include Marfan's syndrome and Huntington's disease (see DEGENERATIVE BRAIN DISEASE).

People with Marfan's syndrome have long thin limbs, fingers, and toes. The syndrome is caused by a defect in one of the genes that controls the production of collagen, a substance found in connective tissues. Death may be caused by sudden rupture of the aorta as result of weakening of the connective tissue in the aorta's wall.

Symptoms of Huntington's disease begin between the ages of 25 and 55 years. The symptoms begin with clumsiness and lead to uncontrollable muscle spasms, incontinence, personality changes, depression, and eventually insanity. They are caused by a degeneration of the central nervous system and a loss of cells from the brain.

X-linked recessive disorders

X-linked recessive disorder is the name given to inheritance disorders caused by genes on sex chromosomes because there are very few genes on the human Y chromosome and none of the genes on the X chromosome is known to have a counterpart on the Y chromosome. Females carry two X chromosomes, and recessive X-linked traits are rarely carried on both copies. If males inherit a recessive allele, on their single X chromosome, they will express the recessive trait. Thus, some genetic diseases, such as hemophilia, are more common in males; females with a hemophilia gene on one X chromosome are unlikely to have it on the other X chromosome as well.

If an abnormal gene lies on one of the X chromosomes of the mother, half her sons are likely to be affected, and half her daughters will be carriers. If the abnormal gene is on the father's X chromosome, all his sons will be normal and all his daughters will be carriers.

The genes that control color vision are carried on the X chromosome. About 8 percent of males in the United States have one of the two X-linked color-blindness conditions.

Hemophilia is the most common X-linked disorder. In hemophiliacs, the blood is deficient in a protein called factor VIII, which is essential for blood clotting. The blood does not clot properly after a minor injury or bruising. Bleeding after minor surgery, such as a tooth extraction, may continue for days or weeks. However, symptoms can now be averted by treatment with infusions of a clotting factor.

TRIPLE REPEAT DISORDERS

New molecular technology has uncovered a totally unexpected type of mutation that causes genetic disease in humans. The mutation is a triplet of DNA bases (bases are the most basic building blocks of DNA), repeated many times, one after another, called a triplet repeat.

Triplet repeats are now known to cause about a dozen human diseases. In general, the higher the number of repeats, the more severe the symptoms and the earlier in life the symptoms appear. Huntington's disease is an example of a triplet repeat disease. In Huntington's disease, there are triplet repeats in the Huntington gene, which codes for a protein of unknown function. In a normal Huntington gene, there are about 20 repeats. In an individual with Huntington's disease, however, there are 36 to 180 repetitions.

A CLOSER LOOK

X-linked dominant disorders

There are only a few dominant X-linked conditions, and most occur in females. Male fetuses with these rare disorders tend to die before birth. One example is oral-facial-digital syndrome, in which the person has a cleft tongue and palate, no teeth, fusion of the fingers and toes, and mild retardation. Women who are affected by this disorder pass it on to half their daughters; afflicted boys die before birth.

Multifactorial disorders

While single-gene disorders are devastating to the families involved, they are rare in populations as a whole. Conditions such as diabetes, asthma, common cancers, heart disease, and psychiatric disorders pose a much larger threat to public health. These diseases are called multifactorial because they are due to mutations to many genes.

Environmental factors also affect the likelihood of developing a multifactorial disease. Identifying the genes involved in multifactorial disorders is difficult, particularly as researchers do not know whether the genes are inherited in a dominant or recessive fashion. It is difficult for researchers to separate the environmental component from the genetic component. As a result, researchers often use identical twins, which share exactly the same genetic heritage, but sometimes different lifestyles, as a basis for their scientific investigations.

Genetic contributions to a few polygenic diseases (those controlled by a group of genes) have been identified. For example, researchers have identified a number of genes that control cholesterol levels in the blood (see BLOOD). Variations in these genes affect the risk of heart disease.

Mitochondrial disorders

Mitochondrial disorders are rare genetic disorders caused by mutations in nonchromosomal DNA, located in compartments of the cell called mitochondria. Essential for generating energy for the cell, these organelles are inherited only from the maternal side and do not follow Mendel's rules of inheritance. Diseases are quite variable and often have delayed onset. One example is Leber's hereditary optic neuropathy (LHON), in which vision is affected.

P. DAVIS

See also: ALZHEIMER'S DISEASE; ANEMIA; BIOETHICS; BLOOD; CELL BIOLOGY; DEGENERATIVE BRAIN DISEASE; DNA; GENETICS; HUMAN GENOME PROJECT; MENDEL, GREGOR; MUTATION; PREGNANCY AND BIRTH; TWINS AND MULTIPLE BIRTHS.

Further reading:

Blackford, S. L., ed. 2001. *Gale Encyclopedia of Genetic Disorders.* 2 vols. Detroit: Gale Group.
Khoury, M. J., W. Burke, and E. Thompson, eds. 2000. *Genetics and Public Health in the 21st Century: Using Genetic Information to Improve Health and Prevent Disease.* Oxford: Oxford University Press.
Milunsky, A. 2001. *Your Genetic Destiny.* Cambridge, Mass.: Perseus Pulishing.

SINGLE NUCLEOTIDE POLYMORPHISMS

Every human is 99.9 percent identical at a genetic level. Yet, within that 0.1 percent variation lies the key to the varying susceptibility of humans for certain multifactorial genetic diseases. These hot spots of variation are called SNPs (single nucleotide polymorphisms; see DIMORPHISM AND POLYMORPHISM). They are variations that occur when a single letter (base) in the genetic code is altered.

Many geneticists believe that identifying SNPs will be able to reveal the risks of dying from many common diseases and possibly reduce them. Publication of the first draft of the human genome identified millions of potential SNPs. The disease risk of a small number of SNPs have been identified. For example, a SNP in the apolipoprotein E gene is associated with varying predisposition for late-onset Alzheimer's disease (see ALZHEIMER'S DISEASE).

A CLOSER LOOK

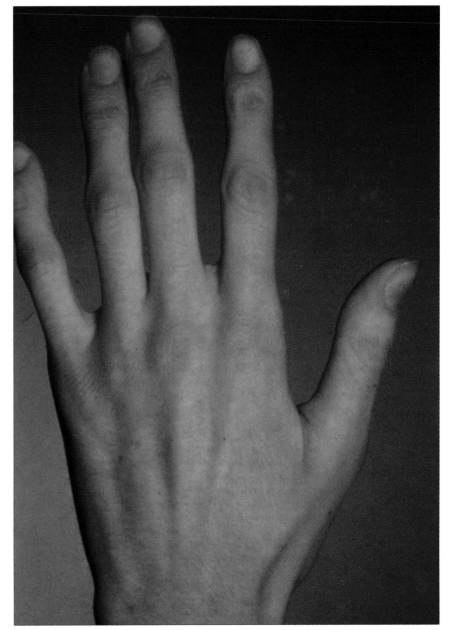

Marfan's syndrome is caused by a defect in the structure of collagen that leads to long thin fingers, as shown in the picture above. This hereditary disorder of connective tissue is characterized by abnormal elongation of the bones and often by eye and circulatory defects. It is named for a French pediatrician, Bernard-Jean-Antonin Marfan (1858–1942).

GENETIC ENGINEERING

Genetic engineering is the alteration of an organism's genetic material to change its characteristics

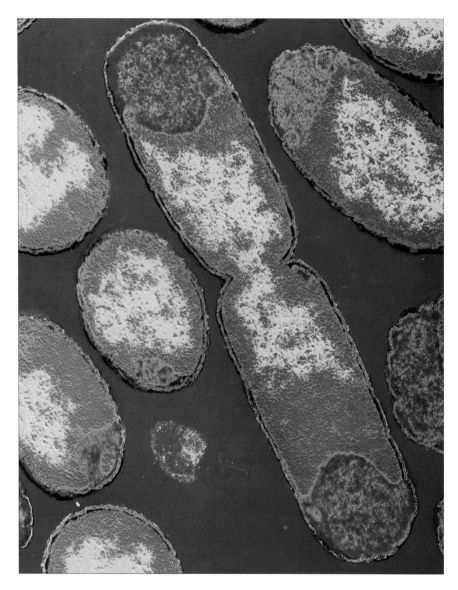

Escherichia coli, *a human intestinal bacterium, was one of the first organisms to be genetically altered in a laboratory.*

CONNECTIONS

● **GENE THERAPY** is a type of genetic engineering.

● **SELECTIVE BREEDING** is the process by which plants and animals are bred for specific characteristics.

Crops resistant to disease, tomatoes that stay fresh longer, and mammals that glow under UV light—all are examples of genetic engineering, the manipulation of an organism's genes. In this process, a foreign gene is introduced into the genome that changes an organism's physical characteristics in some way. The DNA of this organism is called recombinant DNA, in which DNA from two different sources are joined together artificially. While most discussions restrict the term *genetic engineering* to techniques involving recombinant DNA technology, this article also includes, for example, the domestication of the dog and plant breeding.

Genetic engineering has seen great advances in the last few decades, yet there is nothing particularly new about the idea of altering an organism's genetic makeup: people have been influencing the genes of plants and animals for thousands of years. The oldest genetically engineered animals are probably dogs, bred from wolves; humans heightened the animals' natural abilities as hunters, protectors, and companions. Furthermore, human societies have also been selectively breeding plants with desirable traits, as part of the process of agriculture. The biggest difference between breeding methods and recombinant DNA engineering techniques is that the latter makes possible gene combinations that could never occur by mating: DNA can be introduced from a different organism, species, or even kingdom.

Cut and paste

Recombinant DNA procedures are a form of molecular cutting and pasting that employs naturally occurring enzymatic proteins as both scissors and glueing agents. The scissor proteins, called restriction endonucleases, occur in microorganisms. To protect themselves from attack by viruses, microorganisms carry restriction endonucleases that cut foreign DNA strands at specific sites to produce fragments of defined length. The enzymes identify a particular sequence of base pairs (building blocks of DNA) and snip the DNA only at these so-called recognition sequences within the virus. The microorganism's genome remains unharmed. Purified restriction endonucleases are currently available from an enormous variety of bacteria, each capable of cutting DNA strands into fragments of different lengths because they have different recognition sequences. The ends of these DNA fragments can be glued together with another bacterial enzyme, DNA ligase. These DNA glue enzymes normally play a role in both DNA replication and DNA repair, sealing nicks produced by both processes. Ligases recognize only the ends of DNA fragments.

DNA that has been cut with particular restriction enzymes sometimes creates "sticky" ends that readily join up with the matching ends of other pieces of DNA. With the help of DNA ligases, they attach to each other so easily that it does not matter if the two DNA molecules have come from very different organisms. Thus, genetic engineers have been able, for example, to insert human genes into bacteria and get the microorganisms to produce human proteins such as insulin and blood-clotting factors.

Duplicating DNA

Researchers wishing to isolate a particular gene are faced with a problem. Genes occupy only a tiny

CORE FACTS

■ Genetic engineering raises many social and ethical issues.
■ Advances in DNA technology have revolutionized genetic engineering.
■ Many scientists believe agriculture and medicine have benefited greatly from genetic engineering.

proportion of the chromosomal DNA; with the average gene taking up only 0.007 percent of the total genome, the isolation of a gene becomes the hunt for a needle in a haystack. Researchers have several techniques to overcome this problem and can now copy vast quantities of a specific gene.

DNA cloning (copying; see CLONING) uses plasmids, small circles of DNA naturally present in bacteria. Plasmids usually carry genes that are helpful to bacteria. For example, some plasmids carry genes for antibiotic resistance. With restriction enzymes, a scientist snips the plasmid so that the circle becomes a linear fragment with two sticky ends. With the same restriction enzyme, the scientist also snips the DNA that contains the gene he or she wants to copy. These fragments of DNA with sticky ends easily join up with the plasmid DNA, forming a complete circle once again. When the engineered plasmid is inserted back into its bacterial host, the bacterium divides and multiplies as usual, creating new copies of the plasmid (with its new gene). Copies of the gene can then be isolated and transferred to other organisms. Alternatively, the bacteria can be stimulated to produce copies of a useful protein encoded by the new DNA.

Sometimes, getting a cloned gene into a new organism is difficult because certain details of gene expression vary between different cell types. To reduce cellular incompatibility, biologists can use yeast cells, which are more closely related to human cells, rather than bacteria, as hosts for human genes. Scientists have also built artificial chromosomes, miniature versions of whole chromosomes, that can carry much more DNA than a plasmid vector, enabling very long pieces of DNA to be cloned.

Since the late 1980s, genetic engineering has been revolutionized by another technique, polymerase chain reaction (PCR), which is performed completely in vitro (in a test tube). PCR is an extremely easy method to produce abundant quantities of DNA that is normally very scarce or impure so that it can be examined in the laboratory. The technique allows tiny quantities of DNA to be amplified (copied many times) in a few hours, whereas DNA cloning takes several days.

PCR makes use of an enzyme called DNA polymerase that is capable of producing copies of a DNA template as long as short sequences of DNA, called primers, are bound to it as a starting place for DNA synthesis. By using a set of primers placed strategically at the ends of any double-stranded fragment to be copied, DNA polymerase can produce an exact duplicate. The copying process is automated by using a cycling waterbath that raises and lowers the temperature in the DNA synthesis reaction. A heat-resistant DNA polymerase is used, and after each cycle of copying, the temperature is raised to separate the DNA strands and then lowered to begin another cycle of priming and DNA synthesis. As long as the primer DNA is kept in excess, the DNA fragment is copied in a chain reaction that makes over 1,000 copies in 10 cycles and over 1 million copies in 20 cycles.

Analyzing DNA

After cutting DNA into pieces using restriction enzymes, a scientist can sort and analyze the fragments with a technique called gel electrophoresis (see ANALYTICAL TECHNIQUES). DNA molecules are slightly negatively charged. When an electrical current is applied to a gel containing DNA pieces, they move toward the positively charged end of the field. Smaller pieces move faster than large pieces, so fragments can be sorted by size. Two of the most common types of electrophoresis are agarose and polyacrylamide gel electrophoresis. After electrophoresis, DNA may be stained to show the pattern of bands. The size of each band can be estimated from the distance it moved in the gel, and this information can be used to make DNA maps.

Sometimes, researchers transfer the DNA from the gel to a membrane of nitrocellulose. The membrane is then treated with heat or chemicals to denature the DNA (cause the strands to separate). Because the DNA is now single stranded, it readily

The process of gene cloning, shown below, using recombinant DNA techniques, enables scientists to produce identical copies of genetic material.

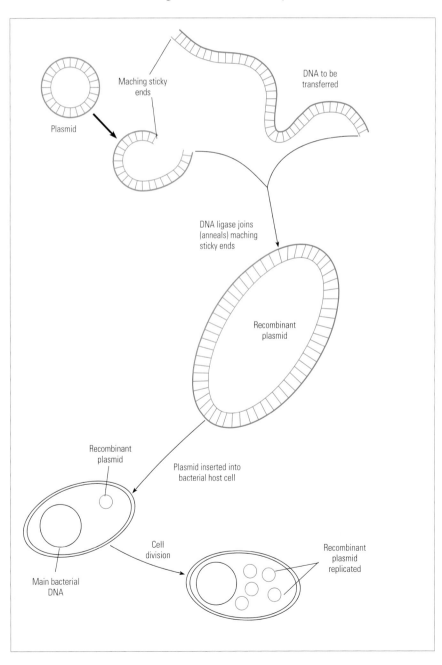

Plasmid

Maching sticky ends

DNA to be transferred

DNA ligase joins (anneals) maching sticky ends

Recombinant plasmid

Recombinant plasmid

Plasmid inserted into bacterial host cell

Main bacterial DNA

Cell division

Recombinant plasmid replicated

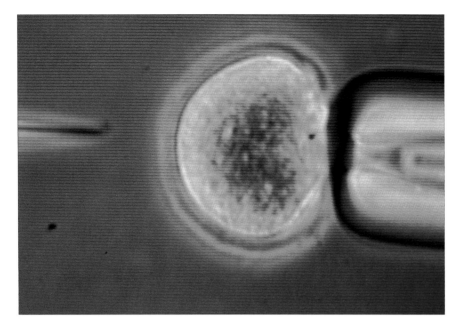

The process of microinjection enables genetic material to be introduced into a cell so that it can be incorporated into the existing genetic material.

The diagram below shows how the use of restriction enzymes to cut the DNA of two individuals results in fragments of different length. The differences become apparent when the fragments are subjected to electrophoresis; the variability of fragment size is useful in DNA fingerprinting and the mapping of human genes.

joins up with any complementary strand of DNA, each A with T and each G with C. Scientists use small pieces of DNA (called probes) that are tagged with radioactive or fluorescent markers to locate a particular gene of interest from the many bands on the membrane. This process is called Southern blotting after E. M. Southern, the scientist who invented it.

These types of DNA analyses have many applications. DNA patterns from different samples can be compared for similarity. This approach is used in forensic science to compare DNA extracted from blood samples found at a crime scene with DNA from the blood of a victim or a suspect, a technique called DNA fingerprinting or DNA profiling (see FORENSIC SCIENCE). Identical patterns strongly suggest identical sources, since everyone's DNA is unique, except for identical twins'. A similar test can be performed for paternity or maternity testing.

DNA sequencing

One way of describing a particular strand of DNA is to list, in order, the succession of bases—adenine, thymine, guanine, and cytosine—of which it consists (see DNA). The most widely used sequencing method was invented by British biochemists Frederick Sanger (b. 1918) and Alan Coulson. Scientists usually refer to this process as the Sanger method. The Human Genome Project, a global scientific collaboration, has identified the whole sequence of the human genome. It is hoped that this genetic know-ledge will help find new disease treatments.

Sequencing of the human genome was completed much earlier than expected thanks to leaps in automation and sequencing technology. A privately funded version of the human sequence was generated by Celera Genomics of Rockville, Maryland, in only three years of effort, even more quickly than the public version. The private group used powerful computer technology to sort and analyze DNA fragments into a sequence. They also used publicly available data generated by the Human Genome Project to build their version of the human genome.

Sequence analysis

DNA sequence information has many uses, such as to explain gene function or clarify evolutionary relationships between different organisms. Because some DNA is thought to mutate at a constant rate in some organisms, scientists are calculating when species emerged on Earth. One group of studies tracks mutations in mitochondrial DNA, inherited from mother to child. Mitochondrial DNA analysis suggests that humans originated in Africa and spread to Europe, the Middle East, and Asia. Sequence data has also helped scientists find the origin and spread of certain viruses, such as HIV. The vast quantities of sequence data being generated have also led to the birth of a new field, bioinformatics, in which computers are used to manage and analyze genetic data.

The future of genetic engineering

The possible uses of genetic engineering are staggering in their variety, and scientists are thinking up new applications every day. The accessibility of DNA technology has also made genetic engineering widespread. For example, Chicago-based artist Eduardo Kac commissioned French scientists to introduce genes for green fluorescent protein (genes originally isolated from jellyfish) into the developing embryo of an albino rabbit. The recombinant rabbit, named Alba, produces the fluorescent protein and glows green when exposed to blue light. Kac considers Alba a new form of art. Beyond the art world, genetic engineering has given researchers the power to understand the molecular machinery of cells and viruses, to diagnose and treat human disease, and to produce novel organisms with attributes that are useful to people.

Agriculture

In 2001 a total of 5.5 million farmers planted genetically modified (GM) crops in some 124 million acres (50 million hectares) of arable land. In North America commercial GM production is common, while in Europe it is still prohibited. The main aims have been to increase yields and tolerance to adverse weather conditions such as droughts and cold winters.

Scientists have already sequenced the entire rice genome with such improvements in mind, and the sequencing of other plant genomes is under way. Much effort has gone into creating plants that can withstand herbicide sprays that kill adjacent weeds. Many fruits and vegetables such as melons have been engineered to stay fresh for more than a month in cold

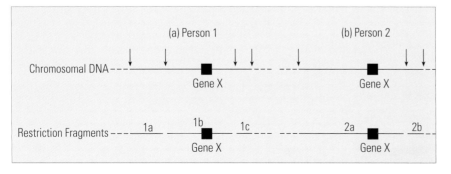

storage. A GM grape containing a silkworm gene that protects it against Pierce's disease, a fungus that ravages vine crops, is currently being tested. Other crops are being developed to contain higher levels of specific nutrients than are found in nature.

Transgenic animals

Scientists first produced transgenic animals (those that have had a foreign gene introduced into their genome) in 1980, using tiny syringes to inject foreign genes into mouse embryos. Genes have also been inserted into much larger animals, such as pigs, goats, sheep, and cows. There are many reasons for creating such animals. For example, medical researchers need laboratory animals with various genetic diseases similar to human disorders, such as cystic fibrosis and diabetes, so they can discover their causes and cures. In addition, "knockout" mice, in which a single gene is disabled, can enable researchers to discover the role of a particular gene. Transgenic cows and goats can be engineered to produce medicines in their milk, providing a novel approach to drug delivery.

Biotechnology

Biotechnology means getting microorganisms and other types of cells to produce useful substances. Some biotechnological processes go back centuries, for example, the use of microorganisms to make bread, wine, and cheese. These products make use of fermentation, in which microorganisms, usually yeasts, consume sugars and produce carbon dioxide and alcohol as by-products of their metabolism.

More recently, bacteria engineered to contain the human gene for making insulin now produce human insulin in great quantities for the treatment of diabetes. Bacteria also make the antiviral agent interferon and a blood-clotting factor for hemophiliacs, who are unable to clot their blood normally.

Genetic engineers are also making more efficient natural microorganisms that can clean up oil spills and other toxic substances from the environment. New kinds of microorganisms can produce particular antigens for vaccines, such as the rabies vaccine for foxes. Scientists are even developing a bacterium that can prevent tooth decay.

Ethical issues in genetic engineering

Many of the moral, social, and public policy issues that have arisen in connection with genetic engineering are not really about genetic engineering as such. For example, much controversy surrounds the introduction in the United States of a genetically engineered version of bovine growth hormone (BGH), which, when injected into cows, induces them to give more milk. The three main arguments against it have been: (1) that it will harm the cows, making them more subject to disease and stress; (2) that it will be very expensive and thus favor large-scale dairy operation and drive small dairy farmers out of business, and (3) that excess BGH may be secreted into the milk and affect young children. These arguments would be the same if BGH were produced by some method other than genetic engineering.

Another set of issues specific to genetic engineering involve questions about whether a newly created organism will be capable of passing its new gene(s) on to another organism and, if so, whether the gene might cause harm. These concerns are expressed frequently in connection with agricultural genetic engineering, mainly because plants are constructed by nature to exchange genetic material. These worries have centered particularly around plants that have been altered to resist herbicides. What if any of them passed that ability to nearby weeds? The new herbicide-resistant weeds would be a far worse problem than the original weeds they were trying to get rid of.

The possible ill effects of passing on new genes is also an issue for other types of organisms, especially humans. These worries center around gene transfer between generations. New screening techniques being applied in pregnancy can detect diseases in the developing fetus. If detected, parents can choose abortion. Opposition comes not only from those who oppose all abortion, but from those concerned that aborting a fetus with a disease or birth defect is a form of eugenics. However, opposition is usually based on a theoretical moral viewpoint rather than practical quality-of-life issues.

Many people are not sure that they want to know what genetic future awaits them. Others are concerned about the potential uses of this information. Will it be kept confidential? Employers may not want to hire people they perceive to be unhealthy. Insurance companies and health maintenance organizations may want to charge some people higher premiums.

Gene patenting has also raised concerns. At present, a number of genome companies have filed patent applications for thousands of DNA sequences. There is a fear that DNA sequence patents could stifle research and make treatments and tests expensive. For example, a company owning a sequence for a potential drug target might demand that researchers who wished to produce a drug based on that sequence would have to pay a fee. The companies argue that gene patents offset development costs. However, the patenting of rice sequencing genomes is morally indefensible when it prevents the cultivation of types of rice by growers who have been doing so for centuries.

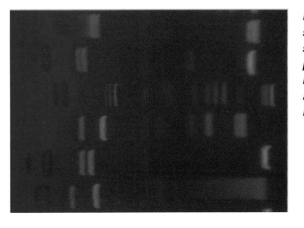

By understanding gene sequences like those shown left, with the pink bands representing base pairs, gene therapy and antiviral drugs may be developed.

Eugenics

In 2000 doctors in the United States specifically selected a new baby boy from among 15 healthy embryos because he had the right bone marrow to help his older sister who had a rare disease. Some argue that such an event paves the way for the re-emergence of eugenics—the study of human genetics and of methods to "improve" the inherited characteristics, physical and mental, of the human race. The first half of the 20th century saw extreme coercive application of such principles by governments, ranging from enforced sterilization of the insane and restricted immigration in the United States and other nations to the Holocaust of Nazi Germany. Even up till 1994, marriages in China involving people with certain disabilities and diseases were prohibited.

Englishman Francis Galton (1822–1911) conceived the term *eugenics*. In 1865 he published two short papers on hereditary talent and character," which influenced genetics in two ways. First, with these papers Galton founded biometry, the mathematical and statistical approach that dominated genetic science until the coming of molecular biology in the last half of the 20th century. Galton stressed that basing scientific ideas on single isolated observations could be very misleading. Instead he urged a statistical approach and rigorous data analysis.

Second, he also argued that "the power of man over animal life, in producing whatever variety of form he pleases, is enormously great. It would seem as though the physical structure of future generations was almost as plastic as clay, under the control of the breeder's will. It is my desire to show, more pointedly than, so far as I am aware has been attempted before, that mental qualities are equally under control." Galton had analyzed biographies of outstanding men, which revealed, he said, that they were related to each other far more often than chance would lead one to expect. These studies persuaded him that

human talent and achievement were strongly influenced by heredity. He went on to suggest a utopian (ideal) society in which the "best" people receive taxpayer subsidies to mate and produce children, which were then educated at public expense.

These notions were the foundation of eugenics, an idea that grew into a political and social movement, much of it damaging, in modern history. The eugenics movement was a program for genetically improving human populations, either by discouraging the propagation of the unfit (negative eugenics), or encouraging propagation among those who are healthy, intelligent, and of high moral character (positive eugenics.) Thus, eugenicists advocated artificial selection against the genetically handicapped and in favor of the types of people they considered desirable.

After the atrocities committed by the Nazis in World War II (1939–1945), in which thousands of people were sterilized and millions murdered, the eugenics movement disappeared. Because the study of genetics was in its infancy at the height of the eugenics movement, the steps its supporters advocated did not rest on good science. For example, sterilizing the mentally retarded does little to eliminate mental disabilities because most forms of mental disability are not inherited.

Advances in human genetics and DNA technology have raised fears that that the eugenics movement will return. It is now possible to take a number of prenatal tests to screen for genetic diseases, such as Down syndrome. Some fear that biotechnology may eventually go beyond preventing disease to engineering traits such as intelligence and physical beauty. Such a world could create a genetic underclass, where those with undesirable genetictraits are discriminated against. There may also be unforeseen consequences that cannot be reversed.

In all, efforts to increase the supply of good genes are not likely to work, particularly as the notion of a good or bad gene is highly subjective. Many so-called bad genes may be good in some circumstances. For example, in the homozygote condition, two recessive genes that lead to sickle-cell anemia are crippling and fatal. In the heterozygote, a single sickle-cell gene protects against malaria, one of the most common causes of death (see GENETICS).

P. DAVIS

Genetic engineering has been used in biotechnology to improve naturally occurring yeasts, single-celled fungi that have been used in the process of fermentation for thousands of years.

See also: ANALYTICAL TECHNIQUES; BIOTECHNOLOGY; CLONING; DNA; DOMESTICATION; ENZYMES, FORENSIC SCIENCE; GENETICALLY MODIFIED FOODS; GENETICS; HUMAN GENOME PROJECT.

Further reading:

Evans, J. H. 2002. *Playing God? Human Genetic Engineering and the Rationalization of Public Bioethical Debate.* Chicago: University of Chicago Press.
Nelson, G. 2001. *Genetically Modified Organisms in Agriculture, Economics, and Politics.* San Diego: Academic Press.
Stock, G. 2002. *Redesigning Humans: Our Inevitable Genetic Future.* Boston: Houghton Mifflin.

GENETICS

Genetics is the study of how the information needed to make an organism is stored and transmitted

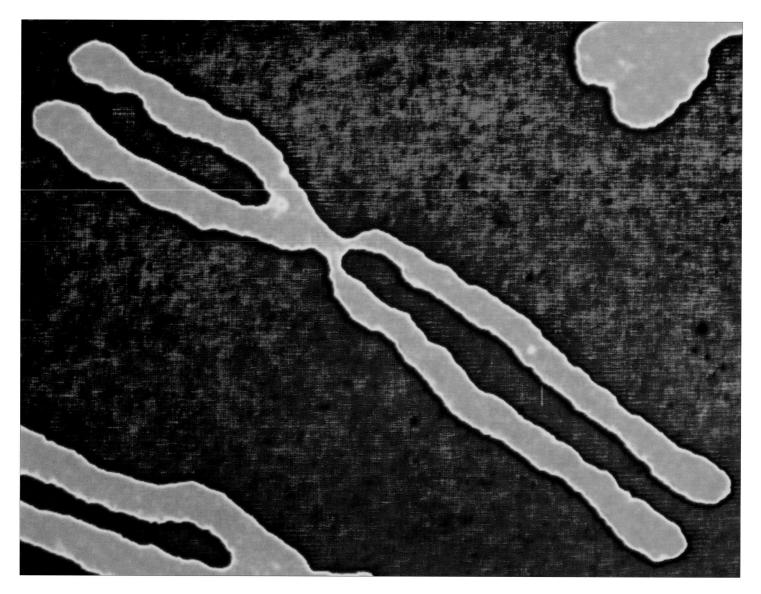

Chromosomes contain genetic material (DNA). The nucleus of every human cell contains 46 chromosomes.

CONNECTIONS

● The **HUMAN GENOME PROJECT** has uncovered the sequence of every human gene.

● **GENETIC DISEASES** are determined by a person's genetic makeup.

Anyone who has ever wondered why some people have blue eyes and some have green has been thinking about genetics, the science of heredity. Geneticists study how information needed to make an organism develop and function is passed down from one generation to the next. The information is stored in cells as long strands of DNA (deoxyribonucleic acid). The DNA in cells is organized into units called chromosomes (see CHROMOSOMES). Some segments of chromosomes encode directions for making proteins. These segments are called genes. Other segments are regulatory regions, telling the genes when to turn on and off. Then entire instruction set needed to produce an organism is called its genome (see HUMAN GENOME PROJECT).

Understanding genes gives scientists insight into both the construction and function of living organisms because proteins are a fundamental structural element of all cells. In addition, proteins are the main components of the enzymes necessary for biochemical reactions in the cell.

The birth of genetics

In the last few decades scientists have discovered what genes are and how they work, but they have known about the effects of genes for a much longer period. The Hippocratic medical essays, composed in Greece 2,600 years ago, discuss the inheritance of physical traits and diseases. The modern era of genetics dates from 1865, when an Austrian monk and science teacher, Gregor Mendel (1822–1884), published *Experiments in Plant Hybridization* (see MENDEL, GREGOR).

CORE FACTS

■ Genetics is the study of how the information needed to make an organism is stored, transmitted, and expressed.

■ Genetics is a powerful tool for learning how living organisms are constructed and how they work.

■ Modern genetics dates from 1865, when an Austrian monk and science teacher, Gregor Mendel, published his article *Experiments in Plant Hybridization*.

TERMS USED IN GENETICS

allele: one of two or more alternate versions of a gene. For each gene, an individual inherits two copies that may be identical or different alleles

chromosome: a unit of genetic material in the cell containing a double-stranded DNA complexed with proteins

DNA: the universal genetic material that carries the code for all living cells

diploid: a cell containing a pair of each chromosome

dominant gene: an allele that is expressed and that can suppress the effects of other (recessive) alleles with which it is paired

gamete: a sex cell that joins with another cell to form a zygote

gene: a length of DNA that codes for a protein

genome: the whole set of genes for an organism

genotype: the complete genetic makeup of an organism

haploid: a cell containing a single set of unpaired chromosomes

heterozygous: (of an organism) having two different alleles of a given gene

homologous chromosomes: a pair of chromosomes that are the same length and have the corresponding genes along their length

homozygous: (of an organism) having identical alleles of a given gene

locus: the site of a gene on a chromosome

meiosis: specialized cell division that produces gametes

mitosis: nuclear replication process that produces more identical cells

phenotype: the observable properties of an organism that are produced by the expression of genes

recessive: describing an allele that is expressed in an organism only if it is paired with another recessive allele, not with a dominant one

trait: a characteristic that is controlled by one or more pairs of genes

zygote: the single cell that is the result of the union of two gametes.

Mendel used ordinary garden pea plants in his experiments, selecting pure varieties that differed in a single trait, such as color (yellow or green) or whether the seed was round or wrinkled. He crossbred them and counted the number of each type in subsequent generations. He concentrated on traits that were, luckily, governed by a single gene. The term *genetics* was coined in 1883, and news of Mendel's work did not reach others until after 1900.

Sexual and asexual reproduction

The science of genetics rests on the knowledge that any living organism is simply the latest in a chain of other organisms, its ancestors. This uninterrupted chain stretches backward, generation on generation, to the beginning of life on Earth. Living things age and die, so for life to continue, an organism's attributes must be passed on to the next generation. There are two main types of reproduction, sexual and asexual. In both, the parents must ensure that the complex process to create a whole new individual is carried out accurately and efficiently.

In asexual reproduction, the parent creates a copy of itself that is genetically identical to the parent (its clone). Asexual reproduction occurs in bacteria and fungi, and is also used commercially to propagate many plants by means of cuttings.

Most animals, many plants, fungi, protists, and some bacteria create new individuals through sexual reproduction, in which a new organism is created by the joining of two specialized cells called reproductive cells (also called germ cells, or

gametes). In animals, the male gametes are usually called sperm, and the female gametes are usually called eggs (ova). In plants, the male and female gametes form from pollen and ovules, respectively.

When two gametes combine, they form a single cell (zygote) that eventually develops into a new organism. This organism is not genetically identical to either parent but receives half its genes from each parent. For the zygote to end up with the right amount of DNA, each gamete must have a half measure of DNA. An organism's gametes are therefore haploid, and all the rest of its cells are diploid. So frogs, for example, have 26 chromosomes in their diploid body cells and 13 chromosomes in their gametes. Haploid gametes are created by the specialized process of cell division called meiosis.

Meiosis

Meiosis occurs only in the reproductive organs. Diploid precursor cells undergo meiosis to produce haploid gametes. Meiosis differs from mitosis, the nuclear replication process that creates two identical diploid daughter cells during normal cellular reproduction. In mitosis the entire genome is duplicated, and then each of the two newly divided daughter cells ends up with one set of chromosomes. In meiosis the cells divide twice but only duplicate their genome once, the result being four haploid cells. In any diploid cell, the chromosomes have matching pairs of chromosomes that are the same length and carry the same sort of genetic information. They are called homologous chromosomes. During meiosis, before the cells divide, the homologous chromosomes line up against each other and exchange genetic material. This exchange (called crossing over, or recombination; first observed in 1931 by Harriet Creighton and Barbara McClintock in their studies of corn meiosis) creates chromosomes that are a mixture of the precursor cells' maternal and paternal DNA. The homologous chromosomes then separate, and one of each pair migrates to one end of the cell, which then splits to produce two diploid daughter cells with recombined chromosomes. In the next stage of meiosis, the daughter cells divide once more, but the chromosomes do not replicate during this division. The result is four haploid cells, each with a unique mix of paternal and maternal genes.

Classic Mendelian genetics

Mendel drew conclusions from his experiments with pea plants. He began selecting plants that bred true for single traits, for example, purple-flowered plants that produced only purple-flowered offspring. When crossed them with true-breeding white-flowered plants, purple flowers predominated in the next generation (called F1, the "first filial" generation). This pattern persisted in each of the traits he studied. Therefore, in a cross of true-breeding round peas and true-breeding wrinkled peas, round peas predominated in F1, and in crossing tall with short, the next generation of peas all had tall vines. In true-breeding purple-flowered plants, both genes coded for purple flowers, and in true-breeding white-flowered plants, both genes coded for white flowers. However, when a purple-flowered plant was crossed with a white-flowered plant, purple flowers were produced. So Mendel called the trait that predominated *dominant* and the trait that was hidden by the dominant one *recessive*.

When Mendel crossbred the F1 peas with each other, the next generation (F2, the "second filial") produced peas that mainly possessed the dominant trait, but some displayed the recessive trait. In other words, the recessive trait was not lost. Despite the fact that the F1 looked identical to the dominant true-breeding parent, it was not genetically identical. In the F1 cross, the ratio of dominant to recessive traits was about 3 to 1: three-quarters had purple flowers, and about one-quarter had white flowers; three-quarters had round seeds, and one-quarter wrinkled seeds; three-quarters had tall vines, and one-quarter had short vines, and so on, for each of the traits he studied. These experiments showed that while two dominant genes or one dominant and one recessive gene produced the dominant trait (purple flowers), two recessive genes were needed to produce the recessive trait (white flowers).

Mendel hypothesized that traits, such as flower color, were determined by something transmitted from parent to offspring, which he called an "element" and is now called a gene. The genes, he decided rightly, do not blend or influence each other when in the F1 hybrid generation. Instead, they segregate (separate) and pass separately into the reproductive cells that will form the next, generation, F2. They act as particles. This is Mendel's law of segregation.

It is easy to see how this pattern of inheritance occurs if letters are used to represent genetic traits, using capital letters for dominant traits and small letters for recessive ones. For example, if one assigns the gene for flower color the letter *P*, where *P* represents purple, and *p* represents white. A new organism arises from the union of two reproductive cells, one from each parent, so that it gets two copies of each gene, one from each parent. The true-breeding purple-flowered pea can be represented by the letters *PP* and the true-breeding white-flowered pea by the letters *pp*.

Phenotype and genotype

When true-breeding peas *PP* and *pp* are crossed, each of their offspring has purple flowers, but possesses one parent's gene for white flower color and the other parent's gene for purple flower color. Their appearance (called phenotype) is that of a purple-flowered pea, but their genetic makeup (called genotype) includes a gene for each color. Thus, the genotype of the F1 generation is *Pp*.

Most genes come in more than one form. The different forms are called alleles. Mendel's peas possessed alleles for both purple and white flower color. The true-breeding peas, with the two identical alleles (either *PP* or *pp*) are called homozygotes.

The *Pp* peas, the ones with both types of alleles, are called heterozygotes, and the phenotype of their flowers is purple, because purple is dominant. However, recessive white flower color can reappear in the next generation, the F2 generation, even though it has not appeared in the F1 generation.

The F1 parents cannot breed true as their own parents did because now they are carrying and can pass on both kinds of alleles. Their alleles segregate when reproductive cells are formed; half the reproductive cells carry the *P* allele for purple flower color, and half the *p* allele for white flower color. When a reproductive cell from one F1 pea combines with the reproductive cell from another F1 pea, three results are possible in the F2 generation.

If one reproductive cell with the *P* allele combines with another reproductive cell with this same allele, the result is a homozygous *PP* offspring, with a purple-flowered phenotype and genotype. On average, this combination happens 25 percent of the time (in one F2 pea out of every four).

If a reproductive cell with the *P* allele combines with a reproductive cell with the *p* allele, the result is a heterozygous *Pp* offspring, with a purple-flowered phenotype (because the purple allele is dominant). On average, the chances of this combination are 50 percent: about half the F2 offspring will be heterozygotes with purple flowers.

If a reproductive cell with the *p* allele combines with another reproductive cell with this allele, the result is a homozygote with a *pp* genotype, so the phenotype will be white flowers. One in four of the F2 peas are expected to have white flowers.

On average, in the F2 generation, the phenotype separates into three-quarters purple flowers and one-quarter white flowers. The ratio of the genotypes is one-quarter homozygous purple (*PP*) to one-half heterozygous purple (*Pp*) to one-quarter homozygous white (*pp*).

Punnett squares

A diagram called a Punnett square, named after the geneticist R. D. Punnett, is often used to figure out

Cells undergoing meiosis. Reproductive cells that give rise to new individuals develop from the division of specific cells in the body of the parent in a process called meiosis.

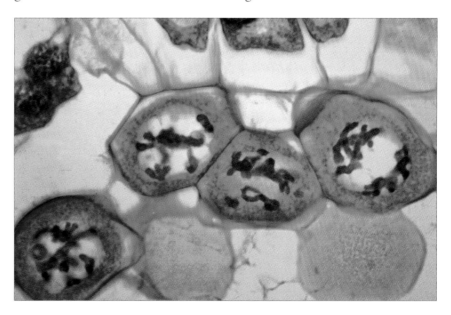

inheritance patterns. The symbols for the possible types of male reproductive cells are written across the top of the square, and the possible types of female reproductive cells down the left; the possible combinations of genes than can occur in their offspring are then entered in the boxes (see Figure 1 opposite).

If one considers a gene with two alleles, such as the pea flower example, the Punnett square for the F1 generation will look like the square in Figure 2. In this simple example, both parents are true-breeding homozygotes, so each can produce only one type of gamete. As a result, they produce only one type of offspring: heterozygotes (*Pp*).

A Punnett square listing the possible genetic combinations that can occur in the F2 generations looks like the square in Figure 3. In this example, there are one-quarter homozygous purple genotypes (*PP*), one-half heterozygous purple (*Pp*) genotypes, and one-quarter homozygous white (*pp*) genotypes.

Mendel put forward another hypothesis about how genes worked and verified it by making a test cross. He reasoned that if one of the purple-flowered F1 hybrids (*Pp*) was crossed with one of the white-flowered parent pea plants (*pp*), the next generation should have equal numbers of only two types of peas: purple-flowered heterozygotes (*Pp*) and white-flowered parent pea plants (*pp*). This test cross allows a geneticist to test for the heterozygous condition. In a test cross, the phenotype and genotype ratios are the same, 1 to 1. The Punnett square for the test cross looks like that in Figure 4.

Mendel studied the inheritance of combinations of traits (dihybrids) in pea plants. For example, he crossed true-breeding plants with smooth yellow seeds and wrinkled green seeds to produce dihybrids (double heterozygotes) that all showed the dominant smooth yellow seed phenotype. When Mendel crossed the dihybrid, he found that the progeny seeds produced were in the ratio 9 smooth yellow to 3 smooth green to 3 wrinkled yellow to 1 wrinkled green. This ratio was expected only if each trait assorted independently of the other. Mendel proposed a second law based on this observation, called the principle of independent assortment.

However, Mendel's results may be too perfect to reflect the sometimes exasperating statistical results of plant breeding in the real world. As a result, some think Mendel may have changed his experimental data to fit his hypothesis, for example, by omitting results that appeared to be wildly wrong. This contention cannot be proved, but if true, his conduct was misguided and even unethical. Despite this possibility, Mendel remains recognized as a great scientist who achieved brilliant insights into the fundamental biological system of genetics.

Factors complicating Mendelian inheritance

Geneticists have observed that simple Mendelian rules do not seem to apply in many instances because a number of processes obscure normal inheritance. For example, genes often have more than one

Mendel studied seven different traits (characters) of the pea plant. Dominant and recessive alleles control the appearance of the seeds, pods, and stems.

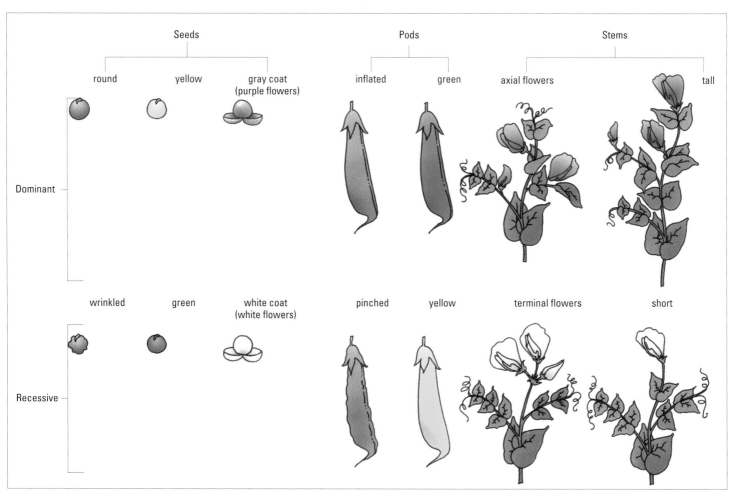

phenotypic effect, a process called pleiotropy. In the genetic disease Tay-Sachs, for example, a recessive allele of a single gene causes multiple symptoms (mental retardation, blindness, and loss of muscle control).

Differences in the expression of a trait may also be caused by variation in the environment, as demonstrated in the case of fur coloration in Siamese cats. These cats are homozygous for a mutant allele of a fur color gene that produces white fur all over the body, except on the extremities—the paws, tail, and nose. The pigment-producing enzyme that the gene codes for works best at low temperatures. Therefore, the parts of the body that are farthest from the animal's warm core are darkest.

Sometimes, a gene at one locus alters the expression of a gene at another locus. In the mouse, for example, at the B locus, the genotype *bb* is brown and *BB* or *Bb* is black. However, if the mouse is homozygous *cc* at another locus, C, the mouse is albino (has no pigment), regardless of its genotype at the B locus. The genotype *cc* is said to be epistatic to alleles at the B locus. Epistasis, in which two loci are involved, is not the same as dominance, in which one allele is dominant to another allele at the same locus. The basis for epistasis is the fact that enzymes encoded by genes act in successive metabolic reactions where the loss of one enzyme activity due to genetic mutation can inhibit the formation of an end product, despite the fact that the remaining enzymes in the pathway are functional.

Linked genes

A chromosome may carry many genes. During meiosis, the chromosome is passed through the generations as a single unit. This situation presents a paradox for one law of Mendelian inheritance. How can genes physically linked on chromosomes be segregated independently, as Mendel suggests? The answer is that linked genes do not segregate independently. They are usually inherited together. Two genes can segregate independently only when they are present on different chromosomes, as were the traits Mendel was fortunate enough to choose. Perhaps Mendel accidently chose some linked traits for some of his crosses, but if he did, the data were never presented. Because linked genes are segregated together, the traits seen in the parents are overrepresented in the progeny, and the results would deviate from Mendel's rules.

Although at first glance gene linkage appears to eliminate certain mixtures of maternal and paternal allele configurations, the process of genetic recombination (crossing over) during meiosis ensures that offspring will inherit new combinations of traits. During crossing over in meiosis, homologous chromosomes exchange segments containing genes. As a result, the linkage between two genes may be broken and new hybrid chromosomes carrying both mother and father combinations generated. The recombination process ensures that the deck of cards (the alleles from both parents) is shuffled despite physical gene linkage. The discovery of linked genes and recombination due to crossing over has formed

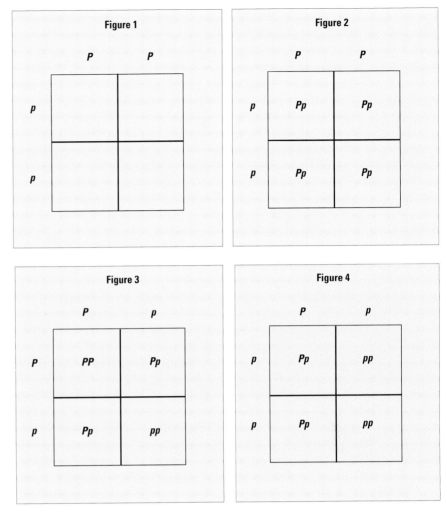

the basis of a method for the construction of genetic maps, which are ordered lists of genes along a particular chromosome (see HUMAN GENOME PROJECT).

The reasoning behind this method is that the further apart from each other two genes are, the higher the probability of recombination between those genes. Some genes are far apart on chromosomes, and crossovers between them occur frequently. Therefore, using recombination data from crosses, it is possible to assign relative positions of genes on chromosomes.

Linkage maps of genes, based on recombination frequencies, depict the order of genes on a map but cannot give precise locations of genes. Other methods enable geneticists to make physical maps of chromosomes that locate genes in relation to physical features on the chromosome.

Polygenic inheritance

Mendel looked at characteristics with two distinct phenotypes, such as round or wrinkled peas. However, many characteristics, such as human height or skin color, vary continuously. These traits are polygenic (controlled by several genes). For example, if three genes, *A*, *B*, and *C*, control human height (in reality, many more than three genes control this trait), for each gene, there is an allele for tallness (*A*, *B*, or *C*) and an allele for shortness (*a*, *b*, or *c*). Also, each allele shows incomplete dominance to the other allele. Therefore, an *AABBCC* person would be

Punnett squares: Figure 1 shows the alleles present in the male gametes across the top of the square and those present in the female gametes down the left side. Figures 2, 3, and 4 show the results of different crossings.

EXTRANUCLEAR GENETICS

Although most genes tend to be found on the chromosomes, a small amount of genetic information is located in other areas of the cell. One location of extranuclear genes is within mitochondria. In plants there are a number of different organelles, called plastids, that also contain extracellular DNA.

Extranuclear genes do not follow Mendelian principles because they are not inherited according to the same laws that govern the distribution of nuclear genes during meiosis. In most plants, plastids are transmitted from the cytoplasm of the (female) ovum and none from the (male) pollen. Therefore, a number of plastid genes involved in pigmentation or photosynthesis depend on maternal inheritance.

In mammals, mitochondrial genes are always passed down by the mother. The egg carries 100,000 mitochondria. A whole sperm contains 10,000 mitochondria, but most are in the tail. Since only the head of the sperm, containing nuclear DNA, fuses with the egg, few male mitochondria are donated to the zygote. A new IVF technique called intracytoplasmic sperm injection (ICSI) raises some concerns over the inheritance of mitochondrial DNA. In ICSI, a whole sperm, including the mitochondria that power its tail, is injected into the egg, so the resulting zygote and therefore human would have paternal as well as maternal mitochondrial DNA. Although children produced by this method appear to be normal, it remains to be determined whether the injection of male mitochondrial DNA has any long-range effects on health. Scientists have discovered that mutations in mitochondrial genes cause a number of rare genetic disorders (see GENETIC DISEASES) that might have been circumvented by in vitro replacement of the defective mitochondrial DNA with that from a female donor.

extremely tall, an *AaBbCc* person would be of intermediate height, and an *aabbcc* person would be small.

However, because the alleles have an additive effect, people with genotype *AaBbCC* and *aaBBCc* would also be of varying intermediate heights. Environmental factors also interact with the expression of a polygenic traits. For example, western European countries have seen significant height increases in the population over the past 150 years, mainly because of improved nutrition. Taking both environmental and genetic factors into account, it becomes obvious how a smooth gradation in a polygenic character within a population can occur. A number of common diseases, such as cancer, are also influenced by genes acting at multiple loci (see GENETIC DISEASES).

Population genetics

This article has described how the genes of two sexually reproducing organisms behave when they interact. Population genetics is the study of the effects of dominance and recessiveness on the characteristics of a group of interbreeding organisms. It describes the genetic composition of populations, including human populations, and the reasons why the genetic composition of populations changes. It is useful, for example, to get an idea of how common a certain genetic disease is and whether it is increasing or decreasing in frequency. Population genetics is particularly important for finding out about human genes because scientists cannot control the breeding of humans to perform experiments on inheritance of traits.

A group of interbreeding organisms is called a Mendelian population, whose reproductive cells go to produce the next generation. The sum total of

alleles in this population is called the gene pool. For example, the percentage of reproductive cells in the gene pool that possess alleles *A* or *a* depends on how frequent those alleles are in the parental generation whose reproductive cells form the pool. If most of the parental population have genotype *AA*, then they will create comparatively few reproductive cells carrying the *a* allele, and the next generation will have very few individuals of genotype *aa*.

If mating in this population is completely random, then any sperm has an equal chance of fertilizing any egg, and the proportion of alleles will determine the proportion of genotypes in the next generation.

In the square shown in Figure 5 (opposite, below), p symbolizes the proportion of *A* alleles in the gene pool, and q symbolizes the proportion of *a* alleles. These proportions are called gene frequencies. If the gene frequencies in the parental generation are known, it is possible to figure out the proportions of both the genotypes and the phenotypes in the next generation. Looking at the Punnett square in Figure 5, p^2 (that is, p x p) symbolizes the *AA* genotype, 2pq symbolizes the *Aa* genotype, and q^2 (q x q) symbolizes the *aa* genotype. Because the proportions of *A* and a must add up to 100 percent to account for all the reproductive cells in the gene pool, p + q must equal 1. These proportions can be figured out using the following formula instead of using the Punnett square:

$$(p + q)^2 = p^2 + 2pq + q^2 = 1.0$$

This formula is the Hardy-Weinberg law, named after British mathematician G. H. Hardy and German physician W. Weinberg, who discovered the law independently of each other in 1908.

The Hardy-Weinberg law is the foundation of population genetics. It predicts that, if certain conditions are met, the gene and genotype frequencies will not change in subsequent generations. So, although the number of dominant alleles in a population is high, they cannot drive recessive genes out of existence, and the homozygous recessive genotype will remain in the population at a stable probability from generation to generation. This stable state is called a genetic equilibrium (see DIMORPHISM AND POLYMORPHISM). Some of the conditions that determine whether there is a genetic equilibrium include
1. Mating is random.
2. Each genotype can survive and reproduce as well as any other.
3. There is no migration of genes into or out of the population.
4. There is no mutation, that is, genes do not change from one type of allele to another.

In the real world, these ideal conditions are impossible to achieve. Mating is not random; for example, similar people tend to marry (called assortative mating). Not all genotypes are equally viable; some, in fact, lead to early death. Some degree of migration occurs in most breeding groups. Genes are

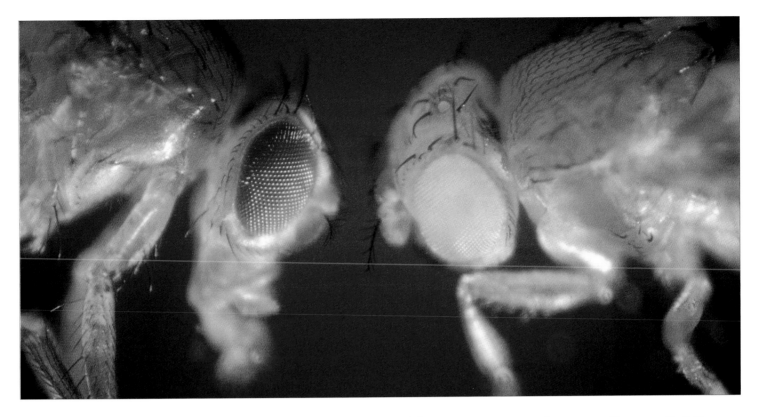

also subject to mutation by a host of factors, such as the ultraviolet rays of the Sun. Even so, the Hardy-Weinberg formula is still a remarkably good tool for predicting the relative percentage frequencies of specific genes between two different generations.

However, the Hardy-Weinberg equilibrium is never perfect. Small changes in gene frequencies do occur over many generations, and as a result, populations change. When there are enough changes, new species may be formed. This process is called evolution, and the major force leading to these changes is natural selection. Chance events are also important for changing gene frequencies in a population, particularly in a small population. This phenomenon is known as random genetic drift, and some geneticists believe that it is as important a force in evolution as natural selection. Mutation and migration also change gene frequencies. Population geneticists can measure these forces and predict their effects.

Mapping human migrations

Population geneticists have used genetic data on human population to understand human migration patterns. Because DNA undergoes mutations, it accumulates variations that can be counted and studied. The more similar the DNA of two individuals, the more recently they share a common ancestor. Geneticists can now use the study of DNA mutations to develop a molecular "clock." They estimate how long it takes for a certain amount of mutation to occur and on this basis, calculate genetic differences between the two people they are studying and how much time has passed since they shared an ancestor.

In recent years, geneticists have used these methods to understand migration events in early human evolution. In particular, genetic tools have been used to address one of the most contentious subjects in human evolution: the emergence of modern humans. Until the emergence of DNA technology over the last few decades, human evolutionists had to rely on fossil remains. At the ends of the scale, two theories prevail: the Out of Africa and the Multiregional hypotheses. Both theories agree that humans originated in Africa; the argument is about when they left Africa and spread around the world.

In the Multiregional hypothesis, *Homo erectus*, the precursor to modern humans, left Africa between one and two million years ago and became established around the world. These populations then persisted and evolved into modern groups of *Homo sapiens*. In this model, the Neanderthals, who lived in Europe, the Middle East, and Asia from about 130,000 to about 35,000 years ago, are the direct ancestors of humans living in these areas.

The Out of Africa hypothesis proposes that after the first migration of *H. erectus*, there was a second migration of fully evolved modern humans

The genes of fruit flies (Drosophila melanogaster) often mutate. The fly on the left, with a red compound eye, is the natural fly, or wild type. The fly on the right, with white eyes, short wings, and bristles on its head, is the mutant.

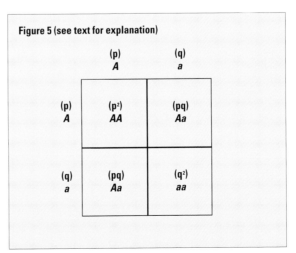

Figure 5 (see text for explanation)

	(p) A	(q) a
(p) A	(p²) AA	(pq) Aa
(q) a	(pq) Aa	(q²) aa

MULTIPLE ALLELES AND CODOMINANCE

Mendel looked at genes that have two alleles. However, most genes have more than two alleles present in a population. At one extreme, the *MHC* gene, which codes for a protein involved in immune recognition, has hundreds of different alleles. In the ABO blood group system in humans, there are four possible blood groups (phenotypes): A, B, AB, O. These letters represent recognition factors found on the surface of red blood cells: A (factor A only), B (factor B only), AB (factor A and B), and O (no factor). Matching blood types are necessary for successful blood transfusions. The genes for the A factor and the B factor are codominant, that is, in the heterozygote both alleles are expressed. In this case, the person's red blood cells have both A and B factors on their surfaces.

(*H. sapiens*) from Africa about 100,000 years ago. These modern humans replaced the global populations of humans that had migrated from Africa one to two million years ago. In this view, modern humans from Africa did not interbreed with groups such as the Neanderthals, but replaced them.

A pioneering study in 1991 on human evolution used genes from mitochondrial DNA (mtDNA) as a molecular chronometer. Since mtDNA is inherited via the mitochondria (tiny organs in the cell responsible for making energy available) in the egg, changes in mtDNA sequence reflects evolutionary changes in the maternal lineage (see box page 826). MtDNA also mutates 10 times faster than nuclear DNA and so is useful for looking at recent evolutionary history. Analysis of mtDNA from the entire global population suggests that all people are descended from an

African woman who lived around 200,000 years ago. This hypothetical woman is nicknamed Eve.

This study also showed that the greatest genetic variation occurred in African populations. This discovery was taken to indicate that the oldest populations are located in Africa and that Eve must have lived in Africa. Many experts have disagreed with these findings. Some researchers argue that the molecular clock is inaccurate; others criticize the methods used to construct evolutionary trees. Yet others maintain that the early African population was larger than the other populations in the study, and its greater size promoted the accumulation of more genetic variation.

Many more genetic studies have taken place, using the entire mt genome rather than a single gene, nuclear genes, and Y chromosome data. The majority of studies agree that African DNA shows the most genetic variation. Dates for the emergence of modern humans differ, but support a recent migration from Africa. Dates vary for a number of reasons, including statistical methods and the individual evolutionary history of the gene examined.

In another attempt to resolve this issue, geneticists sequenced the DNA of some Neanderthal fossils. Their analysis indicated that the Neanderthal individual was genetically very different from modern Europeans, further support for the out of Africa model. However, recent analyses of DNA from the oldest fossils of modern humans show it differs as much from present-day humans' as from Neanderthals' DNA. These results have heightened the debate over human evolution and origins. An intermediate model for the origins of modern humans is most likely. In this scenario, a recent migration from Africa is probable, but there may have been some genetic mixing between these modern humans and non-African archaic groups.

Scientists are also using genetic data to study more recent migration patterns. Studies of Australian aborigines, who have dark skin, show that they are far more closely related to the Chinese than to dark-skinned African populations. Similarly, researchers have identified three distinct groups of Native Americans: the Inuit, the Canadian Na-dene, and the American Indians of the United States and Central and South America.

P. DAVIS

See also: CELL BIOLOGY; CHROMOSOMES; CLONING; DIMORPHISM AND POLYMORPHISM; DNA; GENE THERAPY; GENETIC ENGINEERING; McCLINTOCK, BARBARA; MENDEL, GREGOR; STEM CELLS.

CLONES AND CLONING

The terms *clone* and *cloning* are well known from science fiction books and movies. Within genetics, these terms are confusing because they can be used in different contexts (see CLONING).

When applied to cells, a clone is a group of genetically identical cells that are descended from a single parent cell that has replicated. Bacteria reproduce by making clones of themselves. The term can also be applied to DNA. In this context, cloning means to create a very large number of copies of a single piece of DNA (using a technique called PCR, or polymerase chain reaction, for example; see GENETIC ENGINEERING). When applied to multicellular organisms, the term *clone* means that the organisms were created by asexual reproduction and are therefore genetically identical to their sole parent; new plants grown from cuttings rather than from seeds would be considered clones.

The term *cloning* may also refer to a laboratory technique. Called nuclear transfer (see STEM CELLS), this technique involves transferring the nucleus of an adult cell into an egg that has had its nucleus removed. The resulting cell then has all the genetic material and biochemical machinery it needs to become an embryo. This technique was used to produce the cloned sheep Dolly in 1997.

The essential point that underlies these different meanings is that the genetic material created in the cloning process is always the same as the original genetic material from which it is derived, no matter how many cells, pieces of DNA, or organisms are produced.

Further reading:

Griffiths, A. 2000. *An Introduction to Genetic Analysis*. New York: W. H. Freeman.
Gonick, L., and M. Wheler. 1991. *Cartoon Guide to Genetics*. New York: Harper Perennial.
Jones, S. *Introducing Genetics*. 2000. Icon Books.
Olson, S. 2002. *Mapping Human History: Discovering the Past through Our Genes*. Boston: Houghton-Mifflin.
Ridley, M. 2000. *Genome*. New York: HarperCollins.

GERMINATION

The germination of the wheat seed (Triticum sp.) shown above is an example of hypogeal germination. The emerging radicle and plumule can both be seen.

CONNECTIONS

● Seed dispersal (see **SEEDS AND SEED DISPERSAL**) and **COMPETITION** can be deciding factors in successful germination.

● Changes in the atmosphere may result in a seed breaking its **DORMANCY**.

● Reliance on **PHOTOSYNTHESIS** marks the end of successful germination.

Germination marks the start of growth of a new generation of plants. It usually occurs only under certain conditions: the temperature, moisture, and oxygen levels must be right. Many seeds are shed from the parent plant and then lie dormant (inactive) in the soil, and so germination often follows a period of dormancy lasting months or years. Once the conditions are suitable, the plant embryo begins a rapid burst of growth. Organs such as roots, stems, and leaves start to form. The result of germination is a new seedling.

Seed structure
Each seed consists of a seed coat (the testa), an embryo, and a supply of food to keep the embryo alive during its dormancy and to nourish it while it develops into a seedling during germination. At one end of the embryo is the radicle, which grows to form the seedling's primary root; at the other end is the plumule (epicotyl), which forms the shoot and first leaves. In between are the cotyledons (or cotyledon in monocotyledons), often called seed leaves (see DICOTYLEDONS; MONOCOTYLEDONS). The two main locations for food storage in seeds are the cotyledons and the endosperm. The endosperm is the tissue formed by the union of one of the two sperm nuclei from a pollen grain and the two polar nuclei of an ovule. (The embryo is formed from the union of the other sperm nucleus and the egg nucleus.) Some seeds store food in the perisperm, which is derived from the nucellus, the layer of the ovule between the integuments (the outer covering that becomes the testa) and the female gametophyte (embryo sac).

Germination is the initiation of growth in plant seeds

Dormancy
Dormant seeds exhibit little metabolic activity and no growth. Many factors can cause a seed to be dormant, and these vary among different plants. Some seeds have a hard, thick seed coat that keeps out oxygen and moisture, both of which are necessary before the seed can germinate. A hard seed coat may also stop the radicle from pushing out into the soil. The hard coating must therefore be softened or broken for germination to begin.

The seeds of some plants are shed before the embryo is mature, and the embryo needs time to develop inside the seed before it is ready to germinate. Other seeds need certain environmental conditions, such as very high or low temperatures. Most seeds need a period of low temperatures to break their dormancy. Scientists do not yet fully understand exactly how chilling works in this way. However, they have found that in some seeds the enzymes needed during germination increase during chilling, as do the levels of plant growth promoters such as gibberellins (see DORMANCY).

How germination begins
Once dormancy has been broken, the seed can germinate as soon as conditions are favorable. Many seeds will germinate when they have water, a favorable temperature, and oxygen. Most seeds are very dry—their water content is between 5 and 10 percent—and by remaining dormant until there is sufficient moisture in the environment to allow germination, the seeds increase their chance of survival.

The seeds of many plants will germinate only if the temperature is within certain limits, to make sure the resulting seedling will have a good chance of survival. Some seeds need fluctuating temperatures before they will germinate. If there is a gap in the vegetation, there will be a large difference in temperature at the soil surface between day and night. If the ground above the seed is covered in established plants that will provide competition for the seedling, this plant cover insulates the earth, and, thus, the daytime and nighttime temperatures are more alike. A seed that needs fluctuating temperatures will not germinate under closed vegetation conditions.

Other seeds respond to light. This response is dependent on the seed's depth in the soil: a seed that

---

CORE FACTS
▪ Germination is the beginning of growth in plant seeds.
▪ Germination often follows a period of dormancy.
▪ Various environmental conditions may be necessary to break dormancy and initiate germination.
▪ Germination may be epigeal (the cotyledons rise above the ground) or hypogeal (they remain below the ground).

is too far down may use all its food reserves before the shoot can reach the surface. Plants that need light to trigger germination often have small seeds. The type of light may also be important. After passing through leaves, sunlight has a lower proportion of light in the red end of the spectrum, and so the ratio of red to far-red radiation is very much lower beneath a canopy of leaves than on open ground. In many seeds, germination is inhibited by light with a low red to far-red ratio, and they will germinate only in the open. Again the seedling will have less competition from other, more established plants.

The process of germination

In the first stage of germination, the seed takes in water very quickly; this stage is called imbibition. This process is reversible, and most seeds can be repeatedly dried and rehydrated without being killed. As the germinating seed takes in water, it swells and often bursts the seed coat, after which the process is irreversible. Once the coat is split, the embryo can take in water and oxygen even more readily, and respiration speeds up. By the time imbibition has finished, the seed has usually doubled in size.

During the next stage of germination, the large food storage molecules in the seed are broken down into smaller units by various enzymes. Starch is converted to sugars by enzymes called amylases, fats are broken down into fatty acids and glycerol by lipases, and proteins into amino acids by proteinases and peptidases. The end products are transported to the seedling's growing points, the radicle and the plumule, where the sugars provide energy and the amino acids are used to build new proteins. The seedling will die if it dries out at this stage.

The radicle breaks through the seed coat and pushes down into the soil, where it anchors the new plant and starts to take in minerals and water. The plumule then emerges from the seed and breaks through the surface of the soil. Which part of the seed breaks the surface first and when the shoot development occurs may vary. The variations are described in greater detail in the following sections.

As soon as the young leaves are able to photosynthesize and manufacture food and the root system is absorbing water and minerals from the soil, the young plant is self-sufficient.

Some scientists consider germination to be over once the shoot emerges from the soil. Others think germination ends when the seed's food reserves have all been used up and the seedling has to survive solely by photosynthesis.

Variations in germination

There are two main types of germination, depending on whether the cotyledons stay buried in the ground or are raised out of the soil. In some plants, such as garden beans (*Phaseolus vulgaris*) and onions (*Allium cepa*), the cotyledons are raised above the ground. This process is called epigeal germination. In others, such as peas (*Pisum sativum*) and all the grasses, including wheat (*Triticum* spp.), corn (*Zea mays*), and barley

*The diagram below illustrates epigeal germination of the green bean (*Phaseolus vulgaris*), in which the cotyledons are raised above the ground.*

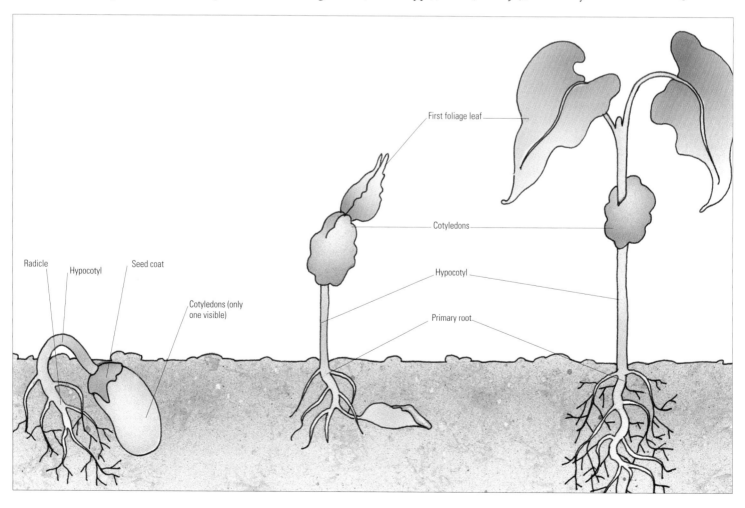

Radicle Hypocotyl Seed coat Cotyledons (only one visible) First foliage leaf Cotyledons Hypocotyl Primary root

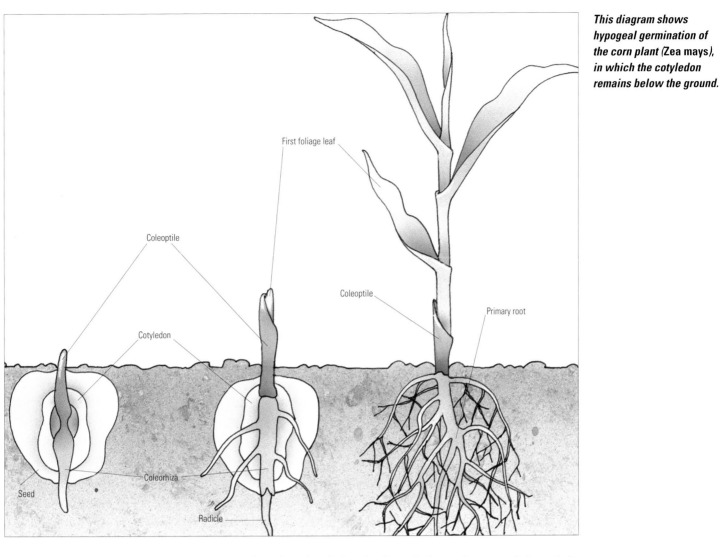

Coleoptile

First foliage leaf

Coleoptile

Cotyledon

Primary root

Coleorhiza

Seed

Radicle

This diagram shows hypogeal germination of the corn plant (Zea mays), in which the cotyledon remains below the ground.

831

(*Hordeum vulgare*), the cotyledons remain buried, and the process is called hypogeal germination.

Epigeal germination

The green bean (*Phaseolus vulgaris*) is often used to demonstrate germination because of its large seeds and seedlings and because it germinates very quickly. Once the seed starts taking in water, it takes just a few hours for the seed coat to burst. After two or three days, the radicle emerges and grows down through the soil. Over the next few days, the radicle continues to grow and to sprout secondary roots. The plumule starts to emerge around the sixth day, and a day later it has formed a hook that forces its way up through the soil. Around the tenth day, the plumule has broken through the surface, carrying its cotyledons with it. The hook straightens out and grows rapidly. A day later, the cotyledons open out, and the first true foliage starts to grow. Finally, after around 12 days, these first leaves are photosynthesizing, providing food for the growing plant. The seedling is now well established.

Hypogeal germination

Corn (*Zea mays*) is an example of a plant that carries out hypogeal germination. In all grasses, the emerging radicle and plumule are enclosed in protective sheaths. Once germination begins, the seed takes in water and swells. Around four days later, the coleorhiza (root

sheath) breaks through the seed coat, and the radicle emerges and grows down into the soil. The coleoptile (the sheath protecting the plumule) appears around day seven. The coleoptile breaks through the soil surface. After another two days, the first leaf has emerged, followed by a second leaf. The radicle continues to grow and produces secondary roots. After around two weeks, the seedling has a well-established root system and leaves. The cotyledon stays in the ground.

K. MCCALLUM

See also: DICOTYLEDONS; DORMANCY; FLOWERS AND FLOWER STRUCTURE; MONOCOTYLEDONS.

Further reading:

Baskin, C. C., and J. M. Baskin. 1998. *Seeds: Ecology, Biogeography, and Evolution of Dormancy and Germination*. San Diego: Academic Press.

THE ROLE OF PLANT GROWTH REGULATORS

The levels of plant growth promoters, such as gibberellins, and plant growth inhibitors, especially abscissic acid, play an important role in germination and subsequent growth. In laboratory experiments, researchers have shown that gibberellins break dormancy and initiate germination, whereas abscissic acid induces dormancy and prevents germination.

GESTATION

Gestation is the development of an embryo into a fetus within its mother, resulting in the birth of live young

The South American sea lion (Otaria byronia) has a gestation period lasting about 12 months.

CONNECTIONS

● **MONOTREMES,** like platypuses, reproduce using a combination of reptilian and mammalian processes. The **FETUS** develops in the uterus, after which membranes and a shell form around the embryo. An egg is then laid next to the female's abdomen. After hatching, the offspring attaches itself to the mother's mammary glands.

A baby elephant and a human infant have more in common than might be thought from appearances. In both cases, the fertilized egg (zygote) develops inside the mother's body, and the young are born live. This process of internal development of zygotes is known as gestation. Species that gestate and give birth to live young are known as viviparous, and they include a wide variety of animals. Internal zygote maturation is uncommon among insects, fish, and reptiles but is found in all but a few mammalian species. The only mammalian order that lays eggs is the monotremes, a group that includes spiny anteaters (*Tachyglossus aculeatus*), echidnas (*Zaglossus bruijni*), and duck-billed platypuses (*Ornithorhynchus anatinus*) (see MONOTREMES). As gestation is the general rule among mammals and the exception among other organisms, the term usually refers to internal zygote maturation in mammals.

Implantation and development of the placenta

Once a mammalian egg is fertilized and has traveled down the fallopian tubes, the zygote attaches to the lining of the uterus and a placenta starts to form. This process is known as implantation. The placenta is the zygote's lifeline, bringing its blood close to that of its mother and providing a means by which the mother delivers food and oxygen to her developing zygote and takes away its waste products. The structure of the placenta varies widely among mammals; the greatest differences are found between marsupials and placental mammals.

CORE FACTS

■ Gestation is the rule among mammals and the exception among other animals.

■ Special cell layers surround the developing fetus and protect it from the mother's immune system.

■ The placenta, the fetus's lifeline, brings the fetus's blood close to that of the mother and allows gas, nutrients, and waste exchange to take place.

■ Marsupials have modified the reproductive processes of the monotremes by eliminating egg laying, retaining the fetus inside the mother for a longer time, and completing development attached to a nipple in the mother's pouch.

■ Placental mammals, unlike marsupials, have a highly developed placenta, which enables gestation to be maintained for longer periods; the resulting offspring are therefore born much larger and more highly developed than those of marsupials.

• **The marsupial placenta:** Marsupials include pouched animals, such as kangaroos and opossums. In all marsupials, except bandicoots, the recently fertilized egg, now developed into a hollow ball of cells known as a blastocyst, does not implant itself directly in the endometrium (the uterine lining) but settles in a shallow depression in the mucosal lining of the endometrium. The yolk sac of the egg expands to form a primitive placenta, known as a choriovitelline placenta, as the outside of the blastocyst (the chorion layer) is in contact with the outer layer of the endometrium. Because there is no close contact between the blood supply of the mother and the developing zygote, the zygote is nourished by uterine "milk," secreted by the mucosal lining of the endometrium and absorbed by the blastocyst.

• **The eutherian mammal placenta:** The group Eutheria comprises the placental mammals and includes all mammals except marsupials (of the group Metatheria) and monotremes (of the group Prototheria). The eutherian placenta is far more developed than the marsupial placenta. The blastocyst actually digests its way into the endometrial lining of the uterus and then forms a so-called chorioallantoic placenta. The outer layer of the blastocyst, the trophoblast, develops little fingerlike projections, called villi, that push farther into the endometrium to form a strong bond with the uterus. The villi, in addition to providing a strong anchorage for the fetus on the uterus, also greatly increase the surface area of this connection. Around the site at which the villi implant, the uterus becomes highly vascularized—it develops a web of blood vessels that carry nutrients and oxygen to the fetus and remove waste products.

When the villi of the trophoblast first embed themselves in the wall of the uterus, there are a number of barriers that separate the mother's blood supply from that of the zygote. To get from the mother to the zygote, nutrients must pass out through the walls of the uterine blood vessels, through a layer of connective tissue, past the outer layer (epithelium) of the uterus, and finally through the epithelium of the zygote's chorion. In humans and other primates, the endometrial lining of the uterus is completely destroyed at the site of implantation, and thus, the chorionic villi make direct contact with the mother's blood vessels. The fewer the barriers between mother and zygote, the greater the efficiency of transfer of nutrients and other chemicals from the mother's blood to that of the fetus. For this reason, pregnant women should not drink alcohol, smoke, or use drugs (including most prescription medications) during pregnancy.

Gestation in marsupials

The pattern of gestation differs significantly between marsupials and other mammals. In marsupials the young are usually born after about four to eight weeks' gestation. The length of the gestation period is not strongly influenced by the body size of the parent animal. For example, a red kangaroo (*Macropus rufus*) can weigh as much as 132 pounds (60 kg), the size of a human, but it has a short gestation period of only approximately one month.

However, the comparison between marsupials and placental mammals is somewhat misleading. When the baby marsupial is born it is extremely underdeveloped, weighing less than $\frac{1}{30}$ ounce (1 g). The baby marsupial is born a fetus, with a large mouth, strong forelimbs, and practically no abdomen or legs. Using its strong arms, the baby crawls up its mother's belly, and attaches its mouth onto one of her nipples. The baby's jaw sucks on the nipple, which expands to fill the mouth cavity, and thus the infant is locked onto its mother's teat, where it stays for some months.

While many marsupials have pouches in which this development takes place, others, such as the North American opossum (*Didelphis virginiana*), have infolded skin on their bellies that covers but does not encapsulate the young locked onto the teats. In truth, gestation in marsupials should be measured as the time spent in the mother's uterus plus the time spent attached to one of her teats.

*Newborn Virginian opossums (*Didelphis virginiana*) attached to the mother's teats.*

The white rhinoceros (Ceratotherium simum) has a gestation period of 17 to 18 months.

Factors affecting gestation time

Gestation length in placental mammals is extremely variable. While there are no rules governing the length of gestation across all species, there are discernible patterns. Generally speaking, there is a strong correlation between body size and gestation length across families of placental mammals. The shortest gestation lengths are found among species of rodents, with hamsters having gestation lengths of two to three weeks. In contrast, elephants may gestate their young for nearly two years. However, size alone does not explain much of the observed variation in gestation length among mammals.

Despite extensive research, no single factor has been found that explains the observed variation in gestation length, either between or within families of mammals. In addition to the body size of the mother, several factors appear to be important. Animals in which infants have a high degree of cephalic development (the head forms a large proportion of the body mass) are known to have a relatively long gestation. Animals that have a relatively low metabolism for their body weight also tend to have longer gestations, but this connection is weak. Another perhaps more important factor affecting gestation length is the degree of development of the young at birth. Those animals that give birth to well-developed, active young have a long gestation period.

Gestation and hormones

Before implantation can occur, the lining of the uterus must be prepared by the thickening and development of blood vessels and by the development of endometrial glands, the secretions of which aid implantation of the fetus. Endometrial development is first triggered by estrogens and continues through prolonged exposure to progesterone. These hormones are first secreted by the ovary, under the control of the pituitary gland and the hypothalamus. Later on during pregnancy, the placenta itself in many species takes over secretion of these and other hormones necessary for the maintenance of gestation. If the placenta does not produce these hormones, the pregnancy may fail, as a lack of progesterone terminates pregnancy.

Nonmammalian gestation

There are a number of nonmammalian groups in which fetuses develop within the mother's reproductive tract. Many of them develop within eggs, using the egg's yolk for nutrition, a process called ovoviviparity. Viviparity, where fetuses are actually fed by the mother, occurs in a number of nonmammalian vertebrates, such as the elasmobranch fishes (sharks and rays), which have gestation periods of up to two years. Most cases of viviparity among reptiles and amphibians occur in harsh environments (for example, very hot and dry areas or those with many predators) where external development in a shelled egg would have little chance of success.

In viviparous amphibians, the embryos are fed with secretions from the oviducts (the reproductive tract of the female), while in live-bearing lizards and snakes, the embryos obtain nourishment from a primitive placenta, major components of which are the yolk sac of the egg and the wall of the mother's oviduct.

True viviparity is rare among invertebrates. One important exception is the tsetse fly (*Glossina* spp.), a carrier of sleeping sickness. In this fly, a modified oviduct feeds the single, developing embryo. In viviparous scorpions (of the class Arachnida, order Scorpiones), the embryos are fed through a sort of umbilical cord, which links the embryo directly to the mother's digestive tract.

J. GINSBERG

See also: ABORTION; EGGS; EMBRYO; FERTILIZATION; PREGNANCY AND BIRTH.

Further reading:
Hickman, C. P. 2000. *Integrated Principles of Zoology.* 11th ed. Columbus, Ohio: McGraw-Hill Higher Education.
Kosco, M. 2000. *Mammalian Reproduction.* Clarion, Pa.: Allegheny Press.

GILLS AND SPIRACLES

Gills and spiracles are parts of the
respiratory systems of animals
such as fish and insects

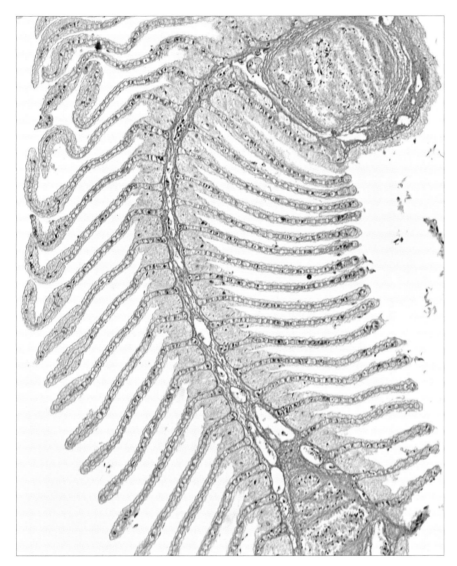

*Cross section of a fish gill
filament, showing the
secondary lamellae.*

CONNECTIONS

● Most **AMPHIBIANS**
have gills in their early
development. Some
keep them as adults
and are aquatic.

● Apart from using gills,
LUNGS, and spiracles,
many small animals
breathe through their
SKIN, in what is called
cutaneous respiration.

Without respiration there can be no life. Respiration is both the act of breathing and the process by which an organism exchanges gases with its environment. Respiration provides cells with the oxygen they need to break down glucose for the production of energy (cellular respiration), and it removes the resulting waste, carbon dioxide. All animals have similar respiratory requirements, and there are three basic types of respiratory organ: gills in aquatic animals, lungs in land and some aquatic vertebrates and invertebrates, and spiracles and tracheae (singular, trachea) in insects and some other arthropods. Each type of organ must have three elements so that gases can be exchanged: a surface (membrane) that allows exchange of gases; a mechanism that ensures rapid exchange of oxygen and carbon dioxide; and an ability to distribute incoming oxygen to the body fluids and expel outgoing carbon dioxide.

All respiratory structures work by the physical process of diffusion, and the amount of gas exchanged (diffused) across them is proportional to the surface area of the respiratory membrane and to the gas concentration on each side of this membrane. Thus, the larger the surface area and the higher the difference in concentration on opposite sides of the membrane, the more gas is exchanged between body fluids and the air or water being breathed.

In some small invertebrates (animals lacking a vertebral column), such as jellyfish and roundworms, gaseous exchange takes place by diffusion across the whole surface of the body, a process known as cutaneous exchange. Because a respiratory surface must remain moist, these animals must live in water or damp places. Animals that breathe only through their skin have a low metabolic rate and so need only a small amount of oxygen. Hence, they have no need for specialized external respiratory structures to increase gas exchange.

Cutaneous respiration is limited when the body surface is covered by a shell or is thick and bulky or when the animal is large. Larger bodies have a proportionately smaller surface area available for gas exchange compared with smaller bodies. However, the surface area can be increased by changing the body shape. For example, a bundle of branched filaments (threadlike projections of the body surface) provides more surface area than a smooth ball.

The vertebrate gill

Fish have highly developed gills, located on both sides of the foregut (front of the alimentary canal). They have slit-shaped openings to the outside leading from the pharynx (canal between the mouth and the esophagus) so that water passes from the pharynx, over the gills, and out through the gill slits. Rigid bony or cartilaginous gill arches stop the gills from sticking together. Around each gill arch are many pairs of filaments, forming a V (the whole structure resembling two combs placed back-to-back at an angle). On each side of the filaments, thin, fingerlike secondary lamellae extend outward, exposing the blood that runs close under the surface to the dissolved oxygen in the water.

CORE FACTS

■ Animals breathe in oxygen and expel carbon dioxide using one of three main types of respiratory organs: lungs (found in land vertebrates), gills (aquatic animals), or spiracles and tracheae (insects and other arthropods).

■ A successful respiratory system needs a membrane that allows rapid gaseous exchange and an ability to distribute oxygen to and dispel carbon dioxide from the tissues.

■ Gills are highly folded, semipermeable membranes with a large surface area that maximizes contact between the oxygen-containing water and the animal's blood.

■ Fully aquatic animals have proportionately larger gill surface areas than those living in intertidal zones.

This diagram shows the location and structure of fish gills and how they are adapted to the efficient uptake of oxygen.

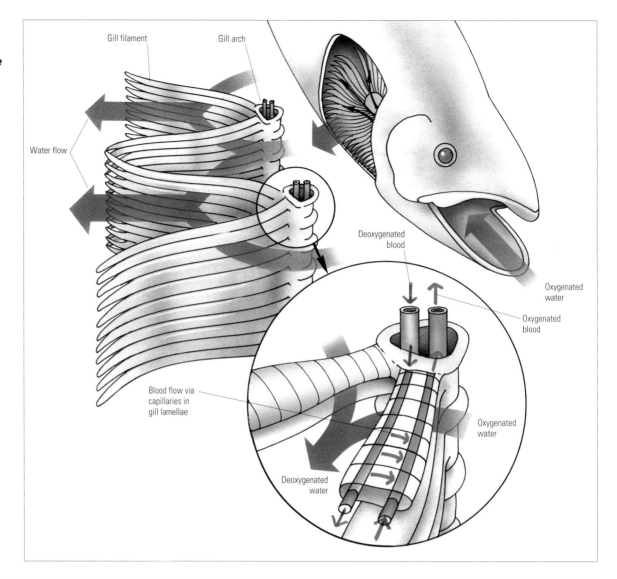

Gill filament

Gill arch

Water flow

Deoxygenated blood

Oxygenated water

Oxygenated blood

Blood flow via capillaries in gill lamellae

Oxygenated water

Deoxygenated water

THE EVOLUTION OF VERTEBRATE GILLS

Evidence from ancient invertebrate fossils suggests that major invertebrate phyla coexisted in the warm Precambrian seas about 570 million years ago, although invertebrates' earlier history can be established only indirectly, as fossil records are poor. The fossil records of vertebrates are younger and more complete.

Lancelets (Cephalochordates) are ancient but extant small, warm-water invertebrates that have proved crucial in understanding the morphology and evolution of chordates—the phylum of animals that includes the vertebrates and is defined by having an elastic supporting skeletal axis (notochord) and dorsal nerve cord (see CHORDATES). Although lancelets respire through their thin skin, one of their key characteristics is a pharynx with gill slits, which are used to collect food by filtering water. Cilia around the mouth and opening of the pharynx draw in water, which then passes over the pharyngeal slits into a chamber known as the atrium and exits through the atriopore.

The function of gill slits in the lancelet is thought to resemble that of ancestral vertebrates. Primitive vertebrates breathed mostly through the skin, as do some modern lungless salamanders. The vertebrate gill probably originated as a feeding device, as in lancelets. Water was filtered through the mouth, organic matter was extracted and swallowed, and the water exited through the gill slits.

Over time, the need for protection, particularly against predators, led to the evolution of increasingly thick skin, some also armored or covered with scales. This skin functioned poorly for respiration. At the same time, other demands encouraged the development of larger, swifter animals that expended greater amounts of energy and had a greater need for oxygen to power their metabolism. In response to these needs, gill slits evolved to take over the new respiratory demands, and the gill surface area increased in size and blood supply.

Fish are thought to have evolved in fresh water. Chrondrichthyes (which include sharks and skates) became sea dwellers early in their development, while bony fish (Osteichthyes) developed in fresh water and spread to the seas much later.

Some primitive bony fish adapted to freshwater bodies in which oxygen was depleted by evolving swim bladders that served as lungs, promoting oxygen extraction from the air rather than the water. The most highly adapted of all, lungfish, can exist in water that has too little oxygen to support other fish by rising to the surface to gulp air.

In their early stages of development, amphibians resemble fish, in that their larvae (tadpoles) live in water and breathe through gills. Later they become lung-breathing forms with limbs. Some salamander-like amphibians, like their aquatic larvae, remain gilled.

EVOLUTION

Arteries called the afferent (incoming) branchial (gill) arteries supply blood to each gill arch. Within each arch the afferent branchial artery branches to each of the filaments. Each branch divides repeatedly to supply the secondary lamellae. In the secondary lamellae, blood enters fine capillaries close to the surface, where oxygen is absorbed from and carbon dioxide is lost to the water. The oxygenated blood then enters efferent (outgoing) gill arteries, which unite to form the dorsal aorta that supplies the fish's tissues.

As the fish pumps water through the gill chamber, the gill filaments present a large surface area to dissolved oxygen. Owing to the very high number of folds in the membranes of the gills, they can make up 60 to 75 percent of the total surface area of an adult fish. This fact, combined with an adaptation that causes the blood in the lamellae to flow in the opposite direction to the water being pumped past them, results in very efficient gaseous exchange.

Fish gills also help solve the animal's need to keep the salt concentration in its body fluids at the correct level by providing a surface for excreting salt (see EXCRETORY SYSTEMS). Osmosis is a process by which water moves from an area with a high concentration of water to an area with a low concentration of water through a semipermeable membrane. Thus, marine fish lose their body water to the more salty water surrounding them and so must drink to replace this lost water. Freshwater fish take in water from their dilute surroundings and must urinate frequently to get rid of the water gained by osmosis.

Invertebrate gills

Among invertebrate animals that have gills are mollusks (such as bivalves, squids, and snails), which have soft bodies, generally enclosed in a shell; arthropods (crustaceans and many aquatic insects), which have segmented bodies and jointed legs; and echinoderms (sea stars, sea urchins, and sand dollars), which have bodies radiating from a center with a tough skeleton just under the skin.

Perhaps the simplest form of invertebrate gill is found in echinoderms. These gills, called dermal (skin) branchiae and papulae, are protrusions from the body wall surrounding the internal organs.

Most aquatic mollusks typically have gills called ctenidia (derived from a Greek word meaning "comb"). Blood passes through gill filaments via incoming and outgoing blood vessels. Alternately arranged along both sides of the gill axis, molluskan gill filaments have rows of lateral cilia to keep the water moving; squid and octopuses actively ventilate their ctenidia by contractions of the mantle.

Protecting gills from abrasion is critical for species that crawl along rough surfaces or live in mud or sand. To provide protection, the gills extend from their attachment to the body wall into a cavity called the mantle cavity.

Nearly all marine arthropods are crustaceans (crabs, lobsters, shrimps), and their feathery gills are abdominal appendages covered by a layer of permeable exoskeleton (external supporting structure). The gills are usually attached to the upper sides of the legs where they join the body. In the horseshoe crab, *Limulus*, the five pairs of flaplike abdominal appendages form the gills. They are called book gills, so-called because they are folded like book pages.

Habitat and gill type

The number and size of gills correlates with the habits and habitats of different species. Scientists have shown that the amount of gill area per unit of body

This albino salamander (Ambystoma) is a good example of an amphibian possessing external gill structures as an adult.

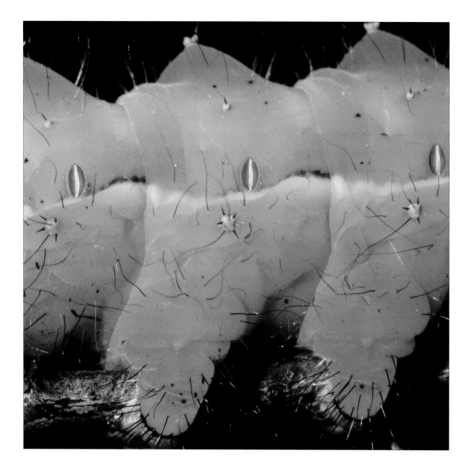

A side view of a caterpillar showing the spiracles (which are orange) along the side of its body. There is one spiracle in each segment.

weight diminishes as decapods (crustaceans with five pairs of legs, such as crabs) move from an existence entirely in the water to one in an intertidal zone and then onto land. Moreover, the area devoted to the gill is greater in active water-living species than in sluggish ones living on the bottom of the sea.

Transition from water to land

Two problems arose in the evolution of aquatic species that retained gills for gaseous exchange but moved into the intertidal zone between the high- and low-tide marks. To adapt to semiterrestrial life, these species had to keep their large soft gills from collapsing when out of water because of the surface tension of water on them. They also had to keep the gills moist and ventilated.

Gill collapse was prevented by methods designed to stiffen the gill filaments. In some, "turgor cells" kept filaments extended at right angles to the central axis. Gill lamellae also became smaller in air breathers because the much larger oxygen content of air (21 percent) than water (1 percent) greatly improved the efficiency of oxygen transport. In turn, this efficiency reduced water loss from the gills by evaporation.

Gills are kept moist and ventilated by various devices that keep water in the gill chamber. For example, after a crab has been in the water, its water-filled gill chamber is stoppered by the crabs' branchiostegites (gill chamber coverings), and breathing is intermittent, so water does not leak out of the gill chamber. However, the crab eventually loses this water and must return to the water to replenish it.

The oxygen supply of the water in the gill chamber is renewed while the animal is on land by circulating air through it. Ventilation of the gills, whether free or enclosed, is accomplished primarily by rhythmic beating of a special pair of appendages, the gill bailers (scaphognathites).

Spiracles and tracheae

Insects, the dominant terrestrial arthropods, have internal tracheae. A tracheal system forms a network of branching and connecting tubes that conveys oxygen directly to the tissues and carbon dioxide to the air. Tracheae are tubes lined with cuticle (hardened skin), thickened in places to form spiral rings to keep the tubes open.

A tracheal system links to the exterior by means of openings called pores, or spiracles (from the Latin word *spirare*, "to breathe"). Typically, there are two pairs of spiracles in the thorax (the middle-body section) and eight pairs in the abdomen (a member of each pair on either side of each segment). There are many variations on this most primitive form.

In many insects, caterpillars, for example, the spiracles are easy to see. Alternate contraction and expansion of the abdomen help drive out deoxygenated air and draw in fresh air. While flying, many insects open the spiracles on the front segment of the thorax and in the abdomen and breathe by ram ventilation, just as a jet engine does.

From the spiracles, tracheae lead inward to a network of smaller tracheoles that penetrate deep into every tissue. There are two main types of spiracles: an open tracheal system, in which the spiracles have no closing device where they connect to the body wall; and spiracles that sit in pits (called atria) equipped with filters of fine hair and a mechanism for opening and closing. Most insects have the second type because they must restrict water loss by evaporation from their bodies.

Spiracles are opened and closed in various ways. The respiratory centers in the insect's nervous system are stimulated by increases in carbon dioxide in the blood and respond by opening the spiracle. In some insects, the spiracles themselves are equipped with receptors responsive to carbon dioxide and open automatically when carbon dioxide concentrations rise.

A tracheal system is efficient for small, active, terrestrial animals because it delivers oxygen directly to tissues. However, it is inadequate for larger animals, since oxygen cannot be supplied by diffusion fast enough with increasing distance along the tracheae to the tissues.

M. DICANIO

See also: ARTHROPODS; CHORDATES; EVOLUTION; EXCRETORY SYSTEMS; FISH; INSECTS; INVERTEBRATES; RESPIRATORY SYSTEMS; VERTEBRATES.

Further reading:
Eckert, R. 1997. *Animal Physiology*. New York: W. H. Freeman.
Willmer, P., G. Stone, and I. Johnson. 2000. *Environmental Physiology of Animals*. Oxford: Blackwell Science Ltd.

GLOBAL WARMING

Global warming is the rise in the average temperature of Earth caused by greenhouse gases

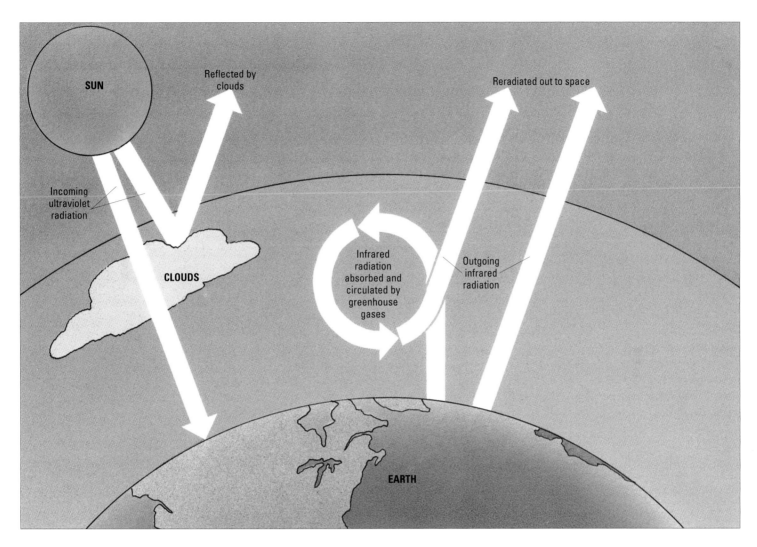

Global warming is the rise in the average temperature of Earth predicted by some scientists. An average surface temperature rise of 1.8 °F (1 °C) by the year 2030 and a rise in sea level of 7 feet (2.2 m) by the year 2100 are both predictions for the possible extent of global warming. An increase of 1.8 °F may not seem like much, but it would be enough to shift crop-growing zones from their present locations, and thus cause soil erosion, desertification, and famine in many areas of the world. The resulting rise in sea level would cause flooding in low-lying areas—in some cases destroying whole cities and even countries. However, scientists by no means agree on the effects of global warming or the role humans play in causing it.

Some people use the term *global warming* interchangeably with *greenhouse effect*, which is believed to be one of the major components involved in global warming. Although the term *greenhouse effect* is often used when refering to a future climatic disaster, the process it represents is a naturally occurring one (see the diagram above). In fact, human life would be impossible without it.

The natural greenhouse effect

Shortwave ultraviolet radiation pours down from the Sun to Earth. Some of this radiation is reflected off cloud and reflective parts of Earth's surface back into space. The rest is absorbed by Earth and reradiated as longwave infrared radiation, or heat. However, heat cannot pass through the gaseous layer of Earth's atmosphere as easily as ultraviolet

In the natural greenhouse effect, shown above, the amount of incoming ultraviolet radiation is exactly balanced by the amount of outgoing infrared radiation. Some scientists think that human activities, by upsetting this balance, are causing global warming.

CORE FACTS

- Global warming is defined as the warming of Earth by greenhouse gases discharged into the atmosphere naturally or by humans.
- The five natural greenhouse gases are water vapor, carbon dioxide, methane, nitrous oxide, and ozone. Human-made CFCs are also potent greenhouse gases.
- Current projections are based on the assumption that the present output of carbon dioxide will double by the year 2030.
- Predictions about the implications of global warming include a temperature rise of 1.8 °F (1 °C) by 2030 and a rise in sea level of 7 feet (2.2 m) by 2100.

CONNECTIONS

- Ozone is an important greenhouse gas present in the **ATMOSPHERE**. Ozone (O_3) is formed when **OXYGEN** molecules (O_2) absorb solar **RADIATION**.

radiation can, and so a large amount of heat is trapped and recirculated. The whole process is similar to the operation of a greenhouse, which allows sunlight to penetrate its glass walls and ceiling but does not let much of the resulting warmth escape.

It is the greenhouse gases (water vapor, carbon dioxide, methane, nitrous oxide, ozone, and human-made CFCs; see box on page 841) that trap some of this outgoing heat and recirculate it through the atmosphere. This circulation of energy warms the air and keeps the temperature of Earth's surface around 59 °F (15 °C) higher than it would otherwise be. This generally warm and very stable climate created by the natural greenhouse effect makes Earth habitable for humans and other animals and provides the energy for plants to grow. However, in the long term, Earth has warmed and cooled in a cyclical pattern over millions of years.

Human activities

Some scientists and policy makers are concerned about global warming because they say that humans may be causing an increase in atmospheric temperature. Human activities, particularly those that have taken place since the Industrial Revolution of the 18th and 19th centuries, have put vastly increased quantities of carbon dioxide and other compounds into the air, leading many scientists to believe that more heat is being trapped by the atmosphere. The result, they say, is global warming. They back their beliefs with evidence that the average global temperature is rising and has been for some time. Other scientists and policy makers argue that any increases in the temperature might well be part of normal long-term fluctuations in Earth's climate cycle.

Ever since it became apparent that change was occurring in the greenhouse effect, scientists have been scrutinizing the greenhouse gases and calculating the amounts of extra greenhouse gases that have entered the atmosphere. Researchers have paid special attention to carbon dioxide, which they have discovered accounts for about one-half of the current additions of greenhouse gases to the atmosphere.

Humans, other animals, and decaying plants have always put carbon dioxide into the atmosphere (see CARBON CYCLE), but carbon dioxide release increased markedly after the beginning of the Industrial Revolution, when humans began burning vast amounts of fossil fuels such as coal, oil, and natural gas. When scientists compare today's atmospheric carbon dioxide (CO_2) levels with those found in ice from Greenland deposited within the last 160,000 years, before the big switch to fossil fuels, they find a modern-day concentration of the gas that is 25 percent higher than before and growing rapidly. Research also shows a distinct correlation in the past between higher concentrations of CO_2 in the atmosphere and higher climate temperatures.

Neither scientists nor policy makers know what will happen if the buildup of greenhouse gases continues at the present rate (a scenario known as "business as usual"). The climatic process is very complex (see box on page 842).

Many current projections are based on an assumption that population growth and human activity will produce the equivalent of a doubling of Earth's present carbon dioxide output by the year 2030. In such a case, the average surface temperature of the globe could rise by between 0.36° and 0.5 °F (0.2° and 0.5 °C) every 10 years. By the year

A potent greenhouse gas, ozone may be formed at ground level by the effect of sunlight reacting with vehicle pollution in urban areas. The ozone mixes up with other noxious gases and soot particles to form a "photochemical smog," as seen in this picture of smog in Mexico City.

THE GREENHOUSE GASES

The major greenhouse gases naturally present in Earth's atmosphere are water vapor, carbon dioxide, methane, nitrous oxide, and ozone.

• Water vapor produces about 75 percent of the natural greenhouse effect. Most of the vapor comes from the evaporation of ocean waters.

• Carbon dioxide (CO_2) is the second most abundant greenhouse gas. It is part of the carbon cycle (see CARBON CYCLE) and is produced naturally by animal and plant respiration (see ENERGY) and by decomposing organic matter. Humans also produce carbon dioxide by a variety of methods: mainly the burning of fossil fuels (coal, oil, and natural gas). Carbon dioxide is also emitted from slash-and-burn tropical deforestation and from savanna fires.

• Methane (CH_4) is produced naturally by the bacterial breakdown of organic matter, mainly in wetland soils and the digestive tracts of ruminant animals, such as cattle. Other sources include organic breakdown in garbage in landfill sites, coal mining, and natural gas production. Compared with carbon dioxide, there is relatively little methane in the atmosphere, but on a molecule-by-molecule basis, methane is believed to be as much as 20 times as effective as CO_2 at absorbing infrared radiation.

• Nitrous oxide (N_2O) is released into the atmosphere by processes that take place in the soil, both natural and as a result of fertilizers used in modern agriculture, as well as from ocean life. Nitrous oxide is also produced by the burning of fossil fuels and vegetation.

• Ozone (O_3) is formed in the atmosphere when oxygen atoms are split by incoming ultraviolet solar radiation. It is concentrated in the lower and middle stratosphere (about 9 to 22 miles, or 15 to 35 km, above Earth's surface), where it forms the so-called ozone layer. This gaseous layer is vitally important to Earth and its inhabitants—it forms a shield against incoming ultraviolet radiation from the Sun, which can damage nucleic acids (which make up the genetic materials DNA and RNA; see DNA) and proteins.

Tropical slash-and-burn deforestation releases carbon dioxide into the atmosphere. As the potential of the soil is poor, little carbon dioxide is reabsorbed through future regrowth on the land.

As well as these natural greenhouse gases, Earth's atmosphere also contains an abundance of human-made greenhouse gases called chlorofluorocarbons (CFCs). These chemicals did not exist before the 20th century. CFCs have several industrial uses, including use as solvents and agents of refrigeration and for blowing foam insulation. Despite being potent greenhouse gases themselves, they do not have much of an overall influence on the greenhouse effect because they destroy the greenhouse gas, ozone (see ATMOSPHERE).

A CLOSER LOOK

2030, the average world temperature would have risen by between 1.26° and 1.8°F (0.7° and 1 °C) above the 1990 average.

Implications of global warming

These temperature changes may seem small; some scientists say they would fall comfortably within the normal range of Earth's climatic ups and downs (although even over a normal range things drastically change). Other researchers who have studied temperature and climate think such a temperature rise could make a big difference, with profound effects on the biosphere and on humans' way of conducting their lives. Possible outcomes of global warming include a rise in sea level and increased levels of precipitation (rain and snow), as well as changes in the distribution of agricultural zones and biomes and habitats.

• **Rise in sea level:** Many nonscientists assume that a rise in global temperature would cause the oceans to rise because of water flowing into them from the melting of polar ice caps. The oceans would indeed rise, and some of that rise would come from melting ice, but it would take many centuries for the ice caps to make much of a difference.

The immediate rise would come from the water already in the oceans. This can be explained by a simple rule of physics: as water warms, it expands, and when ocean waters take up more room, they take it from the places where they meet land, such as coastlines, bays, and rivers.

Estimates vary widely and include a sea-level rise of 1 to 5 feet (0.3 to 1.5 m) by the year 2050, and 7 feet (2.2 m) by the year 2100. A rise of that kind could seriously damage or submerge beaches, residential areas, and industries along low-lying parts of the world's coastlines. Some small island nations would disappear under water completely. For example, the Maldives, a collection of islands in the Indian Ocean, would be entirely immersed by a 6½-foot (2-m) rise.

Established coastal cities would have to spend great sums of money to protect themselves from the heightened sea level. In addition, salt water could enter underground supplies of drinking water near the coasts. A rise in sea level would also severely disrupt lowland agricultural regions, such as the rice paddies in some parts of Asia.

• **More rain and snow:** Warmer oceans would produce greater evaporation of the water in them and, thus, lead to increased precipitation as part of the normal hydrological (water) cycle. The United Nations Environment Program has estimated that if carbon dioxide levels double, precipitation will increase by 4 to 12 percent.

• **Warmer winters and summers:** People in the higher latitudes, which contain much of the developed world, would have warmer winters and summers. The World Resources Institute has predicted that by 2050, following global warming, the number of days per year in which the temperature exceeds 100 °F (38 °C) would increase from 1 to 12 in Washington, from 3 to 21 in Omaha, from 4 to 42 in Memphis, and from 19 to 78 in Dallas.

• **Changes in agricultural distribution:** Higher temperatures and precipitation levels would alter the distribution of agricultural crops. Most commercial crops, such as wheat, maize (corn), rice, oil-producing plants, and vegetables, are fine-tuned through decades of breeding and adaptation to the climates in which they are grown. A hotter climate would lower the yields of these crops in the regions where they are grown, leading to famine in many areas. Higher temperatures may also cause widespread soil erosion and desertification and encourage the spread of warm-weather insect pests.

• **Changes in biomes and habitats:** Trees are sensitive to climate. With a higher average temperature, many tree ranges, such as beech, birch, and sugar maples, would shift north by several hundred miles. Global warming would affect wildlife, too. Throughout the world's history, animal species that were mobile have tried to keep ahead of climate changes. In the Northern Hemisphere, species that prosper in cooler climates have moved north when the climate has warmed and south when it has cooled. Wildlife would try to migrate as a result of global warming, too, but the animals would have more problems than in previous periods of climate change. Much of the modern world's wildlife is penned in by civilization—roads, cities, and farmland—and would find migration difficult or impossible. Scientists fear that human-induced global warming will proceed much faster than the natural warming cycles of the past, and many species will not be able to adapt quickly enough and will become extinct.

Global warming policies

Policy makers have been aware for a number of years of the potential threats that are raised by increased greenhouse emissions. They have spoken out frequently about the problem, and they have commissioned enormous scientific research to get a better idea of what is happening and why.

Nations from around the world attended the 1992 United Nations Conference on Environment and Development (the Earth Summit), an unprecedented international effort to cope with the environmental stresses caused by human activities. One of the important documents that came out of the conference was a Framework Convention on

Climate Change. Representatives of 161 of the world's nations signed the document. It is the aim of the Framework to stabilize the concentration of greenhouse gases in the atmosphere "at a level that would prevent dangerous anthropogenic interference [that is, interference that results from humans' influence on nature] with the climate system."

F. POWLEDGE

This picture shows mobile sand dunes advancing over pine woodlands. In many areas of the world, global warming would lead to similar shifting biomes and habitats.

See also: AGRICULTURE; ATMOSPHERE; BIOMES AND HABITATS; CARBON CYCLE; DESERTIFICATION; ENERGY.

Further reading:

Houghton, J. T. 1997. *Global Warning: The Complete Briefing*. Cambridge, Mass.: Cambridge University Press.
Leggett, J. K. *2001. The Carbon War: Global Warming and the End of the Oil Era*. London: Taylor and Francis Group.

PREDICTING CLIMATE CHANGE

As changes in the greenhouse effect occur, they trigger other changes. Some may increase global warming, while others may decrease it. As a result, it is difficult, if not impossible, for scientists to make hard-and-fast declarations about how much the global climate has changed in the recent past and how much it will change in the future. One of the tools used in measuring and predicting climate change is computer modeling. Scientists use computer programs to divide the Earth's surface into a grid, similar to the longitude and latitude lines on a map or globe, but much closer together. The sections of the grid extend into space or beneath the seas, too. Then the researchers use mathematical equations to represent the temperature and other factors that go into an assessment of climate in each of the boxes. By feeding all the calculations into powerful computers, researchers can assemble an overall picture (or predicted picture) of the climate over a period of time.

These computer models give approximations of climate changes, however; and they do not guarantee that all scientists will agree in their predictions. The interaction of all aspects of the climate system (such as cloud cover, precipitation, and snow and ice cover, for example) are extremely complex. By contrast, computer models are simplified, and the representations of climatic processes within them are approximate and incomplete. As a result, many scientists are unwilling to rely on the climate predictions calculated by computer models, which often differ widely from one program to another.

GRAINS

Grains are the seed-containing fruits of cereal grasses, the most important agricultural plants on Earth

Grains are the most important agricultural crops on Earth. The most common grains—wheat, rice, and corn (maize)—cover about half of the world's croplands. Millions of people rely on grains as their staple food. Wheat, rice, and corn together account for 50 percent of the calories consumed by humans. Grains are also used as animal feed, in brewing, and even to make fuel to run automobiles.

Wheat

Cultivated wheat (*Triticum* spp.) originated in what is now northern Syria, southeastern Turkey, and Iran. People began to domesticate wild wheat at least as early as 7500 BCE. As wild species were domesticated, modern varieties emerged.

CORE FACTS

- Grains are the most important crops on Earth, covering about half of all the world's croplands.
- The most widely grown grains are wheat, rice, and corn.
- The grain is the seed-containing fruit of plants belonging to the grass family, Gramineae, or Poaceae.
- Grains were among the first cultivated plants.
- Grains have a large number of uses: to feed people and animals, to make beer, in the plastics industry, and as fuel for automobiles.

A grain of wheat is called a kernel or wheat berry. It has three major parts: the bran (the outer covering comprising the fruit wall and the seed coat), the endosperm (a food-storage tissue made of starch), and the wheat germ, which lies within the endosperm and is the embryo plant that sprouts when the wheat kernel is sown. If the entire kernel is ground, whole wheat flour (also called graham flour) is produced. If only the endosperm is ground, the result is white (refined) flour. White flour was formerly preferred because it had a longer shelf life, whereas in whole wheat flour the oils in the wheat germ became rancid after several weeks. Whole wheat flour is now treated to extend its shelf life.

Whole wheat flour and foods made from it contain more vitamins, minerals, and protein than white flour. Wheats used in breads and cereals are often enriched with vitamins and minerals—those lost during the manufacturing process—to try to restore the food to its basic nutritional level.

There are several modern varieties of wheat, each with a particular use. Soft wheats, so called because they break into soft fragments when they are ground, are used to make cakes and pastries. Cake and pastry flour is very finely ground and has a satinlike texture. Hard wheats, which have grittier fragments, are made into pasta and breads. Mixtures of hard and soft wheats may be used to

Silos are used to store grain and protect it from weather and pests.

CONNECTIONS

- Grains contain high levels of **FATS AND OILS**, substances required by the germinating embryo.

- Barley, rice, and corn are used in the **FERMENTATION** process to make beer.

- **GENETIC ENGINEERING** has developed wheat, rice, and corn varieties that produce high yields.

WHAT IS A GRAIN?

Scientists sometimes refer to a cereal grain as a caryopsis, the single-seeded, usually dry and nonfleshy fruit of a grass. Grasses are flowering plants and belong to the family Gramineae, or Poaceae. The grain's seed contains the germ, or plant embryo, which holds a supply of oil and protein and an abundant starchy foodstore, the endosperm, to sustain the embryo as it develops during germination. The grain is protected by an outer coating called the husk, or bran, formed from the testa (seed coat) fused to the pericarp (fruit wall). The grain also contains vitamins and minerals, but it lacks the correct mixture of amino acids, calcium, and (except for yellow corn) vitamin A that humans need to stay healthy. Thus, a balanced diet must combine grains with the other foods that supply these essential nutrients.

Endosperm

Germ or embryo

Husk or bran: pericarp (fruit wall) fused to testa (seed coat)

produce all-purpose flour. In addition to various forms of flour, wheat is sold as the whole berry (or grain), cracked wheat (the coarsely ground berry), bulgar (whole-grain wheat that has been boiled, dried, and cracked), and breakfast cereals.

The total gluten content of a variety of wheat affects how it is used. Gluten is a tough, elastic protein substance, which provides the firmness and elasticity for the risen dough used in bread making. Some wheats, such as durum, which is used in pasta, are high in gluten. Generally speaking, the harder wheats contain high-quality gluten.

Rice

The many varieties of rice (*Oryza sativa*) can be divided into two major categories: indica rice, which grows in the tropics, and japonica rice, which is found in more temperate regions and in the cooler, higher parts of tropical areas. Evidence suggests that rice probably originated in Asia; pieces of pottery found in Thailand in 1966 contain imprints of grains and husks of rice dating from at least 4000 BCE. In the early 18th century, rice cultivation began in North America in what is now Louisiana. In the 20th century, the grain was first grown in California's Sacramento Valley.

Rice is grown in several geographic locations, and rice farmers have shown great imagination in adapting their crops to the various environmental conditions. Rice needs plenty of water, so unless it is grown in an area with a rainy season, farmers must create ways to constantly irrigate the land.

Rice paddies are flooded with several inches of water, as rice requires an irrigated system in order to grow. The different varieties of rice are adapted to various water levels.

The processing of the rice grain begins with milling (the mechanical removal of the hard outer husk, or bran). Before milling, the rice is brown. The bran is removed from white rice, along with its protein and vitamins. Rice can be cooked by steaming or boiling, turned into breakfast cereals, made into crackerlike cakes, or processed into alcoholic beverages. The top-selling beers in the United States are made from rice. The husks that are removed by milling are used for cattle feed.

Corn

Corn, or maize (*Zea mays*), is the world's third most important crop in terms of production. It requires a frost-free environment, so its distribution is more limited than that of wheat. Corn is a tall annual plant that, unlike other grains, produces its fruit (the kernels) on cobs. The kernels can be white, yellow, a combination of white and yellow, or even blue, red, and purple in the case of Indian corn.

Scientists believe that people first cultivated corn in Central America. Less is known, however, about the origin of corn. Researchers in Mexico have discovered that a related grass, teosinte (*Zea mays* subsp. *mexicana*), breeds with modern corn, so modern corn may be a descendent of teosinte. Scientists digging in Mexico City have found pollen of the genus *Zea* that is 80,000 years old.

Early cultivators considered corn to be a gift from the gods to humans. They ground, boiled, and parched corn and heated the kernels until they popped, just as people do today. Corn was the source of the flour in tortillas and was made into beer and stronger alcoholic drinks. Some people even used to chew the uncooked grain.

Corn is still grown for these same reasons, as well as for several others. Enormous quantities of corn make up the staple diet of the cattle intensively reared for the hamburger industry. Corn oil is widely used in cooking and in the manufacture of plastics; ethanol produced from fermented corn can be used to power engines that normally run on fossil fuels and is a component of cleaner-burning gasoline.

Other important grains

Barley (*Hordeum vulgare*) was probably domesticated in about 7000 to 6000 BCE. It is mainly used as livestock feed and in the brewing industry. In the United States in 2002, 250 million bushels (8.8 billion liters) of barley were grown, which is equal to about 15 percent of the nation's wheat production of 1.69 billion bushels (59.5 billion liters) .

Oats (*Avena sativa*) have been called the gasoline of the 19th century, because they were the main food of horses. When trains and cars took over from horses as the most common mode of transport, oat production in the United States fell. People still eat oats as a breakfast cereal, and the United States is the world's largest importer of oats, mainly importing the grain from Scandinavia and Canada.

Rye (*Secale cereale*)was first cultivated in 3000 BCE. It has prospered in Eastern Europe, as the plant needs cold winters and warm, dry summers. Europeans bake a thick, dark bread from the grain, that is highly nutritious and lower in calories than wheat bread. Americans buying rye bread in a supermarket are more likely to find a softer loaf containing a mixture of rye and wheat flours. Pumpernickel bread originated in Germany and is made with a very dark rye which is baked at a low heat for a long time. Rye is also used for animal feed and to make alcoholic beverages.

Sorghum (*Sorghum bicolor*), sometimes called milo, is grown and eaten throughout the semiarid tropics, the band of dry, hot land around much of the equator. The grain survives in places where other crops fail to grow, and it feeds people and livestock. The stalks are used for animal fodder, fuel, and a sugary syrup and as a building material.

Pearl millet (*Pennisetum glaucum*)is even hardier. It is grown on an estimated 62 million acres (25 million hectares) of land so poor that even sorghum cannot survive. The ground grain is used to make unleavened bread in India; dumplings, couscous, and beer in Africa; and livestock fodder in other countries. It is also eaten whole as a cereal.

F. POWLEDGE

See also: AGRICULTURE; DOMESTICATION; FRUITS AND FRUIT PLANTS; GRASSES; NUTRITION.

Further reading:
Harlan, J. R. 1998. *The Living Fields: Our Agricultural Heritage*. New York: Cambridge University Press.
Vaughan, J. G., and C. A. Geissler. 1999. *The New Oxford Book of Food Plants*. Oxford and New York: Oxford University Press.

BUILDING BETTER GRAINS

The mention of genetic engineering conjures up thoughts of white-coated biotechnologists working in spotless laboratories to extract genes from one plant and inject them into another. However, people have been manipulating the genetic material of their food plants for thousands of years.

The earliest farmers saved the seeds of a successful year's plants for the following season—plants that did the best job of coping with too little or too much rain, that best coexisted with the local mix of temperature and sunshine, that resisted attacks from insect pests and competition from weeds, and that produced the greatest yield. By so doing, the farmers were selecting the most appropriate genes; arguably an early form of genetic engineering.

More recently, scientists from private industry and the large system of state-operated colleges in the United States have carried on this tradition of isolating plants with favorable characteristics and breeding them with others to produce the kind of seed that growers and consumers want. "Favorable characteristics" can mean many things: a wheat that can easily be harvested by machine; rice that can withstand rainstorms; corn that meets consumers' demands for an attractive mixture of yellow and white kernels. Favorable is most likely to mean a high yield or the greatest quantity of marketable food per acre.

In the 1960s this plant breeding helped save the lives of around 500 million people. Famine was threatening India and Pakistan, and scientists were working feverishly to develop new varieties of wheat and rice that would produce higher yields. They were successful, and the result of their work was called the green revolution. Norman E. Borlaug, who worked on much of the breeding program, won the 1970 Nobel Peace Prize for his efforts.

GRASSES

Aerial view of rice being harvested in Richvale, California. The use of modern machinery and techniques enables U.S. farmers to cultivate grass crops, such as rice, very effectively.

There are more than 9,500 species of grass in at least 650 genera, all grouped under the family name Gramineae, also called Poaceae. Grasses grow practically everywhere—from the tropics, to the Great Plains of the United States and Canada, to the steppes of Central Asia. Some species even grow in the cold Arctic and Antarctic regions.

Of all the different plants on Earth, grasses are probably the most important to humans. The cereal grasses, which include rice (*Oryza sativa*), wheat (*Triticum* spp.), and corn (*Zea mays*), are an important source of food to billions of people. Grazing animals, such as cattle, feed on grasses and are important as a source of meat and dairy products. Grasses also help to keep the soil in good condition for the growth of other crops. Their roots bind the soil together, and thus reduce wind and rain erosion.

Classification of grasses

Grasses belong to the order Poales, within the phylum or division Magnoliophyta (angiosperms or flowering plants; see ANGIOSPERMS). There are two main groups of angiosperms, the monocotyledons (with a single cotyledon) and the dicotyledons (with two cotyledons). The cotyledon, or seed leaf, is the part of the plant embryo within the seed that stores food for use by the growing seedling during germination. Grasses are monocotyledons. The leaves of monocotyledons have veins that usually run parallel to each other.

Grasses can be divided into annuals and perennials. Annuals, such as corn and wheat, complete their life cycle in just one growing season. They grow to maturity, form seeds, and then die. Perennials, such as bamboo (of the subfamily Bambusoideae) and sugarcane (*Saccharum officinarum*), live on year after year. Perennials can reproduce vegetatively (see REPRODUCTION), as well as from seeds. Structures that grow from the parent plant develop into new plants. Grasses may reproduce by means of rhizomes (underground stems). Examples include giant cane (*Arundinaria gigantea*), the popular lawn grass Kentucky bluegrass (*Poa pratensis*), which develops tillers (new shoots and stems growing from the base), and bunch grass (*Schizachyrium scoparium*), which develops stolons (overground stems).

Grass structure

All grasses have the same basic structure. The stem of a grass plant is called the culm. Alternate, linear

CONNECTIONS

● **GRASSLAND BIOMES** are habitats where the dominant plants are grasses.

● Grasses owe their success to their growing **CELLS**, or meristem, which occur at the base of the shoot.

CORE FACTS

■ There are more than 9,500 species of grass.
■ Humans have cultivated cereal grasses for thousands of years, including rice, wheat, and corn. They are the main source of food for people and livestock.
■ Rice is the staple food of about a third of the world's population.

leaves grow out of opposite sides of the culm. The long blade of each leaf is surrounded at its base by a sheath, which is closely wrapped around the culm. The points at which the leaves are attached to the culm are called nodes. The culm itself is usually cylindrical and hollow, except at the nodes, which are solid. In some grasses, such as corn and sorghum (*Sorghum bicolor*), the culm contains a tissue called pith. Some culms can be massive; those of a Chinese bamboo (*Phyllostachys edulis*) may grow 65 feet (20 m) tall and 8 inches (20 cm) thick.

One of the reasons for the grasses' success is that their growing point is at the base of the shoot, not at the top, as is the case with most plants. When animals graze on grass, they remove only the tops of the plant. Therefore the grass is able to regenerate itself. Thus, grazing animals do not generally destroy their supply of food.

Grass flowers

Grass flowers are small, usually greenish, and have no smell. They are wind pollinated (see POLLINATION), relying on the wind rather than animals to carry the pollen from one plant to another.

A typical grass flower, called a floret, has one pistil with two feathery stigmas and three stamens enclosed by two scalelike structures called a lemma and a palea. The perianth (petals and sepals) is reduced or absent altogether. The pistil is the female organ of the flower, and the stigma is the part that receives pollen for fertilization. Pollen is produced by the anthers. These are part of the stamens and are the male organs of the flower (see FLOWERS AND FLOWER STRUCTURE). Sometimes the lemma and palea bear a long bristle called an awn. Individual florets are gathered together into groups called spikelets, which themselves are enclosed by two scalelike structures called glumes. The spikelets are arranged in a flowering head (inflorescence), which varies greatly in form from genus to genus.

A grass seed is actually a single-seeded fruit called a caryopsis, which is almost always dry and non-fleshy. The fruit wall (pericarp) is fused to the seed coat (testa). Inside is the embryo plant and the starchy endosperm, a food store for the embryo.

When grass seeds have formed and matured they are dispersed in several ways (see SEEDS AND SEED DISPERSAL). The size and shape of the seeds will depend on the way in which they are dispersed. In many grass species the seeds are simply carried away by the wind: the seeds are very light and may be carried long distances. Other grass seeds, such as the sandbur (*Cenchrus* spp.), have barbed spines that become attached to the fur of passing animals.

Cereal grasses

Wheat, barley, rice, and corn were cultivated by the earliest civilizations as a source of food. Cereal grasses such as wheat, corn, oats (*Avena sativa*), rye (*Secale cereale*), barley (*Hordeum vulgare*), and rice are still part of the everyday diet. Sorghum and millet (*Pennisetum glaucum*) are a major source of food to

THE CREATION OF TRITICALE

Considerable advances have been made in the area of genetic engineering of plants. A good example is the "creation" of Triticale (X *Triticosecale*), an important cereal grass that was developed by crossing wheat (genus *Triticum*) with rye (genus *Secale*). The new plant, Triticale, is a more nutritious and hardy crop, producing heavy yields and high levels of protein; it showed that new human-made plants could be successfully engineered.

Genetically engineered plants will undoubtedly have a considerable impact on civilization in the future. Growing crops is far more efficient than raising livestock as a means of producing food, and it seems likely that the demand to develop better strains of crops will continue.

A CLOSER LOOK

millions of people in Africa, and sugar cane is of great importance worldwide. Rice is the staple food for about a third of the world's population and is the most important food crop in Asia.

M. BLEIFELD

See also: AGRICULTURE; ANGIOSPERMS; ANNUAL PLANTS; DICOTYLEDONS; FLOWERS AND FLOWER STRUCTURE; GERMINATION; GRAINS; MONOCOTYLEDONS; PERENNIAL PLANTS; POLLINATION; REPRODUCTION; SEEDS AND SEED DISPERSAL.

Further reading:

Clark, L. G., and R. W. Pohl. 1996. *Agnes Chase's First Book of Grasses Explained for Beginners.* 4th ed. Washington, D.C., and London: Smithsonian Institution Press.

The diagram below shows the basic structure of a flowering grass (1), a closeup of a spikelet (2), a closeup of a floret (3), and a floret with palea removed to expose reproductive organs (4).

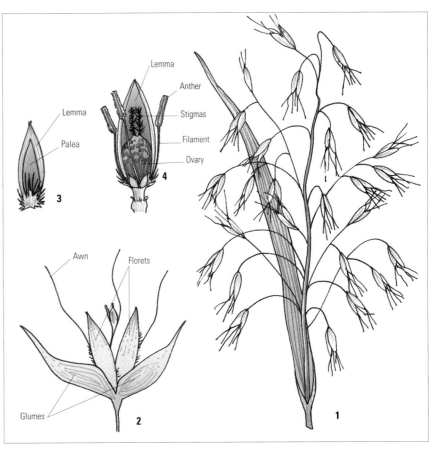

GRASSHOPPERS AND CRICKETS

Grasshoppers and crickets are insects of the order Orthoptera that use sound as a form of communication

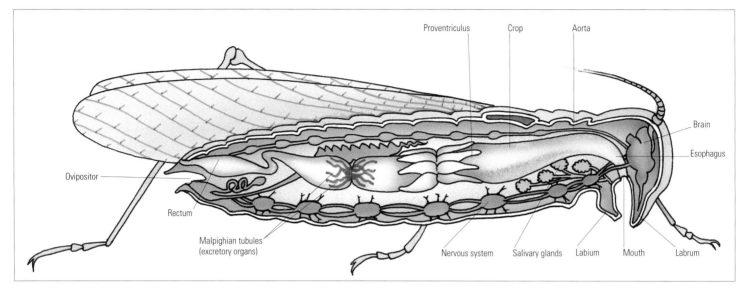

Proventriculus   Crop   Aorta   Brain   Esophagus   Labrum   Mouth   Labium   Salivary glands   Nervous system   Malpighian tubules (excretory organs)   Rectum   Ovipositor

An anatomical diagram of a bush cricket. Grasshoppers and crickets have many features in common.

Male grasshoppers and crickets are some of the world's noisiest insects. They are often heard in fields and meadows, signaling to one another with chirping or rasping sounds. For all their noise, these insects may be very hard to spot, their camouflage providing excellent protection from predatory birds.

Grasshoppers and crickets belong to a large, mostly tropical insect order called Orthoptera, which until recently also included the praying mantids and cockroaches. Although crickets are often given common names containing the word grasshopper, one of the easiest ways to tell the difference between grasshoppers and crickets is to look at their antennae. Grasshoppers have short antennae and are often called short-horned grasshoppers; crickets have long antennae and are often called long-horned grasshoppers.

The approximately 20,000 species of grasshoppers and crickets can be grouped into two suborders. The first, Ensifera, consists of nine different families, including true crickets in the family Gryllidae and katydids and long-horned grasshoppers (also known, less confusingly, as bush crickets) in the family Tettigoniidae. The second suborder, Caelifera, consists of six different families, including short-horned grasshoppers and locusts in the family Acrididae.

Anatomy and lifestyle

Like all insects, grasshoppers and crickets have exoskeletons (external skeletons) and three main body sections: head, thorax, and abdomen. The head has two sensitive antennae, which may be covered with fine hairs.

Grasshoppers and crickets possess five eyes and have good eyesight. They have two large compound eyes, each with hundreds of facets that act as individual eyes, enabling grasshoppers to see moving objects, and three smaller simple eyes that respond to light and dark. They are very wary insects and, if they detect any sign of danger, are quick to leap using their long specially adapted hind legs. Some grasshoppers are able to jump as high as 3 feet (1 m). Mole crickets (*Gryllotalpa* spp.) have adapted to life underground, and as a result have lost their jumping ability and their wings but have developed strong front legs that they use for digging through soil.

Grasshoppers' forewings are straight, thick, and leathery and lie at the side of their body. Their broad, delicate, fanlike hind wings fold under their forewings when the insect is not flying. Most crickets, however, hold their folded forewings over their backs. Compared with other flying insects, many species of grasshoppers and crickets are clumsy fliers, and some species have tiny wings or no wings at all. Most spend their time on the ground or in trees and shrubs.

Camouflage has an important role in enabling grasshoppers to hide from predators. Green grasshoppers tend to live among vegetation; others that live among rocks or on bare ground are dull gray or brown. On the other hand, some grasshoppers are very brightly colored—the coloring warning predators of their distastefulness or poisonous nature. Some of these grasshoppers also defend themselves by discharging an offensive liquid from their mouthparts.

Grasshoppers and crickets have biting or chewing mouthparts (mandibles), which are modified

CORE FACTS

- Grasshoppers and crickets are jumping insects in the order Orthoptera and can be grouped into two suborders: Ensifera and Caelifera. There are about 20,000 species.
- They have powerful hind legs so that they can escape from predators.
- Grasshoppers and crickets undergo incomplete metamorphosis, and the larvae resemble the adults.
- The males are able to produce chirping and rasping sounds to attract a mate and to define their territory.
- Some species are gregarious and travel in swarms.

CONNECTIONS

● Many grasshoppers and crickets use **CAMOUFLAGE AND MIMICRY** to enable them to hide from predators. Some bear a striking resemblance to sticks or living, dead, or diseased leaves.

● These insects also use sound as a form of **COMMUNICATION** between members of the same species and during **COURTSHIP** and **MATING** rituals.

INSECT SONGSTERS

Not all sounds made by grasshoppers and crickets are produced in the same way. Acridiid grasshoppers grate their legs on their wings; crickets in the Tettigonidae family rub their wing cases over one another. The actual sounds depend on which part of the body is used, how many "teeth" it possesses, and the speed at which it moves. Each tooth's impact produces vibrations, which partially diminish before the next tooth strikes and a new chain of vibrations begins. The result is a series of loud, complex trills (pulses of sound). Grillidae wings, during sound production, vibrate at around 5,000 cycles per second.

A CLOSER LOOK

according to the species' diet. Their digestive systems contain a foregut (a mouth, a crop for storage, and a gizzard for grinding), a midgut (stomach), and a hindgut (intestines, rectum, and anus). Most species are phytophagous (plant eating), although some are omnivorous (eating plant and animal matter), and some even catch live prey.

Stridulation

The production of sound (stridulation—derived from the Latin word *stridulus*, meaning "creaking") is a notable feature of the behavior of male grasshoppers and crickets, and it plays an important part in courtship. It also helps the insects define their territory, and as the songs are specific for a species, it helps members of the same species find one another.

Species vary in the way they produce the sounds. There are two basic mechanisms: the first method, used by crickets in the Ensifera suborder, involves rubbing the veins on the bases of their forewings together. On the underside of the wings of the true crickets there is a series of rough teeth, known as the file. Each wing also has a toughened patch known as the scraper. When the wings are moved rapidly, they rub across one another, producing the characteristic chirping sound. Each wing is identical, so it does not matter which lies on top of which.

The second method is used by grasshoppers in the Caelifera suborder. They create friction between ridges (pegs) on the inner surface of their hind legs and pronounced veins on their forewings to produce a rasping sound. One exception is the band-winged grasshopper (*Oedipodinae*), which makes buzzing and crackling sounds by snapping its hind wings together during flight.

To hear the sounds made by other insects, grasshoppers and crickets use auditory organs, called tympana, which are tightly stretched membranes that respond to sound waves. Grasshoppers have their tympana located on the sides of their first abdominal segment, whereas crickets have their tympana on the base of the tibia of their forelegs. The tympana are not sensitive to pitch but can discern intensity and the rhythms produced by members of the same species.

Life cycle

Grasshoppers and crickets have different adaptations for oviposition (laying eggs). Female grasshoppers have a blunt abdomen, which they push into the ground. The abdomen is extended until it reaches some distance below the surface. Several eggs are then

Some grasshoppers, such as this courting pair, are brightly colored, to warn predators that they do not taste very good.

laid (usually between 20 and 120) and are surrounded by a foamy substance, which hardens to provide the eggs with a protective pod. The tunnel made by the abdomen is then covered with loose material.

Cricket species, on the other hand, have a sword-like ovipositor (a specialized organ for depositing eggs) at the end of their abdomen. They use its sharp point to insert the eggs one at a time into soil or plant tissue.

The eggs are generally laid during early winter. They hatch in the spring, and the young grasshoppers and crickets undergo incomplete metamorphosis to become adults (see METAMORPHOSIS).

The developing grasshopper inside the egg is covered by thin serosal skin. At hatching time, an area on the back of its head (the ampulla) swells with hemolymph (insect "blood"). The swelling ruptures the egg, and the vermiform larva wriggles out of the egg and up to the soil surface. Once at the surface, the larva molts its serosal skin to free its legs and antennae. It then resembles the adult in all details, except for the wings, and is known as a nymph. Crickets do not have a vermiform larval stage; a cricket nymph emerges straight from the egg.

The young nymph's soft, moist body dries and hardens, and the insect searches for food. Restricted in its stiff, tight body, the nymph soon needs room to grow, so it molts its cuticle (skin). It hangs upside down from a plant, swallows large amounts of air to expand its body, swells its ampulla, and tears open the cuticle. The nymph then slides out and waits to dry.

The nymph molts a number of times. After each molt, before each new, soft cuticle hardens, the nymph is able to feed on larger quantities of food and increase in size and weight. By the fourth molt, the nymph is about half its adult size and has stubs on its back that will eventually develop into wings. Usually after between five and seven molts, the adult is fully developed and is capable of reproduction and flight. At this stage, hemolymph is pumped into the tightly packed wings to expand them to full size. While grasshoppers have, on average, six nymph stages (called instars) before they reach adulthood, some crickets may have up to ten (see MOLTING).

Flocking nymphs and migratory locusts

Occasionally, grasshoppers, especially spur-throated grasshoppers (*Melanoplus* spp.) and some species of locusts, mass in swarms of many millions and devastate huge areas of crops and other vegetation.

If vegetation is abundant, the females produce more eggs more frequently, and young grasshoppers begin to seek each other's company. Crowding eventually stimulates hormonal changes in the nymphs, which trigger behavioral and physiological changes. The nymphs' coloring may become more striking, and their growth and molting rates may also speed up.

When the food supply becomes depleted, a large group of insects takes to the air and eats the vegetation that lies beneath its path. Different species feed on different plants. Some feed only on grass; others feed on any vegetation in sight.

M. DICANIO

See also: ARTHROPODS; COCKROACHES; EGGS; GRASSLAND BIOMES; INSECTS; LARVAE AND PUPAE; MANTIDS; METAMORPHOSIS; MOLTING.

Mole crickets, which burrow under the ground, have short, shovel-like legs and reduced wings.

Further reading:
Field, L. H., ed. 2001. *The Biology of Wetas, King Crickets, and Their Allies.* London: CABI Publishing.
Grasshoppers and Other Leaping Insects. 2001. Animals of the World. World Book Encyclopedia. Chicago: World Book, Inc.
Naskrecki, P. 2000. *Katydids of Costa Rica.* Volume 1, *Systematics and Bioacoustics of the Cone-Head Katydids.* Philadelphia: The Orthopterists Society.

GRASSHOPPERS IN HISTORY

The ancestors of modern orthopterans may have lived about 300 million years ago, in the Upper Carboniferous period. By the Triassic period, 225 million years ago, winged grasshopper-like insects were abundant, probably resembling modern grasshoppers and crickets.

Grasshoppers and crickets were important to ancient civilizations. A locust is carved on the tomb of Haremhab, a 15th-century-BCE Egyptian pharaoh. Both the Old and New Testaments mention the eating of grasshoppers. Grasshoppers are high in protein and are still part of the human diet even today in some countries. Crickets are sometimes kept in cages as pets in eastern countries.

GRASSLAND BIOMES

Grassland biomes are ecosystems where grasses are the dominant plants

A herd of antelope on the grassy rangeland in central Wyoming.

Grassland biomes are ecosystems where the dominant plants are grasses (family Gramineae, or Poaceae). Grasses are one of the most successful and diverse plants, occupying 25 to 35 percent of Earth's land surface. A relatively recent botanical arrival, they first appeared in the Cretaceous period nearly 70 million years ago, becoming particularly successful in the last 30 million years.

Temperate grasslands

Grasslands are well distributed across the temperate zones of both the Northern and Southern Hemispheres. Although they are called by a variety of names, prairie in North America, pampa in Argentina and Chile, paramo in the Andes mountain range of South America, steppe in Eurasia, veld in South Africa, and outback in Australia, all share many features. Their growth depends on two factors: first, grasslands receive relatively little rain (less than forested areas but more than deserts); second, there are only two seasons: a long, dry season and a shorter, rainy season, with most of the annual rainfall occurring in a period of only a few months.

Nontemperate grasslands

Grasslands in subtropical and tropical zones occur most extensively on the African continent. They are characterized by coarse grasses and scattered tree growth and are typically areas of irregular and infrequent rainfall, alternating with long, dry seasons. In Africa these areas are called savannas, and are bound to the north by subdesert steppes and to the south by equatorial rain forest. The Serengeti is a good example of such grasslands, with a landscape that is transformed from a fairly fertile one in the wet season, to a bleak inhospitable one in the dry season (see SAVANNA BIOMES).

Grasses and grazers

Grasslands can be further subdivided according to vegetation type: for example, whether tall grasses predominate, as in the pampas of Argentina, or short

CORE FACTS

- Grasses are one of the most successful and diverse plants and occupy 25 to 35 percent of Earth's land surface.
- Grasslands are high-yielding ecosystems, which typically support a variety of large grazing mammals.
- Grasslands and grazing animals have evolved together.
- The sequence of grazing, known as a grazing succession, benefits both the grazing animals and the grasses.
- Temperate grasslands generally have two distinctive seasons: a long, dry season and a shorter, rainy season. Most rainfall occurs in a period of a few months.

CONNECTIONS

● Large areas of grassland have been turned over to **AGRICULTURE**, with the native **GRASSES** replaced by domesticated grasses.

● **HUMAN EVOLUTION** is thought by some to have begun in the tropical grasslands, or savannas, perhaps 150,000 to 200,000 years ago.

grasses predominate, as in the steppes of Eurasia. The dominant grass type is important in determining which grazers are likely to thrive in the biome.

In complex grassland ecosystems, grasses and grazing animals have evolved together, and in areas like the Serengeti plains in Tanzania and Kenya, many different grazers, such as buffalo, zebras, antelopes, and rhinoceroses (see UNGULATES), live happily together. After the early rains, grasses grow quickly. There are tall and relatively coarse grasses that provide good forage for zebras. As the zebras eat back the tall grasses they expose lower, finer grasses, which are eaten by the wildebeest, whose teeth and digestive system cannot cope with the coarser, taller grasses. In turn, the grazing by the wildebeest stimulates regrowth, resulting in a carpet of fine, new shoots. These shoots are eaten by Thomson's gazelles (*Gazella thomsonii*). This sequence of grazing, called a grazing succession, benefits both the animals and the grasses. Many of the grass seeds eaten by the animals pass through their digestive systems intact. When the animals move on and defecate, they leave these seeds complete with a ball of dung fertilizer.

Conversion of grasslands to farming

In much of the temperate zone, in areas such as the American Midwest and the Russian steppes, wild herbivores have been all but exterminated and native grasslands turned over to the production of wheat and corn. Although the replacement of native grasses with wheat and corn (both domesticated grasses) seems sensible, some serious problems have resulted (see the box above). Food crops derived from grasses are usually annuals, that is, they complete their life cycle in a single growing season. Temperate grasslands, however, are usually dominated by perennial grasses, which have extensive root systems that support growth from the same plant year after year. These root systems have played an important role in stabilizing the soil. Without the root systems of native grasses, grassland soil is more susceptible to erosion.

The introduction of nonnative species

Grassland ecology can also be disturbed through the introduction of new species. The introduction of cheat grass (*Bromus tectorum*) from the Mediterranean into the American prairies is a good example. Cheat grass tends to grow in a relatively even carpet. When the grass dies back, it leaves a mat of leaves and stems. This mat can spread fire more easily than the dead stems of the native perennial grasses. Fire removes dead plant material and allows light to reach the ground, thus stimulating the regeneration of grasses and small shrubs and bushes.

Native or introduced species of insects can also be critical to grassland stability. In Australia, for example, African dung beetles were deliberately introduced into the tropical grasslands to cope with the dung produced by cattle in the outback. In rainy seasons, the dung of grazing animals breaks down and returns

THE DUST BOWL

The replacement of temperate perennial grasses with annual crop grasses has been a major threat to soil stability, and the results can be devastating. The Dust Bowl, which developed in the prairies of the United States in the 1930s, was caused by a combination of factors, and is perhaps one of the best examples. Many areas were converted to agriculture, but there was insufficient rainfall to ensure that crops grew every year, and in many years the soil lay bare. For example, from 1930 to 1937, rainfall was less than 65 percent of the expected amount. The normal prairie and steppe grasses could have survived this short fall, but not wheat. In addition, other areas where cultivation was impossible were turned over to grazing of cattle and sheep. Overgrazing of natural grasses led in turn to exposed soils. These exposed areas were further destabilized by brush fires, destroying the soil's resistance to erosion. When droughts occurred, winds swept up millions of tons of topsoil and carried it away.

A CLOSER LOOK

vital minerals and elements to the soil. However, for much of the year grasslands are arid, and dung cannot decompose. During these dry periods, therefore, a family of insects called dung beetles (*Geotrupes*) are critical to the recycling of nutrients. The beetles lay their eggs in balls of dung, then bury the dung balls, so returning the dung to the soil. They also reduce problems with cattle pests such as bushflies (*Musca vetustissima*), whose larvae develop in unburied dung.

J. GINSBERG

See also: DESERTIFICATION; GRASSLAND BIRDS; SAVANNA BIOMES; UNGULATES.

Further reading:
Collinson, A. 1992. *Grasslands.* New York: Dillon Press.
Coupland. R. T., ed., 1993. *Natural Grasslands.* New York: Elsevier.

Dung beetles (Geotrupes), seen here with a dung ball, are an example of a deliberately introduced nonnative species. The beetles were introduced to the outback of Australia from Africa.

GRASSLAND BIRDS

Grassland birds are adapted to living in habitats with few trees, and most build their nests on the ground

A truly impressive array of birds inhabit the grasslands of the world, along with a huge diversity of other wildlife. The climate and soil type determine what vegetation will grow and, therefore, the types of birds and animals that are able to live there. Through evolution, these birds have adapted both their behavior and form to make them particularly suited to their surrounding habitat.

Passerines (perching birds) are particularly widespread on grasslands and include larks, starlings, meadowlarks, longspurs, finches, and sparrows. Other common grassland birds are birds of prey, such as owls, eagles, and hawks, and ratites, such as emus, rheas, and ostriches (see BIRDS; BIRDS OF PREY).

Temperate grassland habitats include the prairies of North America, the pampas of southern South America, the velds of South Africa, the steppes of Eurasia, and the outback of Australia. Tropical

and subtropical grasslands include the savannas of southern and eastern Africa (see GRASSLAND BIOMES; SAVANNA BIOMES).

ADAPTING TO GRASSLAND HABITATS
Nesting

Grassland birds have adapted to living in open areas that have few trees or bushes; most of them build nests in shallow depressions in the ground. Typical is the lark bunting (*Calamospiza melanocorys*), also called the buffalo bird. This bird primarily inhabits the Great Plains to the east of the Rocky Mountains of North America, but migrates to the southern United States and Mexico to spend the winter. The lark bunting usually builds its nests on the ground or in low bushes.

Because sound gets lost in the strong winds that often gust across open grasslands, many grassland birds have developed sociable flocking lifestyles—particularly during the nonbreeding season—as an adaptation to overcome the difficulty of finding scattered food resources and for safety against predators. It also enables easier communication between birds. Among these flocking birds are grouse, prairie-chickens, sparrows, weavers, and weaver finches.

Buffalo weavers of Africa (in the subfamily Bubalornithinae) demonstrate the social behavior that characterizes many grassland birds. Because there are few trees in the grassland areas, several birds share a nest. These communal nests are among the most

*A male greater prairie chicken (**Tympanuchus cupido**) displays his sexual availability by raising his head feathers and inflating unfeathered neck patches.*

CONNECTIONS

● Because many grassland birds build their nests on the ground, they need to have excellent camouflage to protect themselves and their young from predators (see **CAMOUFLAGE AND MIMICRY**).

● Not all grassland birds live in one habitat all year round. Depending on local climate, some birds **MIGRATE** during wet and dry seasons or for the winter.

CORE FACTS

- Most grassland birds are omnivorous, feeding on small rodents and insects, as well as on grass seeds.
- The main grassland birds are either perching birds (passerines) or birds of prey.
- Flocking birds (including grouse, sparrows, and weavers) and ratites (including emus and ostriches) are also common.
- Many of the birds build their nests on the ground, and some court without using a branch to perch on.

striking structures made by birds. A nest is built on the strong branch of an acacia tree by several birds (often about eight) working at the same time. In time, the nest grows into a huge mass, within which individual pairs build their nest chambers. The communal nests may be sturdy enough to last as long as a century and can be almost 30 feet (9.1 m) long and 5 feet (1.5 m) deep with as many as 125 entrances.

Weaver finches, which are related to the weaverbirds and inhabit the steppes and savannas of south Africa and Australia, also live in communities. Their almost spherical nests are usually built in bushes or low trees and are always roofed over. In several species, nests are built outside the breeding season, and groups of weaverfinches roost (sleep) in them.

The cutthroat finch and the red-headed finch (of eastern Africa and western South Africa, respectively) do not build their own nests but live in the old nests of other weavers, particularly in the large communal nests of the buffalo weaver.

Courtship songs

Since there are few elevated song perches in their grassland breeding areas, the males of many species must perform their courtship ritual while in flight. Lark buntings, who live in large flocks during the non-breeding season and are highly sociable, are independent during the breeding season. When the males are courting, they rise a few feet above the ground and slowly circle back to the ground, holding their wings above their heads while singing.

Another well-adapted ground nester is the western meadowlark (*Sturnella neglecta*). This blackbird-sized bird has a distinctive flutelike song, and the male defends his territory by singing from tall weeds.

Feeding habits

Most grassland birds feed primarily on insects and other invertebrates (including grasshoppers, beetles, ants, and termites), small rodents, hares, snakes and lizards, and on grasses and seeds. Herbivorous birds (those that are exclusively plant eating) are less common in the grasslands than omnivorous birds (those that eat both plants and animals) because at certain times of the year there is little vegetation for animals to eat on the grassland. For example, the lark bunting feeds on grasshoppers, caterpillars, beetles, ants, and selected seeds, which it finds in abundance on the plains.

The long-billed curlew (*Numenius americanus*) is the largest bird in the sandpiper family and has adapted to feeding on the ground. Its bill is turned downward so that the bird can probe for insects and other tiny animals among crevices in the ground.

In dry and exposed habitats, many grassland birds have adapted their behavior to enable them to live with only a small supply of water. Some Australian weaver finches suck in water by immersing their beaks almost right up to the base. This drinking behavior enables the birds to take in water quickly and, thus, reduce the time during which they are exposed to danger from predators.

VEGETATION IN GRASSLAND HABITATS

Grasslands are too arid or infertile to allow dense forests to develop, but not too harsh to prevent the growth of smaller, long-lived plants. Trees are relatively scarce in these areas, because most are killed by fires that destroy their seeds. Grasses, on the other hand, have their growth areas at the base of their stems, or even below the soil surface, where they are well protected from fire. Because of this fact, the temperate grasslands host a variety of grasses reaching extreme heights (some reaching 10 to 15 feet, or 3 to 4.5 m), capable of supporting the nests of many species of birds. In wetter tropical and subtropical grasslands, expanses of high grasses are interrupted by occasional shrubs and trees, such as acacias.

A CLOSER LOOK

The zebra finch (*Poephila guttata*), which inhabits the dry grasslands of Australia, has adapted to the aridity of its environment to a remarkable degree. It can manage for weeks or even months without directly drinking water by extracting all the moisture it needs from its food. Many other birds, especially arid-land species, also derive much of their water from the food they eat.

BIRDS OF PREY AND RATITES

Two types of birds—some of the birds of prey and the ratites—have completely adapted their behavior and lifestyle to living on open grasslands.

Birds of prey

Birds of prey, including hawks, falcons, and eagles, are more abundant in the grasslands of North and South America than in any other habitat (see BIRDS OF PREY). Reasons for this abundance include the

The burrowing owl (Athene cunicularia) has long legs that enable it to move across rough ground in search of food.

fact that open spaces favor animals with good vision, enabling them to easily spy their prey from the sky.

The ferruginous hawk *(Buteo regalis)* mainly inhabits the prairies and arid grasslands of western North America. When hunting, the hawk swoops from a great height to catch prairie dogs, jackrabbits, mice, and occasionally, grouse and meadowlarks.

Like many other grassland birds, birds of prey build nests. Although most species of owls nest in tall trees, the burrowing owl *(Athene cunicularia)* that inhabits the prairies of North America and the grasslands of western Central America and South America is able to dig its own underground nest chambers. However, it usually makes its home in the abandoned burrows of prairie dogs or ground squirrels and may inhabit the same nest year after year if left undisturbed.

The relative flatness of the prairies and their lack of trees provides few hiding places, so burrowing is an effective strategy for avoiding predators. When it feels threatened, the burrowing owl ducks down into its burrow instead of taking flight.

The burrow provides another benefit for the owl: although the temperature of the temperate grasslands shifts between extremes of hot and cold, it remains relatively constant underground, and the burrows also provide shelter from grassland fires.

Burrowing owls have long legs, which allow them to move across rough ground in search of food. They feed mostly on insects and occasionally on small birds, including horned larks, meadowlarks, and sparrows, as well as some frogs, lizards, and snakes that populate the plains.

The short-eared owl *(Asio flammeus)* is another grassland and marsh bird, found not only in the prairies of North America but also in South America and in Asia and Europe. Although the short-eared owl does not inhabit burrows, it, too, has adapted to the scarcity of trees by making its nest on the ground from dry plant matter.

Plentiful rodents and other small mammals provide the perfect food supply for these predatory birds. The Swainson's hawk *(Buteo swainsoni)* inhabits western North America but migrates to South America for the winter. It feeds on mice, small rabbits, lizards, and grasshoppers, as well as other insects, which it catches in midflight. It also feeds on rodents, by stalking the entrance of its prey's burrows.

Ratites

Some of the more unusual grassland birds are ratites. This group of birds, which includes rheas, ostriches, cassowaries, and emus, have lost their ability to fly, as they spend all their time on the ground looking for food (see FLIGHTLESS BIRDS). Instead they have long powerful legs so that they are able to quickly escape from predators across the terrain.

The emu *(Dromaius novaehollandiae)* is an inhabitant of the Australian outback, while the rhea (in the family Rheidae; also called the pampas ostrich) inhabits the pampas of South America.

The ostrich *(Struthio camelus)*, the world's largest living bird, is found primarily on the African savanna and on the dry South African veld. Its long neck, large stride, and accurate pecking action allow it to gather sparsely dispersed food. As the ostrich feeds with its head down among the vegetation, it is left vulnerable to predators, so it periodically raises its head to scan the landscape. Unguarded ostrich nests are conspicuous from above, so female ostriches have to protect their eggs aggressively from flying predators.

R. PREISER

See also: BIRDS; BIRDS OF PREY; FLIGHTLESS BIRDS; GRASSLAND BIOMES; PERCHING BIRDS; SAVANNA BIOMES.

Further reading:
Kaufman, K. 1996. *Lives of North American Birds*. New York: Houghton Mifflin.
Sibley, D. 2000. *The Sibley Guide to Birds*. New York: Knopf/National Audubon Society.

Golden palm weavers (Textor bojeri) build elaborately woven nests on the branches of low trees.

GROWTH DISORDERS

Growth disorders occur during childhood when something goes wrong with the release of growth hormones

Giants and dwarfs may conjure up pictures of make-believe characters from childhood, but when something goes wrong with the processes that control normal human growth, life can be stranger than fiction. Famous giants include the Alton giant, Robert Wadlow (1919–1940) of Alton, Illinois, who measured 8 feet 11 inches (2.72 m) in height, weighed 495 pounds (222.75 kg), and wore size 37 shoes. By contrast, Dutch dwarf, Pauline Musters (Princess Pauline), the world's shortest woman, measured just 24 inches (61 cm) in height at the time of her death in New York in 1876.

Growth is primarily controlled by growth hormone (also called somatotropin), which is produced by cells in the anterior pituitary gland beneath the brain. These cells, the somatotrophs, synthesize and store the hormone in granules, releasing it periodically in response to hormonal messages from the brain. Growth hormone directly stimulates growth by increasing the synthesis of proteins and breakdown of fats by the body's cells and promoting cell division (mitosis) by causing the liver to secrete another hormone, IGF-1. Many other hormones also participate in the control of growth.

Normal growth

Normal growth is rapid in infancy and childhood. By the end of the first year of life, a 20-inch (50.8 cm) newborn baby may have grown an additional 10 inches (25.4 cm). From the ages of 3 to 12 years, growth is slower but constant. At puberty there is usually a sudden growth spurt, followed by very slow growth in body mass but not height during adulthood. Final full height is usually reached at around 16 or 17 years in girls and between 19 and 21 in boys.

Growth hormone controls the process of growth by stimulating cell division and protein synthesis in soft tissues, bone, and cartilage. It also makes energy available by stimulating the breakdown of fats.

Sandy Allen, pictured above, is a sufferer of gigantism. Her height is due to oversecretion of the growth hormone somatotropin.

CORE FACTS

- Growth is mainly controlled by growth hormone (somatotropin), produced by cells in the brain's anterior pituitary gland. However, other hormones also help control growth.
- Growth hormone stimulates cell division and protein synthesis in soft tissues, bone, and cartilage and the breakdown of fats to produce energy.
- At puberty, a surge in growth hormone causes rapid growth, which slows when the growing ends of the long bones close. Too much growth hormone too early results in gigantism, because the bones continue to grow.
- Dwarfism, which results when too little growth hormone is produced during childhood, may be caused by a genetic disorder, absence of the pituitary gland, or a pituitary tumor, for example.

The sex hormones, released in large amounts during puberty, also have a direct effect on growth. The male hormone testosterone causes the enlargement and development of the sexual organs, muscular development, growth of body hair and growth of long bones. A female sex hormone called estradiol stimulates new bone formation and breast growth, and a woman's adrenal glands also make androgenic hormones, which have effects on growth similar to testosterone. Within a few years of the onset of puberty, this growth spurt slows, owing to the closure of the growing ends of the bones (epiphyses), after which further increases in height are limited.

Proper timing and correct amounts of hormones are crucial: too much growth hormone too early results in gigantism, since the growth spurt is not checked by closure of the growing ends of the long bones. Not enough growth hormone in childhood can lead to permanently stunted growth.

CONNECTIONS

● **ENDOCRINE SYSTEMS** contain the glands responsible for the output of growth-controlling **HORMONES**.

Dwarfism

A deficiency (hyposecretion) of growth hormone during childhood produces a so-called pituitary dwarf if left untreated. These individuals show extremely slow growth as children, while the body is normally proportioned and intelligence is normal. Two-thirds of pituitary dwarfs do not mature sexually.

The reasons that an individual does not produce enough growth hormone are varied: a genetic disorder may be to blame or an unexplained absence or undergrowth of the pituitary gland, or damage to the gland during birth. A benign pituitary tumor can also destroy the hormone-secreting cells. Treatment of pituitary dwarfism is possible if diagnosed early and involves the injection of artificial human growth hormone (see box at right). A similar but more controversial issue is the suggestion that artificial growth hormone could be given to children at the low end of "normal" height.

Abnormally short stature is not always due to a deficiency of growth hormone. In Laron dwarfism, growth hormone levels are normal, but growth is reduced because the tissues are insensitive to the hormone. In this disorder, injection of growth hormone does not work.

The most common form of dwarfism is a hereditary condition, caused by a single, dominant gene, called achondroplasia, in which the individual has shortened limbs, stumpy fingers, and a large, globular head. Exactly how the gene defect leads to the bone-growth disorder is not known. Many achondroplastic dwarfs are stillborn or die soon after birth, but those who survive have normal intelligence and life expectancy and sexual function.

Nonhormonal factors for poor growth include bone disease, chronic malnutrition, diseases in which the supply of oxygen to the growing tissues is insufficient (such as tuberculosis), severe respiratory disease, congenital heart disease, or diseases that prevent the small intestine from absorbing nutrients properly (such as cystic fibrosis and celiac disease). Restricted growth can also be caused by prolonged use of certain drugs, such as corticosteroids and anticancer drugs.

Gigantism and acromegaly

Overproduction (hypersecretion) of growth hormone is usually due to a benign pituitary tumor. In childhood, this results in gigantism. Robert Wadlow's abnormal growth started at age two. He reached 6 feet (1.8 m) in height by his sixth birthday and was still growing at his death at age 22, when he was 8 feet 11 inches (2.72 m) in height.

When hypersecretion of growth hormone first occurs in adulthood, after the long bones have reached maturity, the growth hormone causes an enlargement of cartilagenous regions and soft tissues. Individuals with this condition, called acromegaly, have enlarged feet and hands and show a coarsening of the facial features due to enlargement of the skull and jaw. As with any brain tumor, the symptoms of acromegaly include lethargy and severe headaches.

GENETICALLY ENGINEERED GROWTH HORMONE

Working out the sequence of growth hormone's string of 188 amino acids took 15 years' research. The structure was published in 1971 by C. H. Li, a biochemist at the University of California, and his colleagues. The discovery of the structure of this crucial hormone enabled biochemists to attempt to duplicate it artificially.

Large-scale production of artificial growth hormone became crucial in 1985, when it was realized that some growth-hormone preparations taken from human cadavers were passing on Creutzfeldt-Jakob disease, a rapidly developing dementia caused by a virus, to patients treated with the preparations. The United States and Europe (except France) immediately banned the use of human preparations and switched to genetically engineered human growth hormone.

Recombinant (genetically engineered) human growth hormone (Somatrem) is created by inserting the gene for the hormone into the bacterium *Escherichia coli*, which then produces the hormone in sufficient quantities to be purified and collected. The recombinant growth hormone produced in this way is chemically identical to that produced in the body. The production of recombinant growth hormone is extremely expensive, but there is now sufficient growth hormone for all 10,000 children in the United States who rely on it to grow at a normal rate.

Hypersecretion of growth hormone, whether causing gigantism or acromegaly, can be difficult to correct, since the pituitary gland is buried deep in the brain. However, surgery is increasingly being used to remove the tumor or to reduce gland size. Radiotherapy is also a possibility, although the benefit is gradual, and results may take up to five years to show.

H. BYRT

See also: CHILD DEVELOPMENT; CORTICOSTEROIDS.

Further reading:
Griffin, J. E., and S. R. Ojeda, eds. 2002. *Textbook of Endocrine Physiology*. 4th ed. New York: Oxford University Press.
Roloff, M., and T. Summer. 1999. *Against Tall Odds: Being a David in a Goliath World*. Sisters, Oreg.: Multnomah Publishers.

The most famous of all modern dwarfs were the couple Charlie Stratton (Tom Thumb) and Lavinia Warren, who were both less than 3 feet (90 cm) tall.

GYMNOSPERMS

Gymnosperms are vascular plants having seeds that are not enclosed in an ovary

CONNECTIONS

● Many **TREES** of the division Coniferophyta (**CONIFERS**) have a high commercial value.

● The presence of **VASCULAR SYSTEMS** is an important feature of gymnosperms.

The ginkgo, or maidenhair tree (Ginkgo biloba) of the division Ginkgophyta is often planted in urban parks and along city streets, particularly in the United States, because of its attractiveness and ability to grow in the polluted atmosphere of the city. Male trees are more often planted because the seeds of the female trees are rancid smelling.

within an ovary, and later, the seeds are not enclosed in a fruit, as they are in flowering plants. Instead the ovules are borne on specialized leaves called megasporophylls, which are often grouped together into cones (megastrobili). Similarly, the pollen of gymnosperms is not produced in anthers, as it is in flowering plants, but on specialized leaves called microsporophylls, which again may be grouped into cones (microstrobili). Unlike angiosperms, which make up a single division of plants, gymnosperms are actually an informal grouping of four completely separate divisions (see Classification below). Altogether, therefore, there are five divisions of seed plants, all representing separate evolutionary lineages.

The life cycle of gymnosperms consists of two alternating generations, the gametophyte generation and the sporophyte generation. As in angiosperms, the gametophytes are microscopic and part of the sporophyte plant, rather than free living as in ferns. Also like angiosperms, gymnosperms are dioecious: each gametophyte holding either the male or the female sex cells.

CORE FACTS

■ Gymnosperms are seed-bearing plants with vascular systems. They produce pollen and ovules but not flowers or fruit. Once fertilized, the ovules develop into seeds.

■ The gymnosperms comprise four separately evolved plant divisions, all of which bear exposed ovules.

■ Gymnosperms are a small but diverse group, including some of the tallest and oldest plants on Earth.

Gymnosperms consist of conifers and three other groups and, together with angiosperms (flowering plants), make up the seed-bearing vascular plants. The development of vascular tissue (for the distribution of food and fluids) and seeds (to protect and disperse the developing embryo) are two of the most important characteristics of gymnosperms, which have been in existence for over 300 million years.

Characteristics of gymnosperms

The name gymnosperm means "naked seed," from the Greek words *gymnos* (naked) and *sperma* (seed). It refers to the fact that the ovules are not fully enclosed

Classification

Gymnosperms, along with angiosperms, used to be classified as a class within a larger division called Spermatophyta. Gymnosperms are now regarded as an informal grouping of four divisions that look very different from one another: the Cycadophyta (Cycads), the Ginkgophyta (Ginkgo), the Coniferophyta (Conifers), and the more advanced Gnetophyta.

● **Cycadophyta:** The cycads evolved during the Permian period (290 to 245 million years ago) and were a dominant group of plants, with extensive geographic distribution. Since the end of the Mesozoic era (245 to 65 million years ago), they have been declining, and today only one of the original orders, the Cycadales, survives. It contains three families: Cycadaceae (one genus, *Cycas*), Strangeriaceae (two genera), and Zamiaceae (eight genera). They tend to grow in dry areas in the tropics and subtropics. The cycads have short thick stems and leathery, fernlike leaves. Some cycads are similar to palm trees, in particular, the commonly cultivated sago palm, *Cycas revoluta*. The size of cycads varies from the small Florida arrowroot (*Zamia floridana*) to the large *Lepidozamia hopei*, which can grow to 60 feet (18 m) tall. Cycads grow very slowly, some surviving for over 1,000 years.

Male and female reproductive organs are carried on separate plants, on sporophylls grouped into strobili (cones). The microstrobilus carries the pollen, and the megastrobilus carries the ovules and later the seeds. In some cases the megastrobilus can be enormous. For example, in *Lepidozamia peroffskyana*, the megastrobilus can measure up to 2 feet (60 cm) in length and 1 foot (30 cm) in diameter and weigh as much as 50 to 70 pounds (23 to 32 kg). The microstrobilus can also be large and contain vast amounts of pollen, as much as a pint (500 ml) in some species.

● **Ginkgophyta:** The only living representative of this 200 million-year-old genus is *Ginkgo biloba*, native to China. It is a large tree with characteristic small, fan-shaped leaves, which are divided into two lobes. Male and female reproductive organs are carried on separate plants. The large seeds are borne singly or in pairs on special stalks. They look like fruits but are in fact seeds. The fleshy, rancid-smelling outer coat (sarcotesta) encloses the inner part of the seed, which resembles a pine nut and is edible. Ginkgo is now almost extinct in the wild but is commonly cultivated.

● **Coniferophyta:** Conifers are woody trees and shrus, including such familiar species as larch, pine, fir, spruce, yew, cedar, cypress, and redwood. They are a major source of lumber and paper pulp throughout the world. Most are evergreen, but some, such as larch, are deciduous. The redwoods of the western United States are the largest trees on Earth, capable of reaching heights of over 300 feet (90 m).

There are some 630 species of conifer in 7 families. Conifers often grow in cold northern or mountain regions, where they can exploit the short growing season because they are evergreen and so can photosynthesize during the winter. They are also well adapted to living in dry environments or in areas where water is frozen. The often needle-shaped or scalelike leaves, together with a thick waxy cuticle, or surface layer, cut water loss through transpiration.

Conifers often bear male and female reproductive organs on the same plant, but on unisexual, scalelike sporophylls usually arranged into cones. The male, or pollen, cones are usually small with leathery or fleshy microsporophylls, whereas the female, or seed, cones are usually larger and often have modified, woody megasporophylls, as in pines, or fused and fleshy ones, as in the berries of junipers (*Juniperus* spp.). The yew family (Taxaceae) has female cones with only one ovule, which develops into a seed partially surrounded by a fleshy organ called an aril.

● **Gnetophyta:** The Gnetophytes comprise three families each with a single genus: Gnetaceae, Ephedraceae, and Welwitschiaceae. The genus *Gnetum*, mostly represented by vines in tropical rain forests, is the most advanced and is thought to represent an evolutionary link with angiosperms. This genus possesses broad leathery leaves, angiosperm-like vascular tissues, pollen-producing structures resembling stamens, and ovule-bearing structures that resemble small flowers. The arrangement of veins in the leaves is similar to that in angiosperms.

The genus *Ephedra*, found in Europe, Asia, and the Americas, is well adapted to a dry habitat. These are densely branched shrubs with photosynthetic twigs that bear tiny leaves. Several species are a source of the antihistamine and stimulant drug ephedrine.

Welwitschia, with only one species, *W. mirabilis*, grows in the African deserts and survives the harsh conditions by living mainly underground. These plants grow large, carrotlike taproots, which store water for the plant. The stem, measuring up to 3 feet (90 cm) in diameter, protrudes above ground and bears just two broad, strap-like leaves that continue to grow from the base throughout the life of the plant, wearing away at the tips. Short cone-bearing shoots are produced from between the leaf bases, with male and female cones borne on separate plants.

J. STIRLING

See also: ANGIOSPERMS; CONIFERS; FERNS AND FERN ALLIES; LEAVES AND LEAF STRUCTURE; TREES.

Further reading:
Farjon, A. 2001. *World Checklist and Bibliography of Conifers.* 2nd ed. Kew, London: Royal Botanic Gardens, Kew.
Norstog, K. J., and T. J. Nicholls. 1997. *The Biology of the Cycads.* Ithaca, New York and London: Cornell University Press.

The diagram below shows the structure of female ovulate cones (megastrobili) from Welwitschia *in the division Gnetophyta, showing the megasporophylls (1, 3) bearing seeds, and the inner surface of a megasporophyll (2), showing the position of the seed.*

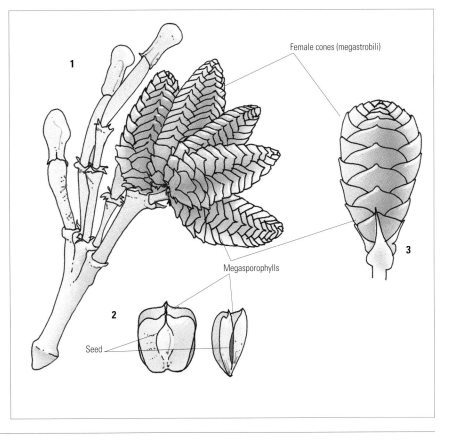

Female cones (megastrobili)

Megasporophylls

Seed

HAIR

Hair is composed of keratinous filaments that protrude from the skin surface of mammals

Hair is produced only by mammals, and its main building blocks are a very tough protein called keratin. Owing to keratin's unique structure, hair always returns to its original shape.

Keratin proteins are made up of strands of corkscrew fibers coiled around each other (see FIBERS). Tiny fibril strands are arranged together in layers to make up these fibers, which are held together by disulfide bonds. The more numerous the bonds, the less flexible the keratin.

Hair plays a protective role for different parts of the body. The head hair of humans and dense fur (comprising long guard hairs and thick underfur) of mammals insulate against extremes in temperature and may also serve as a water-repellent layer. Humans make up for a lack of insulating body hair with a layer of fat beneath the skin.

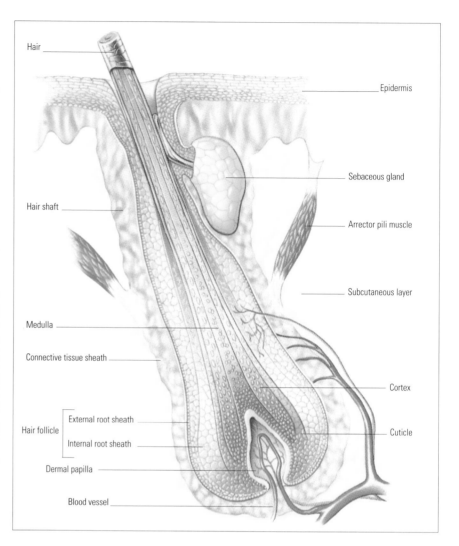

This diagram shows the structure of a hair. Each hair consists of a shaft and follicle, which have a blood supply, arrector muscle, and sebaceous gland.

CORE FACTS

- The growth of hair is a mammalian characteristic. It provides both protection and insulation to control body temperature.
- Hair is composed of strands of keratin, a tough durable protein.
- Dense hair is also called fur, which is present on a large number of mammals; some fur has a high commercial value.

Hair is also a sensitive, tactile organ. A tiny network of nerves surrounds the root of each hair so that when the hair is disturbed, an impulse goes to the brain and is detected. Cats use their sensitive whiskers (modified hairs called vibrissae) on their faces to feel their way through undergrowth at night and to hunt for prey by detecting air currents when the prey animal moves.

How hair grows

Hair starts to grow with an ingrowth, or pitting, of the outer skin layer (the epidermis) into the inner skin layer (the dermis). At the base of each ingrowth, a dermal papilla (a tiny pimplelike projection) forms,

developing into the hair follicle, in which the new hair grows. Associated glands produce sebum (a fatty skin oil) and sweat, which exit via the follicle. The larger the hair follicles, the thicker the hair that grows from them. In humans red-haired people tend to have the thickest follicles.

The dermal papilla is fed by a tiny blood vessel, which brings oxygen and nutrients to the hair bulb (the base of the shaft). It is in fact continuous cell division in the bulb that creates the hair cells. In the root of the hair, above the bulb, the hair cells harden, or cornify. Although this process involves death of the cells, they are still useful to the body. As cornified hair cells get pushed upward by the continuing mitosis in the bulb, they separate from the follicular wall to create the hair shaft.

Hairs also have muscles at their base. A tiny muscle called the arrector pili tucks into the wall of the follicle. When the muscle contracts, it creates a tiny mound of flesh at the base of the hair, and the hair is raised. In humans, this phenomenon is called "goose bumps." This display of hair raising is essential for increasing the insulating effect of hair or fur, and it is also useful as a scare tactic. A frightened cat, for

THE ORIGINS OF HAIR

Little is known about the origin of hair, although the pattern of clusters of hairs suggest that they originally grew in conjunction with scales on the skin of mammalian ancestors. Armadillos have this type of scale and hair arrangement, which allows them to maintain sensory reception in the skin, despite their armor. An alternative theory suggests that hairs are derived from bristles that grew from sensory pits on the skin of primordial ancestors similar to lizards.

CONNECTIONS

- **MAMMALS** produce hair from the epidermal layer of the **SKIN**.

- Rhinoceros **HORN** is actually made up of hardened hair-like fibers.

- **PIGMENTATION** of hair is controlled by the presence of melanin.

example, will raise the hair on its body and tail so that it appears much bigger and more threatening.

Each hair is made up of both dead and dying cells, trapped air pockets, and granules of the color pigment, melanin. Melanin granules are incorporated into the hair as it grows, and hair color depends on the density and distribution of the granules, as well as the number of air pockets. Hair color, like eye color, is the result of inheritance of certain physical characteristics (see GENETICS).

Hair itself is made up of three layers: an outer cuticle of overlapping cells (arranged in a similar way to roof shingles), a cortex (which gives hair its strength), and a central medulla. The medulla is made up of round cells and determines the hair's thickness. In humans, the amount of cortex varies in the hair of people of different nationalities: human Negro hair has the most, Mongol the least, and Caucasian a moderate amount.

Human hair

Humans may think they are among the most hairless of mammals, but the human body is actually covered with tiny hairs, known as vellus hairs (sometimes called peach fuzz). Only the palms, lips, and the bottoms of the feet are entirely free of hairs. In contrast, whales, also mammals, have only one or two bristles on the upper lip.

Humans hair helps protect against chaffing in the pubic area and underarms, and disperses perspiration from the sweat glands in these areas. Hair also seems to capture a person's own scent and plays a role in attraction between individuals.

Human heads are covered with 90,000 to 150,000 hairs, and there are millions more hairs on our bodies. Eyelashes and nose hairs, so-called terminal hairs, protect delicate areas from bacteria, dirt, and other irritants and have a shorter lifespan than head hair. Head hair, undergoing a cycle of growth, loss, and replacement, has a lifespan ranging from 2.4 to 7.2 years. Cycles of hair growth

---

COMPULSIVE HAIR PULLING

It is estimated that millions of people suffer from a little understood impulsive disorder called trichotillomania, which involves pulling out, playing with, and/or eating head or body hairs. The disorder sometimes occurs in very young children but more often begins during adolescence. The impulse to pull hair seems to cease in toddlers eventually, but older children who get the disorder may have it for the rest of their lives. The impulse seems to come and go in waves and may be stronger during stressful times or, among women, during certain stages of the menstrual cycle. Sufferers may make themselves bald, have bald patches, or entirely pull out their eyelashes, eyebrows, or pubic hairs. Some experts believe the behavior stems from vestigial grooming behavior.

THE DIFFERENCE BETWEEN MALE AND FEMALE HAIR

Human hair follicles react differently to hormones in men and women. At puberty, boys develop growth of thick, heavily pigmented hairs on the lower jaw and upper lip; girls continue to grow fine hairs in those regions. In the pubic areas, however, both sexes experience hair growth. As men age, their hair may recede, a process by which the follicles are depleted or lost and the few remaining follicles produce only fine, downy hair.

A CLOSER LOOK

vary with hair type (of which there are several in humans), and therefore the life span of a hair will vary with its location and type.

J. SCHULHOF

See also: FIBERS; GENETICS.

Further reading:

Patent, D. 1995. *Why Mammals Have Fur*. New York: Cobblehill Books.
Prenzel, F. 2003. *The Hair-Pulling Problem: The Complete Guide to Trichotillomania*. New York: Oxford University Press.

This picture shows human hair suffering from split ends—damaged, frayed ends. This condition results from damage to the outer cuticle.

HALLUCINOGENS

Hallucinogens are drugs that trick the brain into perceiving things that do not actually exist

Anyone who sees, hears, smells, tastes, or feels things that do not exist is hallucinating. A hallucination is a state in which perceptions originate within cells in the brain, stimulated by something other than the usual sensory messages from the receptors in the eyes, ears, nose, tongue, skin, or elsewhere.

Hallucinations can be caused by drugs called hallucinogens, many of which are extracted from plants. The main classes of hallucinogens are LSD-like drugs, psilocybin-like drugs, and mescaline-like drugs. Marijuana is also classed as a hallucinogen, although it has various effects. Other drugs, including alcohol, can also produce hallucinations, but are not classified as such since hallucination is not their primary effect.

Seeing begins when light strikes cells in the back of the eye. The messages from these cells eventually reach neurons (nerve cells) in the part of the brain that deals with vision—that is, the occipital lobe of the cortex. The neurons "fire," and the person experiences the phenomenon of seeing (see VISION).

Scientists think that the molecular structure of a hallucinogen fools the neurons into responding as if signals were coming from the eye itself. Hallucinations that affect the other senses are probably triggered by similar processes in other parts of the brain.

LSD

Lysergic acid diethylamide (LSD) was first synthesized in 1938 by Swiss chemist Albert Hofmann (b. 1906). Hofmann accidentally swallowed some LSD and discovered its mind-altering properties. LSD is produced naturally by the fungus ergot (*Claviceps purpurea*) that infects wheat and rye. This powerful drug was originally used to treat alcoholism, autism, and pain in cancer patients. Only one form of LSD is a hallucinogen.

By the 1960s, LSD had become one of the most widely abused drugs. However, many users reported unpleasant or frightening reactions to the drug, called "bad trips." These included dangerous lapses of judgement and mood changes. Physical effects included muscular tremors, blurred vision, nausea, chills, and increased heart rate, blood pressure, and respiration.

Psilocybin

Psilocybin is produced by the mushroom *Psilocybe mexicana*, one of the "sacred mushrooms" of Mexico, used for at least 2,000 years in religious ceremonies. The chemical structure of psilocybin is related to that of serotonin, a neurotransmitter necessary for the transmission of nerve signals in the brain. This structural similarity has led some scientists to speculate that psilocybin mimics the action of serotonin within the sympathetic nervous system, which, among other things, controls the flight-or-fight response. As well as producing hallucinations, psilocybin affects alertness, excitement, and alarm and often leads to nausea.

The dried tops of the peyote cactus, known as peyote buttons, are a natural source of the hallucinogen mescaline.

Mescaline

Mescaline is used in religious ceremonies among Native Americans in the southwest, and formerly by Aztec Indians of Central America. The drug was first isolated from the peyote cactus in 1896. Mescaline can produce startling color visions as well as temporary psychosis, and its effects can last between four and eight hours. It is a controlled substance in the United States, which means its possession and use is controlled by law, although the Native American church is allowed to use the drug for religious purposes and to treat certain medical conditions.

Flashbacks

Some hallucinogens, especially LSD, can distort mental awareness even after the drug has left the body. These episodes, known as flashbacks, may be triggered by marijuana, alcohol, or amphetamines, as well as stressful situations. Flashbacks are often accompanied by extreme feelings of fear, hopelessness, and panic and have led people to commit suicide. Since flashbacks may occur long after the offending drug has left the body, some scientists suggest that hallucinogens may permanently affect brain chemistry.

C. PROUJAN

See also: DRUG USE AND ABUSE; PHARMACOLOGY; VISION.

Further reading:

Barter, J. 2001. *Hallucinogens*. Drug Education Library. San Diego: Lucent Books.
Grob, C. S. 2002. *Hallucinogens: A Reader.* Los Angeles: J. P. Tarcher.

CONNECTIONS

● Many of the hallucinogenic drugs cause symptoms similar to those seen in some **MENTAL DISORDERS**, such as **SCHIZOPHRENIA**. Some drugs, such as LSD, may trigger mental disorders in predisposed people.

INDEX

Headings and page numbers in **bold** refer to main articles. Page numbers in *italics* refer to photographs and illustrations or their captions.